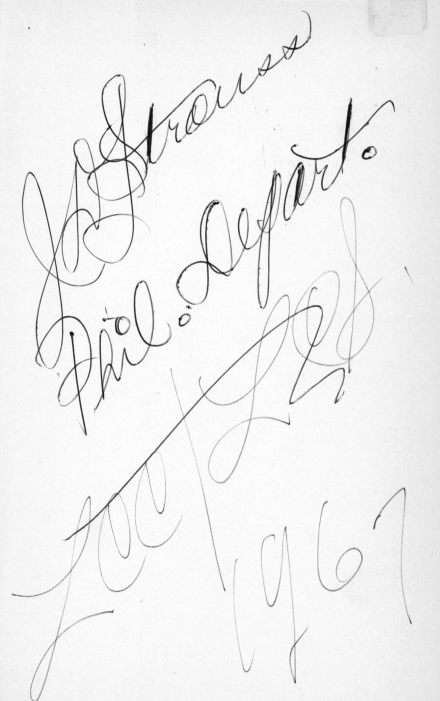

W9-CBA-457

The Church and Social Responsibility

THE CHURCH
and
SOCIAL
RESPONSIBILITY

Edited by

J. RICHARD SPANN

ABINGDON-COKESBURY PRESS
New York • *Nashville*

THE CHURCH AND SOCIAL RESPONSIBILITY

Copyright MCMLIII by Pierce & Washabaugh

Library of Congress Catalog Card Number: 53-8136

Scripture quotations designated R.S.V. are from
the Revised Standard Version of the Bible, copyright
1946 and 1952 by the Division of Christian Education of the National Council of Churches.

SET UP, PRINTED, AND BOUND BY THE
PARTHENON PRESS, AT NASHVILLE,
TENNESSEE, UNITED STATES OF AMERICA

PREFACE

THE THESIS OF THIS BOOK IS THAT CHRISTIAN SALVATION ALSO INCLUDES THE SOCIAL ORDER; THAT THE CHRISTIAN CHURCH IS responsible for the social conditions and must provide redemptive measures for society. This is a study of some of the major social areas in the light of Protestantism's theological convictions.

No single author could have written equally well in each of the areas explored. Each of the fifteen writers of this symposium is a specialist who writes with the insight and generally recognized characteristics of those who specialize. The writers are representative of American Protestantism.

There are many other equally well qualified writers in the various fields who were unable to arrange their schedules to meet the deadline for the symposium.

The diversity of viewpoint in some instances reflects the characteristic independence of thought and action common to Protestantism's religious, economic, and political philosophies. However, the authors are one in the conviction that Christianity must reform the social order, as well as the individual, if "God's will is to be done on earth."

Both the pastor and the thoughtful layman will find this volume a stimulating and rewarding study. Many church groups will want to use this book in social forums and study groups.

The editor is indebted to friends in many Protestant denominations for helpful suggestions in preparing the outline and selecting the authors.

J. RICHARD SPANN

5

CONTENTS

7

PART IV

The Church and the Political Order

PART I

The Social Ministry
of
The Church

1

The Christian Bases of Rights, Freedoms, and Responsibilities

S. PAUL SCHILLING

ON DECEMBER 15, 1952, A NEW SHRINE OF FREEDOM WAS DEDICATED IN WASHINGTON, D.C. THE DECLARATION OF INDE-pendence, the Constitution of the United States, and the Bill of Rights were unveiled in their new home, the National Archives Building. By day they are now on public display in helium-filled cases covered with amber glass to prevent deterioration. At night the entire shrine descends into the protective custody of a fifty-ton, fireproof, bombproof vault specially constructed by the same engineers who built the gold-storage vault at Fort Knox.

The transfer of these treasured documents, which were formerly housed in the Library of Congress, dramatically sym-bolizes the present status of the human rights they eloquently proclaim. Recent decades have witnessed a new affirmation, on a world scale, of fundamental rights and expanded effort in their behalf, but also widespread threats to their preserva-tion and drastic curtailment of their free exercise. The peoples of the earth are demanding as never before a fair chance to live and grow as human beings. Yet at this very time, in many lands freedoms once enjoyed are deteriorating or being buried in the darkness of totalitarian repression or democratic fear.

Here is an area of central concern for Christians and churches who wish to understand and serve their world. What do we mean by human rights and liberties, and by the

11

responsibilities which they imply? What part has Christianity played in advancing them, and what basis do they have in Christian belief? Finally, what can and should we do to secure and extend them?

WHAT ARE RIGHTS, FREEDOMS, AND RESPONSIBILITIES?

A *right* is a claim which belongs to every man as a member of the human family, and without which he cannot become what he is capable of becoming. It is any experience justly claimed because it is necessary to the full, unhampered development of persons in society. A *freedom* is the opportunity to exercise a right. A *responsibility* is an instance of accountability for something within one's control. As it is used here, the word *responsibility* is synonymous with the ethical term *duty*. My responsibility is what I ought to think or do as a person among other persons, sharing a common life, and answerable for my conduct to society and to God.

Rights and responsibilities are complementary. If I am to fulfill my responsibilities, I must have certain rights. Conversely, my claim to these rights entails responsibility for exercising them conscientiously, with due respect for the equivalent rights of others. My duties to others are their rights in relation to me, and their duties to me are my rights in relation to them.

Much current discussion considers human rights out of all relation to responsibilities. Without this context, liberty easily becomes license, and rights themselves are lost in an anarchy of selfishly competing claims. Actually, in an interdependent society mutual responsibilities are more fundamental than rights. The widespread denial of basic human rights makes imperative Christian action to defend and advance them, but rights themselves are secure only when yoked at every point with responsibility.

Until recently human rights in the Western world have commonly meant civil and political rights. These have found definitive formulation in the American Declaration of Independence; the Bill of Rights, comprising the first ten amendments to the Constitution of the United States; and the French Declaration of the Rights of Man and of the Citizen (1789).

These epoch-making statements guarantee freedom of religion, speech, press, and assembly; protection against deprivation of life, liberty, or property without due process of law; trial by jury; and related rights.

The past twenty years have made clearer the importance of the economic and social aspects of life, and this awareness has manifested itself in various statements of human rights. Three may be cited here.

1. In his illuminating work *The Rights of Man and Natural Law*, Jacques Maritain lists three classes of rights: (*a*) the rights of the human person as such; (*b*) the rights of the civic person; and (*c*) the rights of the social person, particularly of the working person. The last-mentioned asserts such economic rights as the right to work, to choose one's work, to organize in unions and other groups, to receive a just wage, to benefit from various forms of social security, and to enjoy the material and spiritual goods of civilization.

2. In 1947 appeared the report of President Truman's distinguished Committee on Civil Rights, *To Secure These Rights*. The first three areas covered survey the contemporary status of the rights to safety and security of the person, to citizenship and its privileges, and to freedom of conscience and expression. The fourth deals with the right to equality of opportunity, including employment, education, housing, health service, and public services and accommodations—rights which are implicit but not explicit in the Fifth Amendment.

3. A historic milestone in man's efforts to safeguard rights and freedoms was reached on December 10, 1948, when the United Nations General Assembly adopted and proclaimed the Universal Declaration of Human Rights. Since then the Commission on Human Rights has labored painstakingly to fashion an instrument through which the nations might commit themselves to further the rights and freedoms affirmed in the Declaration. Current pressing interest in the material conditions of life is reflected in the preparation of two Draft Covenants rather than one as originally planned. One of these deals with civil and political rights, the other with social, economic, and cultural rights. The former specifies, in part, the right to life, liberty and security of the

13

person, liberty of movement, recognition as a person before the law, and fair trial; freedom of thought, conscience, opinion, expression, peaceful assembly, and religion; and prohibition of inhuman and degrading treatment, slavery and forced labor, and retroactive criminal legislation. The latter includes the right to work, appropriate working conditions, and participation in trade unions; to social security; to special protection of expectant mothers, children, and the family; to an adequate standard of living; to health; to education; and to science and culture.

Dr. Charles Malik, chairman of the Commission on Human Rights, describes this new emphasis on the social and economic as "a quiet revolution," "the materialistic revolution of the times." He lists three causes: the increasing impact of Marx; the rise of economically and socially less developed peoples, who naturally accent the material; and the "unimaginative helplessness of the Western world in the face of these two impacts." [1]

This development offers a crucial challenge to Christianity. On the one hand, it threatens to submerge the ends of life in the means. Any view is distorted and partial which imagines that man can live by bread alone, and which in concern for physical necessities excludes the values which impart richest meaning to life.

On the other hand, followers of Him who at Nazareth proclaimed his mission to the poor, the captive, the blind, and the oppressed cannot fail to discern something authentically Christian in this zeal for material welfare. The rights affirmed may be largely instrumental, but they are true rights; and their denial or attainment will powerfully affect the full growth of persons which is sought by the Christian faith. If means are lacking, how shall worthy ends be attained? The theoretical right to life may be a mockery to one who lacks the wherewithal to sustain it, and a free press is not a great boon to one who cannot read. When the hungry, thinly clad, and poorly sheltered ask a decent livelihood for themselves and their families, they are but defining freedom in the terms

[1] "Human Rights in the United Nations," *United Nations Bulletin*, XIII (1952), 253.

most pertinent to them. It ill becomes the comfortable to charge the miserable with materialism. The awakening of the disinherited should rebuke and chasten those who long since should have had imagination enough to sit where they sat and assert for them the rights they now demand.

Fortunately neither type of right need be exalted at the expense of the other; as the proposed covenants recognize, true freedom involves both. They are interdependent, and neither can be fully secured if the other is neglected.

In the above lists much is said of rights but little of responsibilities. The restrictions on liberty which normally call forth such historic statements naturally lead to a preponderant emphasis on rights. However, Article 29 of the Universal Declaration declares, "Everyone has duties to the community in which alone the free and full development of his personality is possible." Likewise the Preamble to both Draft Covenants asserts "that the individual, having duties to other individuals and to the community to which he belongs, is under responsibility to strive for the promotion and observance of the rights recognized in this Covenant."

CHRISTIAN SOURCES

What part has been played by Christian attitudes and beliefs in generating this modern concern for human rights? Here it is important to claim neither too much nor too little for Christian influence, but to examine the record.

Many factors operated in the seventeenth and eighteenth centuries to exalt the liberties of man above all else. Unquestionably powerful was the complex of ideas advanced by various political thinkers of the Enlightenment whose main orientation was not religious but rational. Political formulations of the notion of individual rights were philosophically grounded in such doctrines as the social-contract concept of the state, the theory of inherent natural rights, and the belief in popular sovereignty and the right of revolution. Incalculably influential in the American and French revolutions and the formation of the constitutional governments which followed were the writings of men who vigorously proclaimed these ideas and concretely applied them—thinkers like Locke,

15

Rousseau, Montesquieu, Voltaire, Jefferson, and Paine. The Lockian character of the Declaration of Independence is clearly attested in such expressions as "the laws of nature and of nature's God," "all men are created equal," "certain inalienable rights," "life, liberty, and the pursuit of happiness," and "the consent of the governed." The continuing influence of Enlightenment thought is evidenced in the Preamble of the Universal Declaration of Human Rights, which begins by recognizing "the inherent dignity" and "equal and inalienable rights" of all men.

Interpenetrating these influences have been others specifically Christian, with which we are primarily concerned. Indeed, the origin of the conception of natural rights is to be found in the medieval Christian and Stoic doctrine of the law of nature. The Stoics maintained that there are in the nature of man objective and universal moral standards at least partially discoverable by reason. Through Paul, the church fathers, Augustine, Thomas Aquinas, Grotius, and others, this conception was given a theistic foundation and absorbed into Christian thought. The political theorists mentioned removed the doctrine from its Christian basis, grounded it in human reason, often with a deistic background, and applied it concretely to the rights of man. Christian thinkers largely failed to make this application, but this should not obscure the indispensable service they rendered in preparing the way for it.

The most distinctively Christian impetus toward human rights came more directly, through the impact of the Puritan tradition in England and America. As James H. Nichols has shown, it would not be strictly accurate to speak *in general* of a Christian or even a Protestant basis for democracy. History makes plain that many religious bodies have in fact suppressed freedom. On the other hand, in the sixteenth and seventeenth centuries the Reformed communions were "the most influential . . . champions of popular sovereignty, government by consent, natural rights, the duty to resist tyranny." [2]

Cromwell's brief rule, basically religious in impulse, pointed

[2] *Democracy and the Churches* (Philadelphia: The Westminster Press, 1951), pp. 20, 28.

England toward a new recognition of the freedom of the person and of conscience. In America the most articulate leaders of the revolutionary era were deistic or unitarian, yet orthodox Puritanism—Congregationalist, Presbyterian, Baptist, and Low Anglican—exerted a powerful effect. The largest churches and the most influential clergymen in the colonies were of Calvinist persuasion; they took seriously the duty of the Christian in politics, and their political Bible was Locke's *Second Treatise on Government*. It is highly doubtful whether democratic principles would have prevailed when the Constitution was drafted without the broad popular support springing from a motivation fundamentally religious. "One may even suspect," writes Nichols, "that the cultured rationalist generally restates in abstract terms the fundamental motifs he has heard from the despised and uncultured spokesmen for positive religious affirmations. There is more of creative originality in the latter." [3] Five of these convictions may be briefly mentioned.[4]

1. *The absolute sovereignty of God.* No earthly sovereign has the right to pre-empt the divine rule and claim for himself the allegiance which belongs to God alone. Since the individual is directly responsible to God, he must be free to respond to God's command. Governments must therefore be restrained from compelling the thoughts and actions of citizens, who in case of conflict must be free to obey God rather than man. Constitutional limitations and bills of rights are political means of achieving this restraint.

2. *The sinfulness of man.* Lord Bryce assesses discerningly the influence of Calvinistic theology on the American Constitution:

There is a hearty Puritanism in the view of human nature which pervades the instrument of 1787. . . . It is the work of men who believed in original sin, and were resolved to leave

---

[3] *Ibid.*, p. 40.

[4] These are mainly the views of left-wing Puritans, who were theologically orthodox, but whose political applications of religious beliefs undermined traditional Calvinistic theocracy while laying firm foundations for democracy. Items 3, 4, and 5 are illuminatingly discussed by Nichols (*ibid.*, pp. 32-38).

open for transgressors no door which they could possibly shut. Compare this spirit with the enthusiastic optimism of the Frenchmen of 1789. It is not merely a difference of race temperaments; it is a difference of fundamental ideas.[5]

A major reason for our prized constitutional guarantees of human rights was the belief that men need protection from one another's inhumanity.

3. *The view of the church as a community of mature believers gathered by a covenant to which all consent and to which all are bound.* For participants in a self-governing religious fellowship made possible by the voluntary adherence of each member, united by a common purpose, and enriched by the distinctive contributions of all, a democratic state in which each citizen has duties and rights is a natural political extension of religious belief and practice. The social contract voluntarily entered into by each member of society is thus the political equivalent of the gathered church.

4. *The doctrine of the Holy Spirit as the continuing presence of God in the church, the Counselor and Spirit of truth illuminating its interpretation of Scripture and informing its corporate life.* The New England town meeting, committed to the reaching of decisions through free discussion and open criticism of opposing views, is a natural outgrowth of this Christian conviction, as is democratic government on a broader scale.

5. *The Reformed doctrine of vocation.* This had clear political implications, since the Christian's calling includes that of citizenship. However, he cannot fulfill his religious vocation in politics without freedom to exercise it responsibly, and without the preservation of an area of his life which no government is free to violate. This insistence, advanced by Independents and Levelers in England and by Roger Williams in America, led straight toward the end of theocratic Puritanism and the separation of church and state.

A very different form of Christian influence in behalf of human rights has operated in the past fifteen years. Though

[5] James Bryce, *The American Commonwealth* (Chicago: Charles H. Sergels and Company, 1891), Part I, chap. XXVI, p. 299.

some of the Puritan affirmations still function actively, the underlying factors now emphasized are such principles as the worth of personality, the demands of human brotherhood, the importance of rights to world peace, and the need of freedom for the church to fulfill its divine mission. Ecumenical conferences like those at Oxford in 1937 and Madras in 1938 began a process which was expanded during World War II by interdenominational conferences and commissions in various lands. Recommendations resulting from critical study of the Dumbarton Oaks Proposals by national church groups were an important factor in securing the provisions for human rights in the United Nations Charter. More recently, the Commission of the Churches on International Affairs has maintained a consultative relation to the United Nations Commission on Human Rights.

Theological Foundations

We come now to the question of the theological bases of human rights, freedoms, and responsibilities. From the standpoint of the Christian faith, why should rights and liberties be respected and duties fulfilled? The answer may best be given in three propositions growing out of the Christian view of God, man, and society.

1. *Rights and responsibilities are derived primarily from man's relation to God as manifest in Christ: they are theogenetic.* Man's true destiny lies in the service of God, and can be attained only if man is free to order his life in harmony with the divine purpose.

Ultimately responsible to God alone, man must be free to fulfill his responsibility. The divine will is normative for all; therefore each must be granted the right to obey it in accordance with conscience in all areas of life, and none has the right to lay demands or restrictions on others which would prevent such obedience. Only so can man realize the central meaning of his existence. Furthermore, since God's rule is righteous, those subject to him have both the responsibility for treating one another justly and the right to receive such treatment. "The Lord of hosts is exalted in justice." (Isa.

19

5:16.) This implies the extension to all men of the same fundamental freedoms.

The same conclusions follow from the divine love. In creative and redemptive love God calls us into fellowship with himself. This call is ultimate, and men must be free to answer it; no human agency has the right to exclude any phase of life from its dominion. God's self-giving love constitutes a claim on us which transcends all others, and which involves the right to respond to it in loving service. Moreover, the individual who so responds sees all men as the objects of the same divine concern, hence willingly accords to all the rights he claims for himself. Loving God, he loves those whom God loves and grants to them the freedom which God grants.

In this context it is clear that religious freedom is the most basic of all rights, for it concerns a man's total response to what he deems the ultimate source of value and the most worthy object of devotion. Freedom in this realm carries with it freedom in all others, since free commitment to God implies concern for all the values for which God cares. Obversely, the denial of God or of the right to worship him as conscience dictates undermines all other rights, reduces them to mere conventions or counsels of expediency, and opens the way to tyranny or mob rule. Over the entrance to infamous Buchenwald, it has been said, appeared the appropriate words: "Here is no God."

2. *Concern for freedoms and responsibilities roots also in the Christian doctrine of man.* This concern follows logically from both the sacredness of personality and the universal fact of human sin. Positively, the Christian faith asserts the infinite value of the human soul. Man is a being of eternal dignity and worth, created in the image of God and called to be his son. He is not a means but an end. This is true not of a particular race, nationality, class, or sex, but of man *as man*, hence of *all* men. In the purpose of God each individual is a person with an immortal destiny, having unique potentialities capable of creative realization. As a person he has therefore both duties and rights. He is responsible for developing his capacities to the fullest possible degree. Likewise he has certain rights which all other persons must respect

because without them he cannot become the person God intends him to become.

Christianity also recognizes that man actually falls far short of the divine purpose. He repeatedly negates his own worth, flouts his Creator's will, and injures his neighbor. Men frequently seek special privilege at the expense of others; it is therefore necessary that rights be accorded to all and that laws be universal in application. Only so can men be guarded against their own tendencies to take advantage of one another. The extension to all citizens of freedom of thought, expression, and suffrage provides a needed restraint on the greed and lust for power of those who care little for the common good. Reinhold Niebuhr aptly observes, "Man's capacity for justice makes democracy possible; but man's inclination to injustice makes democracy necessary." [6]

3. *A third important basis of human rights and duties is found in the Christian view of society.* "None of us lives to himself, and none of us dies to himself." (Rom. 14:7.) Rather we are "members one of another" (Eph. 4:25), persons-in-community under God. We are created for fellowship with one another and with God, and we find our highest fulfillment when we think and act as members of God's family. Each individual is a participant in an interdependent community. As such, he is called upon to transcend his own private interests in that service of the common welfare which alone is "perfect freedom." Because man is endowed with certain distinctive talents great or small, he is responsible for making to the community the contribution which only he can make, and without which something will be lacking. To do this, however, he must be free. Freedom is therefore needed not only to make possible the fullest personal growth of the individual, but to enable him to make his best contribution to society and the kingdom of God. It is essential to the growth of moral personality in community.

This is what the World Council of Churches means by "the responsible society": one in which each member freely acknowledges his responsibility to God and his neighbor, and

---

[6] *The Children of Light and the Children of Darkness* (New York: Charles Scribner's Sons, 1944), p. xi.

in which those who exercise power see themselves as responsible to God and the people affected by their acts. Such a society avoids both the irresponsible, amoral use of freedom which marks extreme individualism, and the suppression of freedom inherent in thoroughgoing collectivism.

The result of this freedom-in-responsibility is a kind of spiritual symbiosis. In biology two unlike organisms are symbiotically related when their intimate association is essential to the survival of one or both, as in the case of the alga and fungus which together compose the lichen. Christianity sees humanity as a society of persons so intimately related that the good—and even the survival—of each is inextricably bound to the good of all.

Areas of Action

Christian concern for rights and responsibilities is widespread today. Yet multitudes of church people remain halfhearted or indifferent, while some of the most vigorous champions of basic freedoms are purely secular in outlook. The former leave to governmental or other agencies obligations which for prophetic Christianity are inescapably religious. They thus help to create among ethically sensitive persons the very secularism they often bewail. The latter unnecessarily divorce social action from its ultimate source of meaning and power. When human freedoms are rooted in nothing deeper than an abstract "human nature," they tend to become purely relative and conventional, and the way is open for might to replace right. Fortunately, true Christianity offers a more excellent way than either of these.

To walk in this way requires both education and action. On the basis of distinctively Christian presuppositions like those already discussed, we must endeavor to develop universally applicable principles in terms which will commend them to men of good will everywhere. The church should seek to create an informed conscience, out of which wise laws and treaties may come and without which legislative enactments will be an empty shell. Interpenetrating this task is the vital practical one of translating principles into action. Liberty

22

needs not only discussion and legislation, but living embodiment. This word too must become flesh.

Such action should begin with the Christian community itself. The church will receive and deserve scant attention for its message if it fails to demonstrate respect for human rights. Yet in practice millions of Christians are denied full fellowship because of race; the churches generally follow a pattern of involuntary segregation which violates the deepest principles of the faith they profess. Discriminations based on sex, class, and economic status are likewise widespread. At all levels, but particularly in local communities, we must live as well as preach the truth that in Christ "there is neither Jew nor Greek, . . . slave nor free, . . . male nor female" (Gal. 3:28).

In society at large the plight of freedom is more precarious than at any other period in modern times. Even in the United States liberties are denied, restricted, or watered down in the name of national security. Men who exercise independent and critical judgment must not be labeled subversive or have their reputations jeopardized by sweeping, unsubstantiated charges, with no adequate opportunity for factual reply. Bishop G. Bromley Oxnam has rendered both democracy and Christianity heroic service by exposing the investigating methods of the House Committee on Un-American Affairs. Loyalty oaths, required of public employees in some areas, threaten to undermine freedom of thought and to encourage dull conformity, while their effectiveness in catching the disloyal is open to question. Schools and colleges are seriously threatened when textbooks and faculty members are subjected to unbridled attacks by persons unqualified for intelligent judgment. Under the terms of the McCarran-Walter Immigration and Nationality Act worthy persons should not be unjustly denied entry to our shores and to the new opportunity which America has long symbolized. In areas like these, level-headed, resolute Christian action is sorely needed.

Also demanded is continued and expanded church support of the trail-blazing efforts of the United Nations. It is trying valiantly to express the conscience of mankind in behalf of peoples suffering from glaring discriminations, such as those in South Africa. Through communications to our American representatives, every individual and church can participate in its work.

The road toward acceptance by the nations of the proposed covenants on human rights will be long and steep. The United States government itself has announced that it will not ratify the covenants, because "disregard of the basic principles of human rights is widespread" today, and "the climate of world opinion does not yet seem favorable" to the conclusion of a treaty so comprehensive.[7] Those who recall the important role played by the American churches, led by John Foster Dulles, in securing the insertion of human-rights provisions in the United Nations Charter, will regret the circumstances which now lead him to oppose binding agreements to uphold specific rights. If the climate of public opinion is unfavorable, Christians are called upon to change it, and so to encourage the Secretary of State to go beyond what he now deems possible.

We who are committed to the responsible exercise of human rights have a solemn but thrilling task. If under God we do our work well, the freedoms we cherish will not be insulated from life or buried from view; rather they will become the very air men breathe and the light by which men see as they live and labor together. Charles Malik writes:

The more man awakens, the more he will clamor for his natural rights and fundamental freedoms; and the future does not belong to those who hide their heads in the sand, but to those who, facing the truth in all humility, accept the joyous suffering of transforming the given into the image of the just and true.[8]

This task belongs to none so much as to Christians.

[7] Address of Mrs. Oswald B. Lord, United States representative on the Commission on Human Rights, at Geneva. *United Nations Bulletin*, XIV (1953), 342.

[8] *Loc. cit.*

2

New Testament Sources of the Social Ministry of the Church

Donald T. Rowlingson

THE SOCIAL MINISTRY OF THE CHURCH ROOTS DEEP IN THE HEBREW-CHRISTIAN TRADITION. AS THE EARLIER EXPONENTS of the social gospel confidently affirmed,[1] it is a legitimate and imperative extension of the prophetic movement in Israel which was both fulfilled and transcended in the mission and message of Jesus. The relationship between the two is organic. The fluctuations of biblical and theological thought in our time, however, demand that we define the nature of the relationship carefully.[2] To that end the present discussion will deal first, in the form of two presuppositions, with the perspective from which we may legitimately view the relevance of the New Testament to our day, and, second, with positive aspects of the New Testament message which make a contribution to social ethics.

PRESUPPOSITIONS

The first presupposition is that the definitive contribution of the New Testament comes to us through the *historical*

[1] See the writings of Washington Gladden, Walter Rauschenbusch, Francis G. Peabody, and Shailer Mathews.

[2] Cf. John C. Bennett, *Christian Realism* (New York: Charles Scribner's Sons, 1941), pp. 77-85; *Biblical Authority for Today*, ed. Alan Richardson and Wolfgang Schweitzer (Philadelphia: Westminster Press, 1951); Daniel D. Williams, *What Present-Day Theologians Are Thinking* (New York: Harper & Bros., 1952), chaps. II-III.

Jesus, as he is portrayed primarily though not exclusively in the Synoptic Gospels. This follows inevitably from the fact that Christianity is a historical religion. Its distinctive spirit and genius are determined by the teaching and work of the personality who founded it.[3] This is also to take seriously the biblical theory of revelation [4] to the effect that God's supreme Self-manifestation takes place through finite persons living and working realistically upon the plane of history.

The early Christians whose views are reflected in the New Testament took this presupposition for granted, at the same time that under the guidance of the Spirit they obviously went beyond the historical Jesus in several directions. The most distinctive and all-pervading characteristic of the New Testament is an appreciation of Jesus as "both Lord and Christ" which has at its base a clear recognition of the quality of his earthly life. It is the latter which, from a moral point of view, is the most important causative factor in the rise of the resurrection faith. Also, this fact of Jesus' unmatched character is the ultimate justification of speculative theories about his person which often employ categories of thought foreign to his own. This is the pattern of cause and effect implied in Peter's confession (Mark 8:27-30) and echoed throughout the New Testament (cf. Heb. 2:9, 18; 4:15; Phil. 2:8-11; I Cor. 1:18-25; I Pet. 2:21-25; Acts 10:36-43), alongside the idea with which it is never fully reconciled— that Jesus' exaltation is in some way or other foreordained. The Incarnation is the Word "made flesh" (John 1:14, K.J.V.)— that is, the unique embodiment of divine "grace and truth" in a genuine human being. The very existence of the Gospels, furthermore, proves how important it was to those who most appreciated Jesus' exalted status to make constant reference to the memory of his specific words and deeds in order to define the meaning and to defend the legitimacy of their

[3] Cf. Millar Burrows, *Founders of Great Religions* (New York: Charles Scribner's Sons, 1931); John C. Bennett, *op. cit.,* pp. 124-33.

[4] See Herbert Butterfield, *Christianity and History* (New York: Charles Scribner's Sons, 1950).

discipleship to him.[5] When these facts are clearly apprehended, it does not make sense to affirm, as some do, that the career and personality of Jesus of Nazareth do not matter in the revelation of God's Word. Exactly the reverse is true. Without these concrete facts to give it specific content, the affirmation of the Word made flesh is meaningless.[6]

In order to come to a full understanding of the mind of Christ, we need more than the authentic insights into Jesus' historical career and message which the New Testament yields. We learn much in this respect from the entire New Testament and in addition from all of history and human experience. Elements derived from these sources, however, are as the tree to the seed from which it issues. The historical Jesus as the seed provides the distinguishing marks of the mind of *Christ* as against the mind of Buddha or the mind of Paul or of Luther or of Rauschenbusch or of Barth. In the face of the great diversity of ways in which Christians express their faith, our great need is to discover what has been called "the integrating perspective" or the "structural unity in the Christian view of things." However much may be involved in addition, there is no way to do this adequately without giving the historical Jesus his rightful priority, as the early Christians did.

The second presupposition is that the primary contribution of the historical Jesus is in the form of a *basic core of convictions about God's nature and purpose* which transcend time and circumstance, and which have to be applied creatively in each new social setting. As against specific rules, which can be applied literally and legalistically, Jesus offers vertical vision by means of which any ethical enterprise may be made to conform on the horizontal plane of finite existence to the divine purpose, thus assuring its ultimate success. Like the planets in their relationship to the central sun, all that Jesus teaches in detail about the nature of man

[5] Cf. John Knox, *Christ the Lord* (Chicago and New York: Willett, Clark & Co., 1945); Ronald R. Williams, *Authority in the Apostolic Age* (New York: The Macmillan Co., 1950).

[6] Cf. Donald M. Baillie, *God Was in Christ* (New York: Charles Scribner's Sons, 1948); Daniel D. Williams, *op. cit.*, pp. 105-7.

and of ethical conduct is derived from and sustained by this underlying religious conception. It is with respect to this, and this alone, that "in each of his sayings Jesus expresses himself wholly." [7]

Only as we focus our attention upon this aspect of Jesus' message do the limitations which are inherent in the process of relating it to our time become insignificant. From this perspective it does not matter that his horizon was that of first-century Palestine and that his teaching was directed only to that social and cultural setting. It does not matter that in his teaching there seems to be little system after the manner of books on theology or ethics, or that, even though he made generalizations, the emphasis which he made at any given time was relative to the concrete circumstances of the situation with which he was confronted. It does not matter that, despite his purified prophetism, his concentration upon individual, personal salvation offers no direct precedent for many of the most characteristic features of a social gospel such as we observe in an Isaiah or a Jeremiah and which is so much on our hearts today.[8] It does not matter, finally, that Jesus' world view, like that of his Jewish contemporaries and of his disciples in the early church, was very different from the evolutionary outlook which is normative for most of us.[9] His world view anticipated the sudden interruption of the historical process by divine intervention, probably in the near future, as the means which God would employ to establish his perfect reign.

The key to the solution of the problem of Jesus' eschatological perspective is the fact that the nature of the future hope which any particular doctrine of the last things entertains is determined by the nature of the deity believed in. Eschatologies contain wide variations in details. What is significant is the emphases which characterize any given set of

[7] Maurice Goguel, *The Life of Jesus* (New York: The Macmillan Co., 1933), p. 553.

[8] See Henry J. Cadbury, *The Peril of Modernizing Jesus* (New York: The Macmillan Co., 1937), chap. V.

[9] See Albert Schweitzer, *The Mystery of the Kingdom of God* (New York: The Macmillan Co., 1950), and *The Quest of the Historical Jesus* (London: A. and C. Block, 1945).

ideas, especially with respect to its ethical content and the way in which this is believed to influence the present. These emphases tell us much about the view of God which underlies them and which constitutes the permanent value of the view. In dealing with Jesus' eschatology our task then is to analyze carefully the complex and confusing deposits of his teaching to the end of determining the emphases which he made, so that we are enabled to distinguish the timeless elements of his view of God which are implied even in those aspects of his thought which are time-caught. On that basis the difference between his general perspective on the future and ours, while not less radical, is still not a serious barrier to our quest for his message to us.[10]

This suggests the general conclusion to be drawn from an evaluation of each of the limitations which has been cited. It is not that Jesus is irrelevant to our day or that he is impracticable. Taken together, these limitations simply define the nature of his contribution. With reference to the social ministry of the church this contribution is that of basic insights toward the construction of an active theology of the social gospel, and help in setting goals and establishing dynamics, rather than direct guidance with respect to the mechanics of social reform and reorganization.

THE NEW TESTAMENT MESSAGE

We discover at least four aspects of Jesus' message, reverberating throughout the New Testament, which justify, as they give direction and dynamic to, the social ministry of the Church.

1. Taking the sovereignty of God with deadly earnestness, Jesus interpreted it almost exclusively in *ethical* terms. He assumed that as Sovereign of the universe God had an inexorable purpose for the world of nature and for human relationships which he would at some future time bring completely to fulfillment by eliminating all opposing forces. This

[10] Cf. Thomas W. Manson, *The Teaching of Jesus* (New York: Cambridge University Press, 1939), pp. 245-60; *The Second Report of the Advisory Commission on the Theme of the Second Assembly of the World Council of Churches* (1952).

event would be the coming of the kingdom, the establishment of God's reign. In the interim it was man's sole business to pray for its coming and to seek to meet the conditions of its life by conforming his will to God's will (Matt. 6:10). This central concern for the sovereignty of God, Jesus expressed in the Lord's Prayer, the first great commandment, and in his teaching on sincerity, purity of heart, and humility, all of which he underlined by his own example with Gethsemane as its superb climax. This explains the absolute nature of his ethics. It was not "interim ethics," conditioned solely by his expectation of the imminent end of the age. It was *God's* ethics, portraying in a radical and unalloyed manner the pure will of the Sovereign. The difference may be observed by comparing Paul's eschatologically conditioned advice on marriage (I Cor. 7) with the absolute nature of love as he sets it forth in I Cor. 13. The latter parallels Jesus' outlook. To the extent that the perfect will of God was acknowledged on earth, and when demons were exorcized too (cf. Luke 10:17; 11:20; Mark 3:22-27), one could be aware of the "atmospheric pressure" of the reign of God to be fully established in the future.

The significant thing is that in defining what it meant to do God's will Jesus concentrated exclusively upon moral considerations. As against five possible alternatives this was his emphasis: (*a*) Instead of giving attention to fantastic speculations about the time and manner of the Parousia, as in the normative apocalypticism illustrated by Daniel and Revelation, he urged men to repent and to submit themselves to the moral discipline which would adequately prepare them for a final judgment of a strictly ethical nature (cf. Mark 1:15 and Matt. 25:31-46 as typical).[11] (*b*) Without being an extremist by seeking to eliminate all ritual and ceremony in religious worship, Jesus placed a premium upon the weightier matters of the law—that is, upon its ethical features (Matt. 5:7; 15:5-9; 23:23; Mark 2:23–3:6). (*c*) Believing that intimate fellowship with God was the heart of religious experience,

[11] For the best treatment of Jesus' eschatology in general, see Amos N. Wilder, *Eschatology and Ethics in the Teaching of Jesus*, revised edition (New York: Harper & Bros., 1951).

and God's greatest gift, Jesus viewed its object not as selfish absorption in the Absolute, after the manner of Greek mysticism and the mystery religions, but rather as a stimulus to work more effectively with God upon the plane of human experience in the accomplishment of his moral purpose. He stood in the tradition of Isaiah's call (Isa. 6:1-9) and of Paul's mystical experience (cf. II Cor. 12:1-10).[12] (d) As against the coercion of magic and miracle Jesus staked his cause upon moral persuasion, the vicarious acceptance of the Cross being the decisive and conclusive evidence (cf. Matt. 4:5-11; Mark 8:31-33; 11:1-10; 14:32-42). (e) Although his teaching had political and economic implications, it was centered upon the question of right or wrong in an absolute sense rather than upon that of right or left of some particular issue.

2. The distinguishing mark of moral behavior was *love* for neighbor derived from God's nature as Father. The biological connotation of fatherhood with its counterpart in God's creative activity was far less important to him, as to the Hebrews in general in contrast to the Greeks, than its moral meaning which was implied in the idea of God's adoption of Israel on the basis of the Covenant. The Covenant for him, however, was interpreted in terms of God's taking moral responsibility for *all* men. The result was that, as against the false dichotomy of atheistic humanism, the commandment to love neighbor as self issued inevitably and naturally from his appreciation of God's profound and inexhaustible concern for mankind. Love of neighbor was thus not a rule like that to keep the Sabbath holy. Love was an inner disposition which emerged spontaneously when one had grasped God's gracious magnanimity and experienced forgiveness at his hands. It was man's response to a love which sought him before he recognized or deserved it, as the author of First John also sensed (4:7-21; cf. John 3:16). By the power of a great affection man was inspired to reproduce God's own love for man.

We can be more specific by noting three ways in which the

---

[12] See Albert Schweitzer, *Christianity and the Religions of the World* (New York: Henry Holt & Co., 1939).

meaning of love in human relationships was elaborated by Jesus in a distinctive manner. (*a*) It was the *sole test of right action*. With the intensity with which Paul lifted up agape as the supreme spiritual gift (I Cor. 13) Jesus taught that an inner disposition of good will which bore effective fruitage was the test of ethical living. Because the scribes tended to neglect it, Jesus dwelt almost exclusively upon inner disposition (Mark 7:1-23; Matt. 5:21-48), and his concentration upon the salvation of the soul of the sinner, rather than upon the social consequences of his actions, points to that emphasis (cf. Mark 10:17-27; Matt. 25:31-46). With all that, he never implied that wishing a neighbor well was enough. Love meant fruits consistent with the best interests of the neighbor. It meant service to others rather than being served. As the renowned Parable of the Good Samaritan, itself a parable of Jesus' own behavior, suggests, good will must be implemented by social action. Murder and adultery were not less wrong in deed because the act originated within the mind.

With his intense concern to state God's pure will Jesus apparently gave little attention to the problem of compromise in the face of alternatives which left no ideal choice, but his answer is clear. What may never be compromised in working out any ethical dilemma is the inner disposition of good will and the intelligent appraisal of the effects of conduct upon others. Good will includes the latter by definition.

b) Love in Jesus' view was *inclusive*. Following the highest levels of the Old Testament, Jesus enlarged the conception of "neighbor" beyond the equivalent of fellow Israelite which it connoted in Deuteronomic legislation and in much current practice. This wider definition was presupposed in the commendation of the good Samaritan. Those who passed the victim by did not even practice their own law, let alone love as Jesus understood it. This inclusive quality of love reached its climax in magnanimous behavior toward one's enemy. Indications of a concern for his enemies which the tradition does not elaborate (Matt. 23:37-39; Luke 23:34) make it clear that their best interests governed Jesus' actions even when he felt compelled to criticize them severely (Matt. 23:1-36). When the occasion required it, he was no less severe with his disciples (Mark 8:32-33) and his family. Furthermore, his conception of love forced him to combat the extreme nationalism of Zealot and apocalyptist, as his views regarding the nature of the final judgment most clearly reveal. It would not be a triumph of exclusive national interests, but instead the victory of God's righteousness, Jew and Gentile being judged by the same ethical standard. God had no favored-nation bias. His only interest was in obedience to his moral will. Paul grasped this larger perspective when he envisaged all distinctions of race, nationality, class, and sex as utterly irrelevant when men stood in the presence of God as revealed through Christ.

c) By its very nature love was *aggressive*. God's love forced him to seek the lost sheep until he found it, and in like manner it led Jesus to devote himself energetically to seeking and saving the lost. It compelled evangelism on the part of Jesus and his disciples, and it inspired Paul's mighty campaigns about the shores of the Mediterranean. It caused Jesus to take the offensive against the ecclesiastical and political leaders of Judaism, for their own sakes as well as for the sake of those who were being misled and injured by them. Peace*making*, not peace at any price, was his slogan, whatever the personal cost. Love's demands, when confronted with injustice and need, knew no alternative to

> Ever insurgent let me be,
> Make me more daring than devout.[18]

And when the final crisis came, its issue was the march on Jerusalem, not with the sword, but still with an energetic persistence in the form of vicarious sacrifice which defied passivity in responding to the claims of love.

3. Jesus' conception of God not only defined his ethical ideal; it supplied its *dynamic* as well. God could be trusted with the ultimate outcome of the struggle between the forces of good and evil. This faith in God's final victory is the main religious value of eschatology in general and of that which characterizes the New Testament in particular, whether it

[18] Louis Untermeyer, "Prayer."

be that of Jesus or the flaming apocalypticism of Revelation. Upheld by this faith, and sustained as well by evidences of God's power already at work to achieve his goal, Jesus moved unwaveringly ahead. He was completely mastered by a dream, and "He whom a dream hath possessed knoweth no more of doubting." [14]

A high estimate of man's moral potentialities also emerges from his outlook as a source of morale, because he looked at man from God's point of view as one created in God's image. To be sure, he did not underestimate the limitations of human nature. No man could become good enough fully to merit God's favor. He remained always in the position of an "unworthy servant." Even his most sincere repentance and his most strenuous ethical efforts could not bring or build the kingdom; it was God's prerogative to give it when he saw fit to do so (cf. Mark 1:15; 4:26-32; 9:1; Luke 17:22-37; 12:40; 21:34-36; Matt. 13:24-30; etc.). And if man chose to remain obstinately blind to God's purposes for him, he could conceivably place himself beyond the reach of divine forgiveness and redemption, being "lost" beyond recall. But this realistic view of human nature's limitations was surmounted by a much more positive appraisal. Man at least had freedom to choose for or against God, and that itself bespoke his dignity in God's sight. Jesus' ethical teaching assumed that man was capable of repentance and of a very discerning and imaginative response to God's moral will. Above all else, Jesus' example, which he bade his disciples follow, proves that he thought it made a great deal of difference how seriously and creatively man tried to co-operate with God's moral venture. What is the point of an appeal to spend oneself for one's neighbor, even to a cross, if the capacity to implement that challenge is nonexistent?

This confidence in man, however, was in last resort faith in God. Later reflection upon the crucifixion and resurrection of Jesus came to the conclusion that, long before man deserved it, God had taken the initiative to provide him with access to salvation. His love was expressed in the gift of his

[14] Sheamus O'Sheel, "He Whom a Dream Hath Possessed."

only begotten Son, and his victory over guilt as well as death was manifested in the Resurrection. Jesus anticipated this in the paradoxical way in which he related God's infinite mercy to his demands of ethical perfection, without qualifying either one. Man was incapable by his own efforts alone of fulfilling God's moral demands, but God's grace somehow enabled sinful man to receive forgiveness and to overcome evil with good. Man's part was a sincere response in repentance and a will completely dedicated to obedience, but it was God's grace which made possible their use in constructive ways even while man remained imperfect.

> Our strength is dust and ashes,
>   Our years a passing hour—
> But thou canst use our weakness,
>   To magnify thy pow'r.[15]

4. As for the Church, Jesus apparently did not think of his task as that of creating a nucleus which would evolve in ensuing centuries into an ecclesiastical body on earth. What little the records contain in this area, including the controversial passage about the Church being founded upon Peter (Matt. 16:17-19), must be interpreted within the context of Jesus' first-century eschatological orientation. Yet, simply by what he emphasized, Jesus defined the nature of his Church which was to emerge from his life and work. He was more concerned with the quality of its life than with its organizational forms, as was Paul when he employed the analogy of the body to describe its workings under the headship of Christ. The Church of Christ is essentially a body of disciples who are inspired by their experience of God in Christ to share Jesus' convictions about God and thus to reproduce his ethical values in their fellowship. This is always its distinguishing mark, whatever its denominational or ecclesiastical form.

Jesus also implied something of the relationship of the Church to the world, notably in such figures as that of light and leaven, which was later amplified in several New Testament documents. First Peter contains an inspiring presenta-

---

[15] John Haynes Holmes, "The Voice of God Is Calling."

tion of it, but in no place is it more beautifully and convincingly set forth than in the Letter to the Ephesians. According to this view the Church exists where there is harmony between Jew and Gentile on the basis of their common devotion to God in Christ. Divergent cultural patterns and inherited differences remain, but, as in a great symphony, they are absorbed into the synthetic harmony which expresses the imagination and feeling of the composer of the score. "One new man" emerges from the separate entities which previously existed. It is the divinely ordained destiny of the Church, its supreme privilege and responsibility, by the quality of its fellowship to serve as God's instrument in communicating this harmony to all mankind and thus helping to bring it into being throughout the whole created universe. However imperfectly it was realized, this was in fact the secret of the triumph of the early church in the Greco-Roman civilization of long ago. It will always be the secret of any achievement of the Church which has lasting value.

THE CONTEMPORARY CHRIST

Thus the historical Jesus makes his influence felt in the contemporary impact of his eternal Spirit, inspiring us to go beyond him but not against him. As the contemporary Christ he confronts us with the challenge to undertake a creative venture in human relations, so that ethical love of God's own making may be effectively expressed in current circumstances. We look back to him for guidance and dynamic, but we live and work in the present, and we are amazed to find him pointing to the needs which we confront as those with which he is concerned. He reminds us (Luke 11:29-32), as does Paul (Rom. 1:18-32), that each generation is judged in relation to the opportunities for learning and applying God's will which are peculiar to it, and he adds to this the thought that the effervescent wine of the gospel cannot be confined in old wine skins. In our circumstances this means a social interpretation and application of the gospel which translates Jesus' passion for souls into a realistic and courageous grappling with the problems inherent in the economic and political structure of our society. The full meaning of the everlasting good news is not thereby exhausted, but without it the Church has no word which makes much difference to multitudes of desperate persons struggling to free themselves from a web of socially conditioned frustration and despair. A vague hope of deliverance at some time in the indefinite future is not enough, and apocalyptic hopes of some immediate and final end to human misery apart from human agency but increase the frustration by their failure to mature. Confidence in God's ultimate victory beyond history is indispensable for morale, but this does not exhaust the Christian message either. The contemporary Christ comes *now* to seek and to save the lost. There are tasks which he has set for us to perform in *the present*. Only as his followers rise to that challenge can the modern world learn that Jesus Christ is truly the Saviour of mankind and its only Hope.

PART II

Basic Human Rights
and
The Community

3

The Person in the Community

Joseph Haroutunian

MANKIND HAS ALWAYS FOUND IT HARD TO REALIZE COM-
MUNITY ON THE BASIS OF HUMAN FREEDOM AND DIGNITY,
which are essential for personal existence. Men are perennially
tempted to disrupt community, and society has found it
necessary to devise religious, coercive, legal, utilitarian means
of keeping the members of human societies from disrupting
the bonds of the common life. Priests with their myths and
ceremonies, kings with their underlings and militia, legislators
backed up by police, have sought through the ages to maintain the group life needed for human existence. No wonder
that students of society have regarded communities as entities
formed either by brute force (Hobbes), or by "social contract" (Rousseau), or by some religious inducement (Durk-
heim), directed against some original impulse toward social
conflict and chaos.

Community life has in our time become as difficult as it is
imperative. Because of the increasing interdependence of men
in our industrial world, and the consequent need of increased
organization of human life into group life, this problem has
become one that is decisive to our very existence as well as
welfare. And yet, our generation has found no satisfactory
solution to it. Many nations and peoples have resorted to
totalitarian tyranny, and dictatorship has become a common
means of producing social cohesion. In lands where rule by
coercion is abhorred, community life suffers from disruptive

powers wielded by special interests, and what there is of it is in constant danger of deterioration. "Enlightened self-interest," which is trusted to hold the people together, falls short of that justice required for integration of races and classes into a society of persons. Even among peoples dedicated to "life, liberty, and the pursuit of happiness," or "the greatest good of the greatest number," human dignity and therewith authentic community suffer from a constant corruption, and society vacillates uncertainly between coercion and chaos. The demand for order threatens freedom, and the demand for freedom imperils order. Hence arises the dilemma that while men cannot exist except in community, community life is a difficult and terrifying problem.

The Christian View of Community

When a Christian considers this problem, he is struck by the radical disparity between the biblical view and our common views as to the origin, nature, and problem of community. According to us, community is formed by men desirous to seek their advantage. Self-interest brings men together and holds them together. Hence, lacking enlightenment, they submit to coercion; but when they are enlightened, they associate for their mutual benefit, as in a democracy. The Bible has a different view of the matter. The biblical community is a people called and bound together by God. The Hebrew community exists by an initial call of Abraham and his sons; by the deliverance from Egypt; by the covenant God entered into under Moses with the Hebrew people; by the law of God, by the judgments of God, by the faithfulness of God. The church, which is "the new Israel," is formed by the work of Jesus Christ; by his life and death and resurrection, by his ascension and lordship; by the advent of the Spirit; by the forming of the church as the body of Christ; by the new covenant, the law of love, the judgments of God, and the faithfulness of God. The new community is formed by the forgiveness of sins, or deliverance from sin and death, or reconciliation with God, by the new life in Christ and with one another. The new life is at once the life of the community

and the life of the person. The community is formed by conversion, and conversion is into the body of Christ, or the
Christian community. This community has its origin neither
in a natural affinity nor in a natural necessity, but in God;
in an act of God, and by the will of God.

What then is the nature of community? It is neither a
spontaneous nor a coerced association of men. It is not an
association for promoting self-interest or group interest. Community is the original expression of the life of man under the
law of God. It is a free association by virtue of a common
deliverance and a common covenant with God. It is a mandatory association in that the will of God is the rule of human
life. But its essential nature is signified by obedience to God
and a new regard for the welfare of the members of the community. A community is the scene of the exercise of concrete responsibility for justice according to the law of God.
It lives by men's concern for the dignity of men as members
of a society in covenant with God; by the common enterprise
against the indignities men suffer through injustice and want
and fear. The community, as the person, exists by its regard
for human welfare as defined by the law of God, which is
illuminated by the Bible. Where this law is disregarded,
human dignity is discarded, and we are confronted with
tyranny or chaos. In short, a community is a togetherness of
people made possible by man's restoration to that responsible
existence for which God made him, through Jesus Christ;
which responsibility is at once the exercise of authentic
humanity and the bond of community in which freedom
and order are realized together.

The Problem of Community Today

We must now draw attention to two aspects of the problem
of community which are peculiar to our time. The one has
to do with man's relation to the universe; the other has to
do with our "technological" society. These two have emerged
together, and they influence each other in a decisive fashion.
It is quite evident that faith in God presents a new difficulty
for the modern man. The total scene of human life has
changed. Man who lived in a finite world finds himself in a

world which is indefinitely extended, a world without boundaries and without shape or form. (Bruno, Descartes, Pascal,
Newton, Spinoza, Kant, Hegel, Nietzsche, James, and Dewey
are witnesses to this radical alteration of man's environment.)
In this new world without limits, man is lost, and his mind
is quite incapable of finding "the meaning of life." The setting of society has become an unsociable and mute environment without kinship with man and alien to his ultimate
concern with life and the meaning of history. With the loss
of a cosmos, the inner life of man has become a chaos, and
integration of man or the person has become a mirage. Man
now believes he exists in an ultimate unrelation, and this belief induces an anxiety which makes personal existence and
therefore community radically impossible. (This problem has
been discussed in my book *Lust for Power*, especially chapters 6–7.) Hence, social life has become a matter of preventing dissolution through totalitarian tyranny; and some countries have taken that course out of the modern man's misery.

We cannot go into this matter further in this essay. But
it must be pointed out that unless the church counters this
modern nihilism with the gospel of Immanuel, and learns to
preach this gospel to a people lost in their world, the church
will fail to contribute properly to the making of community
in this generation. This is a problem we have hardly begun
to face. And faced it must be. Let it suffice for the present to
say that the church is called upon to a new single-mindedness
in the preaching of the gospel as grounded, upheld, established in "the fact of Christ," "the whole Christ," as he lived,
died, rose again, and reigns. Jesus Christ came to save the lost
sheep—sheep lost in their world. *He* is the Shepherd. And
when the lost sheep of our day meet him, they shall be found
—they shall be in the fold of God, where there is peace.

More obvious is the second aspect of our problem: the
person in a society dominated by mechanical power. Such a
society imperils personal existence in several ways. It tempts
men to prefer goods to people. It now appears that progress
toward a maximum of prosperity is a cause prior to that of
the enhancement of community. Men lose both taste and ap-
titude for human intercourse illumined by love and under-

standing, and community is changed into organization for the primary purpose of increasing goods made by machines. Thus persons become subordinated to organizations, and people associate primarily for profit. They value not friendship but partnership. They work not by love but by calculation. And everything from education to religion becomes a means of promoting one's power and status. Even freedom, justice, and truth are valued in the context of economic power and lose their significance as exercise of humanity.

The evil consequences of such subordination of human values to economic advantages are all too evident. Men are estranged from one another and lost in the crowds of our urban society. They resent not being treated as human beings, and take vengeance by using others for their interests. They care not for community but for getting ahead of others, not for truth but for advantage, not for justice but for their "rights." Thus men and societies prosper, but they also lose the spice of life, which is in common care and common happiness. It now becomes hard indeed to reconcile power and love, and thus to establish community.

Human selfishness, inflamed by despair about life and destiny, has always made it difficult to be open to the neighbor's needs. Today with increased opportunities, afforded by our industries, for the exercise of selfishness, a human regard for common welfare has become next to impossible. When, as today, men hope to dispel all evil with an increase of knowledge and power, when they are even tempted to disavow human finitude, the temptation to concentrate upon one's own advantage is irresistible. Selfishness no longer appears as a temptation. It becomes "natural," and men practice it with energy even if with a confused conscience. When opportunities for "self-betterment" increase through power and prosperity, it becomes elementary good sense to subordinate others' welfare to one's own and to pursue one's interests with a new singleness of mind. The industrial society thus becomes an acquisitive society, and acquisition becomes the predominant motive of human activity.

Selfishness is now both concealed and confirmed by the formation of groups in pursuit of common ends. Society is broken up into "pressure groups," representing the interests of the several parties in it. Big business, little business; business and labor; labor and farmers; producers and consumers; crafts and professions—all these become organized and form power units, with great economic and political power at their disposal. Each group works for an end which goes beyond the interest of the individual and yet an end which includes the maximum furtherance of the individual's demands upon the commonwealth. Thus selfishness is at once obscured and realized. Society becomes the scene of organized conflict among "special interests" which become chronically incapable of working for the common good. Thus community is constantly sacrificed to partial interests, and justice is overwhelmed by group power.

Under these conditions personal—that is, responsible and loving—existence is suspended, and society becomes an aggregation of "mass men." The mass man is a man who is absolutely loyal to a group interest and exists for its furtherance. He is a man who has become incapable of criticism and whose mind is filled with the prejudices of the group of which he is a part. He no longer has a conscience of his own, and he identifies right and wrong with good and evil as dictated by the advantage of the group. As the group disrupts community, it also cancels the mass man's personality. Thus "special interests" at one and the same time do away with the person and with the community. They violate the freedom of the person while they violate the integrity of the community.

Primal humanity and our democratic tradition have been effective antidotes to the dehumanization threatened by modern "urbanism." Respect for the dignity of man is a deep-rooted impulse in our common life. Twenty centuries of a culture formed by the Bible and "Greek ideals" have produced a "humanism" which is far from spent and ineffective. We still believe in "the rights of man" and defend them with much enthusiasm. Education, politics, business, social life, are still permeated with concern for freedom and responsibility. We may still hope that democracy, in the full sense of the word, will be a going concern for a long time to come.

We cannot, however, overlook the vigor and effectiveness of the forces which put democracy in jeopardy. Our "urban civilization" as a whole represents a powerful threat to responsible human existence. There is much temptation to subordinate freedom of spirit to the pursuit of power and pecuniary advantage. For extra profits and higher wages, for possession and enjoyment of goods, for status and security, men are being constantly tempted to forego the exercise of authentic humanity in a common life of love for their fellow men and the exercise of intelligence for freedom and justice. Our traditional democratic values are becoming corrupted into ideological weapons wielded for furthering special interests. Propaganda is displacing information; emotions are gaining supremacy over reason: fear and anxiety in the presence of power are demolishing wisdom and good sense. Persons are acting as "mass men." It is doubtful if the usual forces making for community—our educational and political institutions—indispensable as they are, will be able to withstand the forces which are undermining both personal and community life.

The Tasks of the Church

1. The church's first task is to be the Church of Jesus Christ. No assumption is more ruinous for the church than that it is already the Church. The church is always in process. It is in process of becoming the Church, the community of believers, the people of God. The Christians are not Christians; they are being made into Christians. They are white men and colored men, Americans and Frenchmen, rich men and poor men, wise men and foolish men—all being converted into Christian men, into human beings who are human beings first, and white and American and rich or poor secondly. The first challenge the Christians have to meet is the challenge of the Son of man that they live as persons. God has established the Church for the end that those who are in it may live the new life of obedience to God's law of love and that thus the seed of the kingdom of God may be planted in the world. The church's doctrine, worship, discipline, social existence, have no other end than the restoration of man to the image of God, that is that true humanity of love for which God has created men. The essential, indispensable, decisive, unendable responsibility of the church, in the face of the challenge made by the world, is to be the means of grace whereby the Spirit of God shall create "the new creature" who has the mind of Christ in faith and hope and love, these three without which we live in sin and for death.

2. *It is the task of the church*, as led by the ministry, *to preach and educate*, so that the several impediments in the way of the Christian's assuming responsibility for the formation of community shall be removed. It has to become clear in the church that the Christian is his brother's keeper; that to be a follower of him who laid his life down for the brethren is to care for the same brethren, to care for their dignity, and freedom, and welfare. A man who is not engaged as a member of the body of Christ in confessing, with his deeds, the dignity conferred by Christ upon his fellow men, acts not as a Christian or a human being, but as one who repudiates Christ and those for whom he lived and died. Christian love is a matter of justice, of obedience to Jesus Christ, of responsibility which must be fulfilled before God, as a matter of life and death. To be a Christian is to be a person. To be a person is to exist in community. So to exist is to love one's neighbor as oneself. So to love is to do justly, to love mercy, and to walk humbly with God.

3. The Protestant churches are in principle congregations of God's people. They are communities first, and institutions secondly. *Their excellence is to be measured by the impetus they provide for the realization of community.* In the churches where men and women meet under God, they meet as human beings, in their condition as "flesh and blood," as beings who owe life to God and live by their hope in God, as "souls" who confront one another in their common knowledge of their freedom in Jesus Christ.

In a sense, the church's essential contribution to community life is its own existence as a community. It is in the "fellowship of saints" that the people exist as God's people and assume the responsibility to love their neighbor as themselves. The worship of God binds them together as God's people.

The gospel and the law—the grace of God in Jesus Christ and the demands God makes upon them through the covenant in Jesus and the prophets—confront them with their neighbor as God's children and the objects of his care. Their association in church life and activity becomes (must become!) a basis for their daily life and activity in the world. When they function as members of the Body of Christ, they learn to become members of the body politic whose end is freedom, justice, and brotherhood. Thus it is that the church contributes and must contribute (if it is to be church) to society in its "secular" dimension.

From a Christian point of view there is no secular life, as there is no life independent of God. Whether in the Church or outside, the Christian has no alternative but to decide for or against God, for or against obedience to God in love. God is everywhere, and everywhere man is under God—even though he deny it. The worship of God is not worship unless it be for obedience—we worship in the church and obey in the world. The church is where by worship we enter into community, but we express our existence as persons in community as we pursue the good life in our political or social relations. In short, the existence of the church, of the congregation of believers, is authenticated in the existence of "community" as characteristic of the totality of human relatedness.

4. *As Christians may not separate the fellowship of the church from their common life, they may not leave their common life out of their church.* Christians need to approach politics as Christians. Hence it is necessary that Christian congregations consider their social life not separately but together, for their mutual assistance and strengthening. As Christians associate in their churches, they need to meet one another with their common problems as citizens. The freedom and mutual love they have in Jesus Christ cannot but express itself in mutual concern and co-operation one with another as they set themselves to obey God in their daily lives. They owe it one to another, as members of Christ's Body, to enlighten one another, to seek one another's counsel, and to act toward a common mind as inspired by Jesus Christ. Therefore, it is hard to see how Christians can escape the responsi-

49

bility of inquiring in common after the will of God concerning their daily duties in the societies in which they participate. Thus, "social education" is a basic responsibility of the church.

But Christian education necessarily has a view to action —knowledge is for obedience, and obedience has to do with particular issues which arise in our public life. *It is inevitable that groups of Christians who consider God's will together should also seek to obey that will at any given time together.* They may not agree always as to what is to be done, but they must act in one or more ways. Christian communities cannot avoid making political decisions; and there is no reason for not acting in common. On the contrary, if Christians are serious about doing God's will, or acting toward the fulfillment of God's purpose at any time, they must increase the efficacy of their actions by acting together as Christians.

We must remind ourselves that personal existence is responsible existence. We are freed for responsibility in our fellowship in the church. Thus we are induced to help one another toward a knowledge of God's will in given situations and to act together as fellow Christians.

Suggested Areas for Social Action

I have said that social education in the church is to be toward particular decision and action in particular situations. However, there is such a thing as the human situation today. God in his providence has confronted us with certain issues which are decisions for personal and community life in our time. Let us consider several of these which place upon Christians an awful responsibility for obedience to God.

The World Upheaval

It is clear that we are living in an age when multitudes of people in our world, especially in Asia, Africa, the Near East, and South America, are filled with a new zeal and hope for a better life; for political freedom, for freedom from feudal oppression, for freedom from want and fear. What Christians do or do not do, faced with this human upheaval in three fourths of the world, will be a measure of their humanity and their obedience to God. There is no escaping our responsibility to love our neighbor as ourselves by giving every needed assistance to these multitudes in search of a life according to the dignity of man under God. If Christians are to do their present duty, they can do no other than to vitalize and increase manifold the Point Four program set forth by the American government. The government needs the sympathy, the understanding, the criticism, the co-operation, of the churches. It will be a calamitous failure on the part of the churches if they remain indifferent to this humane and mandatory undertaking. The Point Four program has had extremely weak popular support. The appropriations for it have been pitifully small. Besides, there is no clarity of motivation behind it. The contribution we might make to the well-being of "backward peoples" is bound to come short of furthering friendship between them and us because of a lack of authentic humanity on our part. The Asiatics, the Africans, and others will no longer tolerate treatment as inferior humanity even in the hands of those who for whatever reasons seek to help them in their quest for freedom and prosperity. No technical and political assistance can take the place of respect for their dignity as human beings as a condition of amity between the East and the West. We are called upon imperatively to treat men of different color, race, or culture from our own as our equals. But where are we to discern such equality except in our common humanity as revealed in Jesus Christ? And how is such humanity to be revealed and to become effective except in the Church of Jesus Christ? It is the present and inescapable responsibility of the churches to exist as communities and to become sources of community life in all the earth. Christians today are responsible for putting all their energy in the service of forces, especially in our government and in the United Nations, working for popular welfare in all the earth and to instill in such forces a respect for human dignity which is indispensable for justice and welfare in our time.

Toward Justice at Home

It is clear that the formation of community abroad is inseparable from the formation of community at home. Every

American Christian needs to be happy over popular well-being in our land. He needs to be jealous for the continuance and increase of community in our land. He needs to be concerned about our failure in humanity, about violations of human dignity, especially with regard to minorities, in our country. The fact is that, in the setting of the world ferment spoken of above, the extent of justice among us is insufficient. While we remain race and color conscious at home and deny equality of opportunity to millions of Americans, we cannot in spite of our great material power, establish our right to lead in the social upheaval of our time. Our respect for persons must remain unconvincing so long as we deal with large segments of our population as though they were not our equals as human beings. Hence it is imperative that the Christians in our land express their participation in communities of believers through a single-minded pursuit of equality for all the peoples in our land. Authentic community in our churches cannot be realized and confirmed without a continual exertion among us toward economic and political equality for all our people.

Here again, there are political and social forces already operative toward such equality. Christians are bound by their common life in the Church of Jesus Christ to co-operate fully with these forces. And they are to do so as men and women being humanized by their life in the Church, as beneficiaries of Jesus Christ and of the Holy Spirit, who is the Author of their life as persons. There will be no authentic community at home, as there will be none in the world at large, unless men be converted into that humanity for which Christ died and established his Church on earth.

Beyond Humanitarianism

Our society contains numerous agencies and institutions whose end is popular well-being. The poor, the sick, the orphans and widows, the old and the weak, people doing our dirty work and people living in our slums, ignorant people and immoral people—all these are objects of attention and help by our government and by sundry charitable organizations. The churches, severally and through federations or councils, have co-operated with the "secular agencies" in improving the lot of the unfortunates among us. Such work shall doubtless go on, and it shall remain a major expression of humanity among Christians. However, humanitarian zeal is a perilous affair. Insofar as the humanitarian excels in pity and prudence rather than in self-criticism, he is less than just and therefore less than human. Insofar as his benevolence presupposes a right to his material advantage and even his moral superiority, it confuses his duty as understood in the light of the commandment "Thou shalt love thy neighbour *as thyself.*" Thus, while the poor are fed and the sick provided with medical attention, human dignity suffers and community life remains impoverished and diseased. The distinction between the privileged and the unprivileged becomes sharp and permanent, and the latter are continually frustrated in their yearning for freedom and opportunity. Thus good is turned into evil, and authentic community and personal life alike are thwarted.

Toward a Maximum Distribution of Power

Hence "social service" cannot be separated from co-operation with the "lower classes" toward the increase of economic and political power among them. The "social revolution" in America is not so obvious and dramatic as it is in Asia or Africa or South America. Nevertheless, the "lower classes" in our country are as determined as those anywhere to achieve the power requisite for their freedom and prosperity. They are being organized for their welfare and have already achieved great gains toward equality. It must be obvious that in principle the organized power of those who have in the past been underprivileged is salutary for the whole of our society. Community means common dignity, which means common freedom and power. The Christian must therefore be in sympathy with the extension of power into all of our society, and he must co-operate with any movement toward a maximum distribution of political and economic power. The chronic antipathy of many Christians in our land toward underprivileged minorities making a bid for power is a sign of failure in the churches to realize both humanity and community. It is time that this antipathy be overcome and that Christians strengthen the arm of all those who are seeking to escape inferiority among us. It is needless to add that unless such humanity be exercised at home, it cannot be exercised abroad.

Summary

The person and the community exist together. They exist by obedience to the law of God, namely, "Thou shalt love thy neighbour as thyself." Such obedience is a fruit of faith which means freedom from bondage to "sin and death" through the work of Jesus Christ and the Spirit of God in the Church. The Church is the nascent community which exists for a common life of dignity and justice. The validity and the vitality of the worship of God is expressed through the Christians' pursuit of justice and freedom in their daily lives, in their economic and political life. To become Christian is to be in the process of conversion to authentic humanity as seen in Jesus Christ, and such humanity cannot be realized without full responsibility for proper action which shall issue in the increase of freedom and justice in the world, both near and afar off, at home and in the rest of this planet, today, especially among races, tongues, and nations which have embraced a new promise of total well-being.

4

The Family in Relation to Church and Community

Donald M. Maynard

IN DEALING WITH THE CHURCH AND SOCIAL RESPONSIBILITY, WE ARE CONCERNED ABOUT DISCOVERING HOW THE CHURCH, as an institution, and its members, as individuals, may more effectively contribute to the building of a society in which everyone shall have an opportunity to live the more abundant life. The church acts as an institution in society—it has a corporate entity, to be sure—and as the body of Christ on earth is more than simply the sum total of its members. Nevertheless, it must not be forgotten that if the church is to assume its responsibility in society, it can do so only as those who make up its membership are socially sensitive, have genuine concern for the welfare of others, and are willing to submerge their personal interests for the sake of larger purposes and to identify their personal interests with the welfare of all. There must be genuine respect for all persons, regardless of race, color, or creed, an ability to see clearly and to analyze correctly the social forces that are shaping society today. There must likewise be an aggressiveness that grows out of a sense of mission—a conviction that something can be done to bring in a more Christian social order—a willingness to experiment.

As I have enumerated some of the characteristics of an individual who is socially sensitive and responsible, let us note that many of them are the qualities that are most likely to be developed within the family circle—if they are to be developed at all. To be sure, we need to guard against an over-enthusiastic or exaggerated appraisal of the influence of the family upon its members. We must not forget that other forces play upon the individual—especially the community and one's associates. At the same time, it is primarily in the home that attitudes are formed and behavior patterns are set. Therefore, in any discussion of the church and social responsibility, we are concerned about family life.

EMOTIONAL STABILITY AND SOCIAL RESPONSIBILITY

Social responsibility that is wise and social action that is intelligent, as a rule, are manifested by individuals who are emotionally stable and mature. To be sure, neurotic individuals sometimes compensate for feelings of inferiority, insecurity, or guilt by enthusiastically participating in social-action projects. Individuals who cannot run their own lives successfully but who delight in trying to run the lives of others are known to us all. But such individuals are likely to become fanatics whose judgment is questionable and whose behavior is erratic. Mature social action is the result of emotional stability. But emotional stability is most likely to be the outcome of a wholesome family life in which an individual feels secure because he has a sense of belonging, because his worth is recognized by members of the group, and because he is accepted for what he is. It is as individuals have respect for themselves that they are capable of having intelligent concern for others. An individual who is tied up in emotional knots, who feels isolated from his fellows, and who is filled with hostility toward himself and others will retard, rather than hasten, a program of social reconstruction.

It is in primary social groups that one's emotional needs are satisfied, and the family is the first and most significant, although not the only, primary group. By a primary group we mean that social grouping in which one feels himself to be an important part, in which he has face-to-face relationships with others in the group, and in which all the members of the group have mutual respect and concern for each other. Secondary groups are those in which one feels himself to be a stranger, groups with which one's contacts are casual, or if more frequent, at least largely impersonal. It is increasingly realized that one must have a vital primary group of his own if he is to be mentally and spiritually healthy. Paul H. Landis reminds us that although many adults spend most of their time with secondary groups, each adult tries to create for himself a primary group in which he receives sympathy and personal attention from others.[1] The phrase "feel at home" is more than a sentimental expression. It denotes something that is essential for wholesome living.

Throughout the remainder of this discussion reference will be made to the importance of primary groups. Our attention now must be directed more specifically to the family as the primary group that more than any other will determine the welfare of civilization. As one writer said, contemplating the return of the soldiers after World War II, if wholesome, happy adjustments can be made at the family level, happiness will be manifest in all the affairs of the country.

WHAT IS HAPPENING TO FAMILY LIFE TODAY?

That changes are taking place in family life, no one can deny. To be sure, families in America differ according to geographical location, race, nationality, and economic class. But even if we refer to families rather than family, it still is true that significant changes are taking place. This is not surprising, however, as the family as a social institution reflects the pattern of culture that exists at a given time and place.

It is more or less inevitable that the transition from an agricultural economy to an industrial, monetary economy should bring a shift in the function and nature of the family system. It is to be expected that in such a shift the family should face many difficulties and endure considerable stress and strain. Furthermore, it is only as we have an understanding of what is happening to the family that we can intelligently plan for the conservation of family integrity in the future. To deal with the family of today and tomorrow as if it were typical of the family of the past makes impossible an understanding of the possibilities and limitations of the family and

[1] See *Social Policies in the Making* (Boston: D. C. Heath & Co., 1947), p. 64.

delays the planning for church and community services that will make the family a vital factor in the world of tomorrow.[2]

What are the changing functions of the modern family as contrasted with those of the family of the past? The most obvious is the change from a producing unit in society to a consuming unit. The family of our forefathers was largely a self-sufficient economic unit in itself. The family grew its own food, made its own clothes, built its own houses. Because of these functions a large family was desired. As members of the family went about their responsibilities, they had experiences of working together, playing together, suffering hardships together, rejoicing in successful experiences. Many children in the family meant that each one had to learn to cooperate with the others, to think of the welfare of the family group as well as his own. As a producing group, members of the family were able to see the product of their labors and receive the satisfaction that comes from an awareness of a task well done. A cellar lined with shelves of canned goods, or a dress made by the mother, gave a sense of achievement that contributed to her emotional health. Working, playing, and suffering together brought a sense of closeness and unity to members of the family—a feeling of belonging and security. To be sure, there were exceptions to what some may consider to be an overidealistic picture, but in substance it is correct.

Today the family is no longer primarily a producing unit. Bakeries, laundries, groceries, restaurants, and clothing stores have made unnecessary the function of production. No longer is it an independent unit in society, but it is increasingly dependent upon others for its welfare; this dependence, furthermore, is largely impersonal in character. Who knows or cares about who bakes your bread, grows the vegetables you eat, or makes the clothes you wear? With the family as a consuming rather than a producing unit, the sense of interdependence among its members is considerably lessened. Mechanical gadgets get the tasks of housework done more quickly and more easily—and are not to be despised—but they make more dif-

[2] See the article "What Is Happening to the American Family?" by Margaret Mead in *Pastoral Psychology*, June, 1950, pp. 40 ff.

ficult the finding of common tasks that will bind members of the family together.

With the decline of the economic function there is also a decline of the secondary functions, such as education, religion, recreation, and protection. Nursery schools, longer hours in the public school, extracurricular activities, and even radio and television are providing much of the education which was formerly the responsibility of the parents. Church schools on Sunday, vacation church schools during the summer, weekday classes in religion, summer conferences for young people, and an increasing number of weekday nursery groups run by the church tend to relieve parents of some of the feeling of urgency they have had in the past for guiding the religious development of their children. No longer is the family dependent upon its own resources for recreation. The Boy and Girl Scout movements, the program of recreation of the public schools and the church, the vast amount of commercialized recreation, again including television and radio, limit the amount of time a family has to spend together in recreational pursuits. Policemen and firemen furnish the physical protection of the household that formerly was the responsibility of the family.

The family, then, has lost many of its historic functions. What remains? Meyer F. Nimkoff names four functions of the family today: reproduction, child care, informal education, and the giving and receiving of affection. He adds, "As a social institution, competing for power with other institutions, the family has suffered a loss of responsibilities, but as a personal institution, serving the psychological needs of its members, the family has probably experienced a net gain."[3]

This transition from an institutional to a companionship family has not taken place without changes in the structure of the family. William F. Ogburn reminds us that the family of today is about a quarter smaller than that of the colonial family; marriage probably occurs later in life, especially for women; many more families are without children; and more

---

[3] *Marriage and the Family* (Boston: Houghton Mifflin Co., 1947), p. 601.

homes are broken by separation and divorce.[4] And an increasing number of families are living in multifamily units, rather than in individual homes.

Our concern is the function of the modern family to meet the psychological needs of the members of the family so that they may become well-adjusted citizens of society. Is the family of today meeting the needs of its members?

It is possible to answer this question with a resounding "No," pointing to the rapid increase in the number of divorces, the appalling amount of juvenile delinquency, the rise of what Carle C. Zimmerman calls "psychopathic personalities," and the high percentages of problems relating to the family that are brought not only to professional marriage counselors but to ministers as well. But this is not the entire picture. Much can be said in favor of the modern family. Nevertheless, it is in a sufficiently critical condition to warrant our consideration of the factors that mitigate against its fulfilling satisfactorily its task of building well-adjusted, emotionally mature personalities. If the church and the community are to serve the family as they should, they must understand the forces that are shaping family life today.

First of all, in an agricultural economy the family as a producing unit is exceedingly important. With the change to capitalistic industrialism, the family as a unit lost much of its significance. As one writer says:

Free, independent family members, mobile families, individualistic rather than patriarchal families, dependent not self-sufficient families, home as consuming centers rather than productive agencies, these were essential to the new industrialism. It is a noteworthy fact that wherever capitalist industrialism has penetrated it has dissolved the family-centered culture ("familism") for the person-centered family ("individualism").[5]

[4] See "The Family and Its Functions" in *Recent Social Trends in the United States* (New York: McGraw-Hill, 1933), I, 661-65. It should be noted that as of 1952, marriages are earlier and families somewhat larger than in 1933, but many feel this is not a permanent pattern of family life.

[5] Reinhardt, Meadows, and Gillette, *Social Problems and Social Policy* (New York: American Book Company, 1952), p. 254.

Another writer takes much the same position when he says:

It may as well be acknowledged at the outset: American life is no longer family-centered. Urban life is built about the individual, not the family unit. Its social life is for the pair, not the family. To find husband, wife, and children at a social gathering one must go to some remote rural area; urban society is stratified by age-groups.[6]

EMPHASIS ON "INDIVIDUALISM" RATHER THAN "FAMILISM"

This emphasis upon the individual and his rights and privileges, wholesome as it is in many respects, has also created many social problems, especially for the family. It has tended to produce a generation whose primary concern is for their own individual happiness, rather than the welfare of others. Teachers and parents who did not fully grasp the insights of the progressive-education movement were frequently unable to distinguish between freedom and license. The child-psychology movement, stressing the importance of meeting the emotional needs of children and suggesting new ways of discipline, was likewise misunderstood by many who falsely concluded that the child must be preserved from any experience that might thwart his wishes. Stress was placed upon children's rights rather than upon their responsibilities. Again, let us remember that this is not the whole picture. The progressive-education movement, the emphasis upon the child and his needs, has done much to develop a generation of young people who are capable of adjusting to the demands of our day. But the emphasis upon individualism has tended to create an atmosphere in which the qualities of unselfishness, self-control, and sacrifice are not exalted. And the family has suffered. Family life will not succeed except as its members are more concerned about the rights of others than about their own, except as they are willing to exercise self-control, understanding, and patience. It is to be hoped that Zimmerman is exaggerating the picture when he says, "Even now it is far from fashionable to find the slightest grounds for asking

[6] Landis, *op. cit.*, p. 227.

an individual to make any great sacrifice to hold his family together." [7]

In our democratic society we have tended to glorify the idea of romantic love and to pride ourselves upon the fact that young people are free to choose their mates on the basis of love. It is rather startling, therefore, to note Margaret Mead's statement that "romantic love puts a premium on choosing a mate in utter disregard of his or her suitability." Free choice did not create such a problem two or three generations ago when one was likely to marry the girl next door and to live in a community in which one had an established position. Today, with the increasing mobility of our population, the situation is entirely different. As Miss Mead says,

Increasing mobility has torn people from their roots, and we now probably have the largest number of marriages that history has ever known of couples who have no visible reason for ever getting together, who share no common background whatsoever, who have no common friends, no common past, not even a dog they can both remember! [8]

Robert E. L. Faris, in discussing the social disorganization of the family, notes that "marriages involving independence from parents, difference of status and background, detachment from community life and responsibilities, and other conditions approved by the romantic tradition, actually have much less possibility of happiness." He then adds, "This knowledge, however, is not as widely distributed and perhaps has less appeal in itself than the romantic mythology." [9]

Although it is perhaps to be expected as a result of the individualism of our day and its emphasis on romantic love, nevertheless it is disturbing to note the widespread acceptance of the idea of divorce as an easy way out of any family difficulties that may arise. Margaret Mead feels that the most serious aspect of the divorce rate is not so much the number of divorces as it is the expectation of divorce. She says, "It seems to me, as an anthropologist, that the most serious thing

[7] *The Family of Tomorrow* (New York: Harper & Bros., 1949), p. 3.
[8] *Op. cit.*
[9] *Social Disorganization* (New York: Ronald Press, 1948), p. 283.

that is happening in the United States, the most significantly important, is that people enter marriage now with the idea that it is terminable." [10] Consequently, in addition to all the other adjustments that inevitably must be made in family life, there is also the constant fear that the marriage itself may be dissolved. A case in point is the more or less flippant comment of a girl asking her minister to perform the ceremony at her marriage to a young man she did not know too well: "If it doesn't work, we'll get a divorce." This attitude toward divorce is also an indication of the decreasing conviction of the religious sanctity of marriage.

POPULATION MOBILITY CREATES PROBLEMS FOR THE FAMILY

Any consideration of family life today must take into account the increasing mobility of our population. There are two types of mobility. Vertical mobility is the shifting of individuals from one class in society to another. The trucker's son becomes governor of his state; the minister's daughter becomes an outstanding columnist, moving in a society foreign to that experienced in her home. The Horatio Alger theme of the poor boy making good is not without its examples today. This process of vertical mobility, however, is creating in individuals a feeling of stress and strain not known to many of our forefathers. As individuals get into new and better occupations, perhaps in communities far away from their homes, they lack that sense of security that comes from following a traditional occupation and way of life. There is contact with divergent social standards, values, and patterns of life. There is the struggle to make good in the new job. Without the support of the primary groups he has known in the past, one is likely to become tense and restless, filled with anxieties and forebodings. It is not strange that Lawrence Frank should suggest that the dominant aspect of home and family life today is the presence of frustrations and anxieties.[11]

Horizontal mobility—that is, moving from place to place —is even a greater problem for the family than is vertical mo-

[10] *Op. cit.*
[11] See Bernhard J. Stern, Ed., *The Family, Past and Present* (New York: D. Appleton-Century Company, Inc., 1938), pp. 251-55.

bility. As individuals move about, there is the likelihood of emotional tensions, feelings of insecurity and fear. Loneliness leads one to seek companionship—almost any kind of companionship. Young people meet, are attracted to each other, and after a whirlwind courtship are married, knowing very little of each other's background. When the thrill of the honeymoon is over and the couple settle down to family life, they discover how little they have in common, and problems arise.

Zimmerman feels that the high mobility of persons is associated with accompanying high mobility of social values. He says:

> Values, provincialism, faith, and beliefs of all types which vary from class to class and region to region, come into constant contact with each other. All ideals are compared with conflicting values and ideals from other sources. Out of this heterogeneous and changing situation arises a general skepticism of all the values of life, since so many are challenged by the constant juxtaposition with the opposite or the new. An increasing number don't know what to believe. Out of this arises a reshuffling of the bases of value systems themselves—from social to individual. More and more the individual sees only his own immediate interest because the social and long term individual values are difficult to visualize.[12]

Needless to say, family life does not prosper when its members are skeptical of all the social values of life and are primarily concerned with their own individual interests.

Space permits only the enumeration of other factors that are threatening the family. The new position of women, with their freedom, their opportunities to have careers of their own, and their lack of training for family life, must be recognized. A president of an outstanding woman's college in the East takes the position that modern colleges are not fitting their graduates for home life. Many women feel that it is largely a waste of time to keep the house clean, to cook meals, and to look after the children.

[12] *Op. cit.*, p. 12.

The influence of multifamily dwellings upon home life is great. They tend to discourage the having of more than one or two children in a family. There is an increase in impersonal relationships with one's geographical neighbors and the feeling that it doesn't make any difference to anyone what happens to the family. The stress and strain that arise from living in close quarters must not be minimized. There is a tendency to find one's recreation away from home. Lack of privacy can be irritating. Elmer H. Johnson, writing on family privacy in a multi-unit dwelling, refers to the experience of two neighboring families who were dining with only the apartment wall between them. One wife asked her husband in a normal tone, "Please pass the ketchup." The husband next door passed the ketchup to his surprised wife.[13]

Other disintegrating forces mentioned by the Conference on Family Life held in Chicago in 1951 are:

The hectic pace of living which leaves us so little time in our homes; our demand for things, stuff, money and materials (that) deaden our spiritual sensitivity; the multitude of organizations that compete with home life . . . the too frequent separations of members of families by their vocational obligations; the decay of our belief in the importance of religion . . . and our cheap philosophy about sex at a personal level.[14]

How the Church May Conserve Family Integrity

As we turn now to a consideration of ways by which the church may help conserve family integrity today, let it be noted that first in importance is its responsibility to furnish individual members or families, and families as families, with a Christian fellowship that is vital and significant—a fellowship, a primary group, in which its members are bound together by understanding, respect, and concern, and above all by a common fellowship with God through Christ. This is what the church is supposed to be—a *fellowship* of believers. Unfortunately, altogether too frequently our churches become only

[13] See "Family Privacy in a Multi-Unit Dwelling," in *Marriage and Family Living*, August, 1952, pp. 219 ff.
[14] See "Christian Family Living in Today's World," advance resource materials for members of the Conference on Family Life, p. 17.

congregations of believers. Landis reminds us that "even the urban church group seems to lack the warm touch of the country or small-town church where everyone shakes hands with everyone else and where all stand about for a friendly chat after the sermon is over. In the city church all feel like strangers." [15]

It is the city church especially, therefore, that must discover ways of providing more primary group experiences for its members. In city churches will be found young married couples and even older couples who are far away from their childhood homes. They do not have the emotional support of grandparents and old friends. The competition to make a living has kept them from making many friends. The church has a responsibility to draw them into its fellowship, to make them significant members of smaller groups within the church. We are learning a great deal about the value of group-work techniques for the conservation of mental and emotional and spiritual health. Let the church provide these smaller groupings—groupings into which people are not "put" but which arise out of common interests and problems. And remember that just as an individual needs others, so do families need contact with other families.

Many of the fellowship groups will be composed of those who are approximately the same age—rightly so. There will be real value, however, if the church can make possible fellowship among families whose members differ considerably in their ages. As young people face the problems of marital adjustment and the guidance of children, it often is a source of strength to have a close relationship with those who are older and more experienced. Miss Mead, noting that sometimes present-day families are accused of having lost their moral fiber, dryly comments that "the family, instead of losing its moral fiber, may have lost grandmother!" [16] Perhaps one of the functions of the church is to provide grandparents for the younger families of the church and community.

Wesner Fallaw, in his significant work *Towards Spiritual*

[15] *Op. cit.*, p. 63.
[16] *Op. cit.*

Security, reminds us that the chief responsibility of the church is to help families become a spiritual fellowship motivated by love and appreciation for each member. He insists that the two spiritual fellowships, that of the family and that of the church, must not be thought of as two separate fellowships. He feels that "the fellowship that is imbued with Christ's spirit as found in the true church and the true family is a single fellowship. It is one, though it is operating in two phases on the human scene." [17] He objects, therefore, to references to the church *and* the family, or church *and* parent co-operation, and stresses the church-family relationship. Although one may feel that his criticism of certain current attempts of the churches to bring about greater co-operation between parents and teachers, for example, is not entirely valid, there can be no disagreement at all with his major thesis that the church must help the family realize that it, the family, is the primary agency for religious living, guidance, and instruction. Neither can there be disagreement with his emphasis upon the importance of helping members of the family face frankly the motives, desires, prejudices, and customs which bind them into rigid patterns of behavior that restrict and sometimes destroy fellowship among families and groups not only in the community but in the church as well.

Fallaw maintains that church-family education can provide the unity and spiritual reality that homes must have if families are to remain families, and it can cure a large part of our social ills and restore spiritual security to lonely and fearful persons. As church-school teachers and parents come together in a continuing fellowship to consider ways by which the family may indeed become a school of Christian living, as under skilled leadership mothers and fathers are helped to "think of every significant choice and major crisis as their opportunity to deliberate and grow as Christians with their children," the family will become less prone to reflect the conventional standards of society and will be more likely to undertake, in daring freedom, to change the social order. A family dedicated to God's will may take a stand against racial dis-

[17] Philadelphia: The Westminster Press, 1952, p. 140.

crimination and local and wider injustices. "We want our children to abide by the Christian ideals and actions that they learn in the church. We know that for most of them to do so, parents must be helped to find Christian fellowship and thus throw their weight against social cleavages, class distinctions, racial discriminations, and merely respectable religion." [18]

Earlier in this discussion attention was called to the fact that this is an age in which the individual and his rights, rather than the family and its rights, are stressed. This is the day and age of age groups. Let us not minimize the importance of age-group activities. They have made the program of the church more vital to boys and girls and young people, and yes, even adults. At the same time, let there be a genuine effort to provide in the church's program more opportunities for the family to be together as a family group. A beginning has been made in our churches in the form of family nights, family recreation, and family camps and outings. Much more needs to be done in this area without, let me emphasize, interfering with the values of the age-group programs. Important as it is for the family to engage in activities together, it is equally important that its members have close contacts with others of their own age outside the family group.

This is not a manual on church-family activities, in the sense that I can here mention all the specific possibilities for such a program.[19] A church that is aware of its responsibility to the family will discover many ways of helping stabilize the family groups in its membership—and even in the community. For example, let us not forget the responsibility of the church to help prepare its young people for marriage—co-operating insofar as possible with community agencies that have a like concern. Courses on boy and girl relationships, on problems of courtship, and on preparation for marriage are of real value if conducted in such a way that they deal realistically, and not sentimentally, with the problems young people face. Young married couples, as they belong to a fellowship of

[18] *Ibid.*, p. 150.

[19] Leaders of denominational and interdenominational family-life programs should be contacted for specific suggestions.

other young couples who may take a course on making marriage successful, in which they face frankly the problems of interpersonal relationships in the home, are likely to gain the assurance that their own problems are not insurmountable. Although such a course, under the guidance of one adequately prepared to help them, is of great value, it should not be forgotten that as young couples themselves interchange some of their experiences and problems, they also receive help. The church should also provide opportunities for them to counsel with the minister or others in the congregation. In a large Midwestern church the pastor, a skilled counselor in marriage and family problems, has a group of young and middle-aged couples whom he has helped gain insights into how to counsel other couples. He has found these couples to be of invaluable help in working with those who need marriage counseling. Frequently they have worked through the same problem that is now the concern of those whom they counsel.

Let us not forget the value of study groups for parents in which parents are helped to deal with the everyday problems in the home and to gain an understanding of how children may become emotionally and spiritually healthy. Genuine interest is manifest when such courses get away from the purely theoretical and get right down to practical problems —such problems in the area of religion, for example, as how to answer questions about God, prayer, or immortality. The church should help its parents understand how to provide their children with sane, wholesome sex education. Problems of discipline, how attitudes are formed, how to deal with jealousy, are all of tremendous concern to parents. Incidentally, it has been suggested that there should be a course for grandparents on modern insights into child guidance, so that they may be of help, rather than hindrance, to their sons and daughters as they deal with their children.

The churches can adapt their church-school curriculum materials for church-family use. It is not necessary for a denomination to have an entirely new set of materials in order to do this. As teachers and parents work together in discovering how the materials may be used to help growing boys and girls, it is inevitable that the experiences of the child in the home and in the church will have unity and integrity. One mother reports that she finds the church-school materials helpful in providing meaningful family-worship experiences during the week.

The church, too, can suggest social-action projects for families, projects that will take the family away from its own immediate concerns and will center its attention upon others. The nature of these projects will arise largely out of the community situation and the larger denominational program.

The church, in working with families, will not forget that although it is dealing with all the families of the church, it is also dealing with specific families. No two families have exactly the same need. Seward Hiltner reminds us that with the family as with the individual, the church must be casework minded.[20]

The church must not limit its concern to its own families, of course. Let it co-operate with all the agencies in the community that are concerned about family welfare. Let it be vigorous in its support of better-housing plans, of more intelligent adoption laws, of attempts to secure uniform state marriage and divorce laws, of efforts to improve the caliber of radio and television programs for children, and of proposals that tend to abolish injustice in any form in the community. Let it co-operate in community family-life workshops, workshops that enlist the enthusiastic support of all the community agencies and organizations interested in family life. In a family-life workshop in San Francisco, for example, representatives of the church participated, and recognition was given to the important part that the church and religion play in family-life education.[21]

Margaret Mead says:

[20] See his chapter, "The Protestant Approach to the Family," in a symposium, *The Family—A Christian's Concern,* published by the Woman's Division of Christian Service, Board of Missions and Church Extension of The Methodist Church.

[21] See Ward Phebe, "A Community Conducts Its First Family Life Workshop," in *Marriage and Family Living,* Winter, 1951.

For the people who feel that the family is in great danger, it is important to realize what a tough institution it is, and how religious and ethical systems the world over have depended on the family. We often hear that religion is the support of the family, but it is equally true that the family is the support of religion and that religious and ethical systems tie themselves into this firmest of human institutions.[22]

We can look forward with confidence, therefore, to the continuing integrity of the family.

[22] *Op. cit.*

5

Race Relations and Civil Rights

Walter W. Sikes

On a Sunday in December, 1952, Neson Cornelius entered a restaurant on Illinois Street in Indianapolis near the Y.M.C.A. where he was a guest and sat down to await service. He was completely ignored at first. Later the manager told him he could not be served. As he arose to go, he remarked, "I am sorry . . . I have come a long way . . . 10,000 miles." On further inquiry the manager learned he was from India and not, as he had mistakenly thought at first, an American of African descent. He then urged him to sit down and be served.

This incident, one of several embarrassing experiences for Mr. Cornelius and quite in keeping with the common practice generally in the United States, led him to terminate his stay in America, where he was on an exchange program subsidized by the Ford Foundation, under the sponsorship of the National Council of Y.M.C.A.'s. He returned to New Delhi to report his impressions of America to his Y.M.C.A. board, which includes Rajendra Prasad, President of India, and to his friends, Premier Jawaharlal Nehru among others. "I have had many pleasant experiences, many courtesies and generosities," he said in recounting this incident, but he added that his experiences and observations of discrimination against people of color made the "one impression that is breaking down all the other impressions I have of this country." He is a Christian, and he was especially hurt by what he saw in our churches. "At this time," he added sadly, "I am completely disillusioned. . . . What is the use of having a church if you do not allow the spirit of Christ to be there?"

This response of Neson Cornelius may seem unjustifiable to some Americans, especially since he admits it reflects only a part of what he saw of race relations in this country. But we cannot ignore this one fact—that race relations have become the most sensitive touchstone by which the political effectiveness, the moral insight, and the religious sincerity of Christendom, especially in America, are being judged throughout the world. Moreover it does not lie within our power to charge off our failures in race relations against a column of worthy achievements. This simply does not make sense to the 1,500,000,000 dark-skinned people in the world, nor indeed to a growing number of the remaining 750,000,000 light-skinned. The treatment accorded members of the colored majority by the white minority is read as a significant symbol of meanings beneath the surface of events that constantly emerge as cruel fact to harass and offend the darker peoples.

At the very time Neson Cornelius was suffering the hurt of these ambiguities in our culture, three events of great importance for race relations were taking place. One was in Washington, D. C., where attorneys were arguing before the Supreme Court five cases originating respectively in three northern states, one southern state, and the District of Columbia, each of which contests the present practice of denying to Negro children the right of attending school without discrimination. Another was in New York City, where the General Assembly of the United Nations was debating, in its respective committees, a number of proposed actions, each tantalizing in its complexity but in all of which this one issue of the rights of colored people was the central consideration. Among these questions was that of whether the United Nations should undertake to curb the color-caste policies of the present South African government; another was whether the "administering authorities" of the "non-self-governing peoples"—new names for old colonial powers and their colonies—should be obligated to continue reporting their policies and practices to the world through the United Nations; and a third was whether the UN should support the demands of certain colored nations, particularly in northern Africa, for self-government and independence. Another simultaneous event was taking place in Kenya, Africa, where members of a secret society with frightening power, the Mau Mau, were carrying on a terrorist campaign to drive the white man out of Kenya. A number of other incidents of similar import could be mentioned—such as the imprisonment of the son of Mahatma Gandhi in South Africa, along with a few thousand others, for resistance against the government for its policies of racial oppression, and the burning of the U. S. Information offices by a rioting mob in the ancient city of Bagdad.

These incidents remind us of the crucial situation in race relations the world over. This is not new, of course, but this age-old problem has reached new dimensions of both depth and breadth in our day. It is rapidly taking on both intensity and extension. These new forms of the "irrepressible conflict" of race and color arise to split political parties in our own land over disagreements for dealing with it; to challenge government agencies with the dilemmas it creates in military forces, in public transportation, housing, and health; to demand review of old legal interpretations and enactment of new laws; and to confront the churches with imperious calls to repentance for conforming their lives to the world of caste instead of being transformed by a renewal of their minds.

THE SICKNESS OF A DIVIDED WILL

If we seek to understand why this crisis in race relations confronts us now in such critical forms, we may begin by noting the most obvious, and to many probably the most urgent, expression of the crisis. It grows out of the fact that the colored peoples of the world, who have been held in various forms of subjugation by the white nations of the West, have now come to the day of deliverance. In the words of Dr. Buell G. Gallagher, they "aspire to a position of freedom from white control and to acceptance in a position of equality. They will endure white domination as long as it is physically necessary to do so and not one moment longer." [1] Both they and we know that the day is approaching when such necessity will end. The tides of history which placed the Western nations in control of Asia and Africa and the isles of the sea are being rapidly reversed. A couple of centuries ago, more or less in particular cases, the civilizations of Asia, after long periods of great cultural achievement, fell into decline. Simultaneously the West was resurgent, with the instruments created by new sciences in their hands with the preponderant military power these gave, and with the lust for political supremacy and for riches as their driving motives. They became the legatees of these decadent civilizations. But now the West is in desperate crisis. And a new spirit of national destiny, a new confidence in their solidarity against the West, a new faith in the justice of their cause, inspire these peoples to seek their freedom and equality now.

The situation is complicated for the West and its urgency greatly increased by two other facts. The first is the dynamic character of Soviet imperialism, which shares—for different reasons—the common aim of these darker races to end the domination of the West in Asia and Africa. The second is that America, thrust into her new role as political and moral leader of the West, has largely forfeited the confidence and respect of these peoples by reason of our policies in dealing with racial minorities at home and colored peoples abroad. We have earned instead their suspicion, distrust, and even hatred.

This, in brief, is what the President's Committee on Civil Rights called the "international reason" for action now to improve the situation as to civil rights for minority peoples. The committee said:

Our position in the postwar world is so vital to the future that our smallest actions have far reaching effects. We have come to know that our own security in a highly interdependent world is inextricably tied to the security and well-being of all people and all countries. . . . We cannot escape the fact that our civil rights record has been an issue in world politics. The world's press and radio are full of it. . . . The United States is not so

[1] *Color and Conscience* (New York: Harper & Bros., 1946), p. 8.

strong, the final triumph of the democratic ideal is not so inevitable that we can ignore what the world thinks of us or our record.[2]

Since this was written, in 1947, the struggle against Soviet imperialism has grown much more intense, and the exploitation by Russia to her own advantage of the discontent of races and peoples held in positions of inferiority has become even more diabolically clever and alarmingly successful. Nor has the record of the United States in international affairs on such issues as mentioned above been effective in countering Communist policies. The contests in the United Nations have frequently found us standing with the minority of old colonial powers—the so-called Christian West—against the Asian, Arab, and Latin American states, supported ominously by the Soviet Union.

The President's Committee on Civil Rights pointed to a second reason why we need to face at once this problem of race relations and civil rights. It is not so obvious as the one just discussed, but it is more important than is generally realized. The committee called it the reason of self-interest or the "economic reason," stated, in part, in these words:

> Economic discrimination . . . imposes a direct cost upon our economy through wasteful duplication of many facilities and services required by the "equal but separate" policy. . . . To the costs of discrimination must be added the expensive investigations, trials, and property losses which result from civil rights violations. In the aggregate these attain huge proportions. . . . What we have lost in money, production, invention, citizenship and leadership as the price for damaged, thwarted personalities— these are beyond estimate.
>
> The United States can no longer afford this heavy drain upon its human wealth, its national competence.[3]

Evidence of this waste has also become more acute since this report was published. One instance of it is particularly disturbing just now. America faces in the immediate future

---

[2] *To Secure These Rights*, Report of the President's Committee on Civil Rights (Washington: U.S. Government Printing Office, 1947), pp. 146-48.
[3] *Ibid.*, pp. 144-46.

the greatest expenditure of material wealth and human resources she has ever had to undertake, save for military defense, if she is to provide educational facilities for her children. Failure to meet this need would be tragic. How we can build and maintain an adequate system of schools is an all but insoluble problem, particularly as long as present demands for military expenditures remain. To undertake to build and maintain in a large part of America duplicate systems of education is unthinkable.

Obviously neither of these reasons explains the present crisis in race relations. Both of them only suggest the expediency of responding creatively to the crisis. They do not state its sources or its nature. A third reason for immediate correction of inequities perpetrated against racial minorities as given by the President's Committee comes closer to the heart of the matter. The committee called it the "moral reason," which may be summed up in these words:

> The pervasive gap between our aims and what we actually do is creating a kind of moral dry rot which eats away at the emotional and rational bases of democratic beliefs. . . . It is impossible to decide who suffers the greatest moral damage from our civil rights transgressions, because all of us are hurt. . . .
> The United States can no longer countenance these burdens on its common conscience, these inroads on its moral fibre.[4]

Gunnar Myrdal and his associates in their definitive study of the Negro-white situation in America cited this tension between our beliefs and our practices as the key to the whole problem. In the two-volume summary of their comprehensive project of research this tension is set forth in these terms: We affirm continually and believe sincerely in human equality; but we have asserted with similar clarity, through the construction and defense of discriminatory social institutions, mores, and traditions, that we are not ready to practice what we affirm.[5] Dr. Ralph Bunche has described the equalitarian faith of Americans in moving words:

[4] *Ibid.*, pp. 139-41.
[5] *American Dilemma* (New York: Harper & Bros., 1944).

Every man in the street, white, black, red or yellow, knows that this is the "land of the free," the "land of opportunity," the "cradle of liberty," the "home of democracy," that the American flag symbolizes the "equality of all men" and guarantees to us all the "protection of life, liberty and property," freedom of speech, freedom of religion, and racial tolerance.[6]

These affirmations, written into the Declaration of Independence, the Preamble, the Bills of Rights, and a series of amendments to the Constitution, and into the constitutions of the several states, not only have become, as Myrdal says, the highest law of the land; they also are a declaration of faith that is prior to and transcends all such political documents. This is the "American creed," the "cement in the structure of this great and disparate nation."

It would be unpardonable arrogance to claim this as an exclusive or original American faith. It did not begin here. We inherited it. It had its roots immediately in the Enlightenment of the eighteenth century in Europe and in English law. More remotely it arose from the two source streams of western culture—that of Greco-Roman philosophy and law, and that of Judaeo-Christian faith and doctrine. In the West generally and in America particularly this double heritage has been made the very foundation of our societal existence and of our personal convictions. Despite the fact, however, that the Western peoples have asserted and sincerely believe in the principle of human equality as against that of hereditary caste, we have never been able to make a clear choice between the two. And here lies the root of the sense of guilt, the anxiety, the fear, and the continual frustration of our ideals of justice which undermine our security and peace. This is the American dilemma. So deeply imbedded in our lives are both these contrary forces that they have pulled us apart. We suffer accordingly from a deep schism of soul.

Color Caste Intolerable and Indefensible

There are four possible choices before us. And we of the West have made, at one time or another, in some fashion or

[6] *Ibid.*, I, 4.

another, all of them. The first two consist in a repudiation of the principle of equality and the assertion of the principle of hereditary inequality. The other two maintain, at least in theory, the equalitarian principle against that of caste.

The first of the four we may call that of inequality in a multiracial society, the second that of inequality in a uniracial society, both of which rest on a caste concept. The other two hold to the concept of equality—the one to equality with segregation of races, the other to equality and integration. Let us note each of these and some of the ways in which it affects race relations and human rights.

The first proposed type of social order, incorporating the principle of caste in a multiracial society, is best seen today in the present government of the Union of South Africa, where the policy of *apartheid*—complete segregation of races —is the organizing principle. It is also advocated by a vociferous minority in the United States, including those who proclaim and defend white supremacy and insist that the Negro should be "kept in his place." Superior and inferior castes live side by side; but all political power, all economic control, and all legal instruments are held by the dominant group and used as means to maintain the lower caste or castes in subjugation. These actions are rationalized by means of an ethic of innate, and frequently of divinely ordained, inequality, maintained by imperious social stratifications crystallized in customs, law, and social institutions, and given emotional support by the subtle symbols of mores and folkways. These devices for maintaining the social stratifications of caste take on a power that overrides all other considerations. They are felt rather than thought. They become the ethos of the caste society.

The second type of social organization, also based on a concept of inequality, seeks to avoid the offenses and perils of a caste-stratified society by isolating the caste groups. This was seriously advocated by many in America a century ago as one way to solve the problem of the Negro slave—deport the Negroes to Liberia or some island of the sea. The same concept was adopted by Hitler, with a fearful difference, and was actually in process of execution in the Third Reich—liquidate the Jews completely.

A current version of this proposal was made in 1949 by the Federated Dutch Reformed Church of South Africa, which supports the governmental policy of *apartheid* but seeks some way to mollify the injustices, insults, and exploitation of those who suffer caste discriminations. The theological ground of this proposal is essentially that of the German delegation to the Madras Conference of the International Missionary Council in 1938, which held, in opposition to the position of the Conference, that "the orders of sex, family, nation, *and race* are divinely established, and therefore the Christian Church is not allowed to dissolve them." [7] The South African Reformed churches declared:

> The traditional fear of the Afrikaner of equalization between black and white has its origin in his antipathy to the idea of racial fusion. The Church declares itself unequivocally opposed to this fusion and to all that would give rise to it, but on the other hand, as little begrudges the native and colored a social status as honorable as he can reach. . . . The policy of trusteeship as exercised at the present time must gradually develop into a complete independence and self-determination for the colored and native in his own community, school and church. [8]

This proposal, further spelled out, states that what the South African Reformed Church desires is complete separation of the two principal castes. The government, which is headed by a theologian of the same church, Dr. D. F. Malan, after consideration of the statement replied simply that it was not practical. The reason is clear. The whole economic and social structure of the caste society rests upon the exploitation of the labor of the subjugated groups. If this were withdrawn, the present system of order and privilege would collapse.

As stated above, the American creed is a repudiation of the concept of caste and an affirmation of the essential equality

[7] J. Merle Davis, ed., *The Economic Basis of the Church*, Vol. V of the Madras Series (International Missionary Council, 1939), p. 553. Italics mine.

[8] Quoted in *Information Service*, Federal Council of Churches, Dec. 17, 1949.

of all men. On this basis we have built a social structure which includes many racial groups. But we have held to a principle of separation between racial groups which has had the effect of caste stratification. The social order which we know is in fact a compromise of the principle of equality. We have affirmed our intention to give members of all minority racial and cultural groups their just rights and privileges. We have generally held that this means equality of opportunity, equality of legal protection, and equal freedom. But we have insisted on segregation. This ambiguous position has been expressed in the famous legal dictum of *equal but separate* accommodations and services for the different racial groups.

The results of this policy for nearly a century may be summed up by saying that in practice it is scarcely distinguishable from the first type of social organization mentioned— that of racial inequality. One of the studies mentioned above, that of the President's Committee, found that the minority groups, especially those of color and more particularly the Negroes, have suffered continuous and severe discriminations which no conception of equality would allow.

The committee laid down the premise that there are four fundamental rights that are essential to the well-being and the security of government. The first of these is the right to safety and security of the person. "Freedom can exist," said the committee, "only where the citizen is assured that his person is secure against bondage, lawless violence, and arbitrary arrest and punishment." The more frequent types of violation of this basic right of minority groups in America are (1) the crime of lynching and the threat of lynching, which always hang over the head of the southern Negro; (2) police brutality, which is widespread; (3) corruption in the administration of justice, especially by extortion of evidence and by exclusion of minority groups from juries; and (4) involuntary servitude perpetrated by the threat of criminal punishment and by freeing convicts into the hands of local entrepreneurs to be worked as serfs.

The second of these basic rights is the right to citizenship and its privileges. This, the committee found, is continually violated in two principal ways: (1) by refusing certain racial and national groups the right of citizenship itself—a discrimination against oriental immigrants that has been considerably modified by recent legislation, and (2) by denying to citizens the exercise of the right to vote and hold office—disabilities that also are slowly yielding to remedial measures.

The third basic right mentioned is the right to freedom of conscience and expression. While the committee confessed that it made no extensive study of our record under the great freedoms which comprise this right—religion, speech, press, and assembly—it did note that "the most immediate threat to the right of freedom of opinion and expression . . . comes from the efforts to deal with those few people in our midst who would destroy democracy" rather than from these enemies of democracy themselves. But violations of this right are not so consistently related to racial discriminations.

The last of the four basic rights cited by the committee is the right to equality of opportunity. The longest section of this study is concerned with this right and the multitude of ways in which it is violated. Violation, in fact, is the general pattern and not the exception in education, health, housing, employment, and public services, whether provided by government or by private enterprise—such as libraries, playgrounds, parks, theaters, community centers, restaurants, shops, hotels, and other accommodations.

These are some of the fruits of our "equal but separate" pattern. Despite the assertion of equality in it, it assumes all the major features of caste societies based on frank assertions of inequality, and it exhibits peculiar irrationalities, moral stultifications, and legal injustices of its own. For example, it is impossible to explain why Neson Cornelius is welcome in an Indianapolis restaurant as a visitor from India but is excluded as an American Negro. Equally inexplicable is the common practice in much of our land that allows two men to sit together at a workbench but prohibits their sitting together in a railroad station, or that permits a maid to spend the day at work in the living room but forbids her to use the front door. This confused pattern makes hypocrites of all who try to follow it and breeds the intolerable burden of conscience which we bear. It may not be—probably cannot be—completely abandoned at once. But it certainly cannot longer be defended.

The only remaining type of society is that based on brother-hood—a society of equality and integration. The conspiracy of events and the logic of our convictions are moving us toward it. This is not to say that such a community of men will emerge regardless of what we do. We must choose it, if it is to come. But it is to suggest that God, by the nature of his creation and by his continual activity in history, has de-creed that no other social order can be successfully established and maintained.

What would be the nature of this integrated community of men? Buell Gallagher has defined it in these words:

The integrationist position is precisely what the Christian ethic requires—that every man, woman and child shall be free to enter into and contribute to the welfare of all mankind, without any restrictions or disabilities based on color caste—and without any advantages because of color or the lack of it?[9]

This position is resisted by some who think it will lead to racial amalgamation. These objectors need to learn that such amalgamation has been going on thousands of years, and no social devices known or imaginable will prevent it where different racial groups live in proximity. Also, the more ad-vanced a civilization, the more racially mixed it is. The only "pure races" are primitive in culture and isolated—primitive because they are isolated. Two prime indexes of civilization are improved means of transportation and of communication. Civilized people get around. Primitive peoples stay put. And wherever peoples meet, they mix. This has been happening between black and white in America since the first slaves landed. Of the fifteen million members of the Negro com-munity here at present, an indeterminate but certainly small number have only African blood in their veins, nor can we know how many or which whites are blood-kin to the slaves of their ancestors, since at least ten thousand pass permanently from the Negro to the white group each year. Several hundred

[9] *Op. cit.,* p. 173.

thousand more could do so and never be noticed. It is by no means certain that amalgamation would go on more rapidly in an integrated society than in a segregated one. In any event, fear of amalgamation can no longer be used as a defense of segregation. The only society consistent with democratic principles or Christian faith is an integrated society.

FROM DECLARED POLICY TO EFFECTIVE PROGRAM

How may we achieve this society and especially what is the role of the church in its achievement?

The courts, particularly the Supreme Court, have made it quite clear within the last decade that equality is demanded by our fundamental law, even if this requires abandonment of segregation. They have opened tax-supported colleges and universities to Negroes and other racial minorities, upheld the rights of these groups to unrestricted accommodations in interstate travel, struck down the legality of racially restricted residential areas, demanded equal pay for Negro and white teachers, and otherwise enforced equality in public policy and practice. They have not yet held that compulsory segregation itself is unconstitutional, but they have shown conclusively that it is impossible to perpetuate it under our constitutional system.

Following the lead of the judiciary, state legislatures have begun to break down legal protections for segregation. In 1949 fifteen state legislatures introduced 149 bills and passed 26 of them into law, and in 1951 eleven states enacted some 14 bills into law, intended to weaken in some manner the pattern of racial caste. Unhappily Senators still have and continue to exercise the power of filibuster, which prevents enactment of significant federal legislation in behalf of civil rights. Despite this fact, however, we may expect legal enactment and judicial interpretation to continue to move toward integration.

What of the churches? The pattern of segregation is more obvious and more adamant in the Protestant churches of America than in any other of our social institutions. In the most recent and most comprehensive study of this problem, by Dr. Frank S. Loescher, his well-documented conclusion is summed up in these shocking words: "Protestantism, by its policies and practices, far from helping to integrate the Negro in American life is actually contributing to the segregation of Negro Americans." [10]

At the level of the local churches Loescher discovers that there are no more—probably much less—than one tenth of one per cent of American Negro Christians in integrated churches, and most of these are in communities where there are exceedingly few Negroes. And the same general pattern prevails for Japanese, Chinese, Indians, Mexicans, Puerto Ricans. [11] The situation is not essentially different in church-supported educational institutions and denominational agencies and associations.

This is fortunately not the whole story. If we take a view of the direction and momentum of the mind of the church rather than of a static cross section of its institutions, there are hopeful signs of an awakening determination to end these unchristian practices. The most obvious expression of this fact is in the declaration of faith and intention by denominational and ecumenical bodies in the last few decades.

Between 1906 and 1929 only six pronouncements by church bodies on race relations are recorded—and these deal chiefly with mob violence in connection with race riots following World War I. In the following decade of the 1930's forty declarations with a total of sixty endorsements were published, but these still concerned themselves with the gross injustices suffered by minority groups, only two major denominations stating that they were opposed to compulsory segregation.

Toward the end of this decade the impact of the ecumenical movement began to be felt in America. In 1928 the Jerusalem Meeting of the International Missionary Council had sounded a revolutionary note in these words:

In lands where different races live side by side full participation in social, cultural, and above all religious interracial fellowship, and the development of personal friendship which such in-

[10] *The Protestant Church and the Negro* (New York: Association Press, 1948), p. 15. Cf. pp. 106 ff.
[11] *Ibid.*, pp. 77-78.

tercourse engenders are the natural expression of our common Christianity, and are obviously to be welcomed as a step toward world wide understanding.[12]

During the last ten years there has been a veritable avalanche of declarations—by denominational bodies, interdenominational councils and agencies, and ecumenical conferences, asserting the Christian imperative to create an integrated society, first within its own life and then in the life of the secular community. Space permits only one quotation from these, made in March, 1946:

The Federal Council of Churches of Christ in America hereby renounces the pattern of segregation in race relations as unnecessary and undesirable and a violation of the Gospel of love and human brotherhood. Having taken this action, the Federal Council requests its constituent communions to do likewise. As proof of their sincerity in this renunciation, they will work for a non-segregated church and a non-segregated society.[13]

This principle and policy were reaffirmed by the Federal Council in 1948 and by the General Board of its successor, the National Council, in 1952. Numerous denominational bodies—national, state, and regional—have made this declaration their own. One may say that an integrated church in an integrated society is the declared policy of American Protestantism.

But declarations of policy are not deeds. This word awaits its incarnation. Only thus can its redemptive power be made manifest. How can the churches give this living word its living deed? It is obvious that we cannot set down here a bill of particular actions. Nor is this required. Libraries are full of such guidance, and every minister either has these helps on his shelves or can easily get them from his denominational headquarters.

[12] *The Christian Mission in the Light of Race Conflict*, Vol. IV of the *Reports* of the Jerusalem Meeting of the International Missionary Council, p. 201.
[13] *The Church and Race Relations* (Federal Council of Churches, 1946), p. 5.

But I do want to mention five areas in which action must take place. The first is the area of the minister's own conscience and will. No "yes-but . . ." theology is adequate. Until the leadership of the church wills to change our unchristian way of life in race relations, how can we hope to see anything adequate happen in or through our churches?

Having committed himself to work for an unsegregated church and an unsegregated society, the minister can in the next place conform his personal and family life to this commitment. He should and can cultivate friendships and associations with congenial members of other races. He can expand this circle by bringing into it others of his church and community. Better race relations must begin in these immediate face-to-face contacts. One who has never cultivated these associations will thus discover a new joy in a rich freedom he has never known before.

In the third place, we can set about making our own churches integrated churches. To be sure, there are situations where an attempt toward integration would be destined to failure because it was artificial. Integrated churches can prosper only where members of two or more racial groups are geographically contiguous and where cultural interests are congenial. There are many such places. But since our churches are, for good or ill, social institutions and manifest in their group lives the sociological features of the surrounding community, integrated churches are likely to prosper only if we also build an integrated society.

The other two areas of action concern this objective. The first of these is the local community. We may begin by seeking to mitigate the evils of segregation and discrimination through such devices as community self-surveys and interracial conferences to examine the body politic and devise appropriate remedies. We will need to move on to break down the psychological and legal barriers among races from which all discriminations spring. It is perhaps better to put new patches on old garments than to let the holes remain uncovered. But the old garment of racial caste cannot hold the new cloth of Christian brotherhood or even of democratic justice.

And finally, we must work unceasingly for the enactment and fair enforcement of legal protections for the freedom of all men—from the county courthouse to the national Capitol. This means political action—intelligent, persistent, and effective political action. Civil rights are a matter of law. And where they are denied to any group, no man's freedom is secure.

Part III

The Church
and
The Economic Order

6

Daily Work and Christian Vocation

Cameron P. Hall

IT IS NEWS WHEN AN ECONOMIST JOINS THEOLOGY AND ECO-
NOMICS OVER AGAINST MATHEMATICS. IN HIS RECENT BOOK
Professor Kenneth Galbraith, formerly of *Fortune* magazine
and now of Harvard University, writes: "Like theology, and
unlike mathematics, economics deals with matters which men
consider very close to their lives." [1] He feels that when these
two subjects are properly understood, their intimacy with
life's daily round is apparent. This study is a confirmation of
this author's statement about their closeness to life.

Daily work is a very human approach to economics; it
focuses upon the individual in the occupation by which he
supports himself and his family. Christian vocation is theology
strikingly related to life; it concerns the meaning that Christians find in the daily work upon which they depend for their
standard of living. We may therefore properly rephrase Professor Galbraith's sentence to read: "Like Christian vocation,
and unlike mathematics, daily work deals with matters which
men consider very close to their lives."

GOD THE CREATOR AND MAN HIS CO-WORKER

Daily work is what men do for a livelihood; Christian
vocation is a way of looking at what they do. Wherein lies

[1] *American Capitalism* (Boston: Houghton Mifflin Co., 1952), p. xi.

a fruitful approach to finding Christian meaning in one's occupation? I propose that we probe for the answer to the question, "Why is a man paid a wage or salary for the work which he does?" In 1952 the American people spent on wages and salaries the massive total of about $275,000,000,000 in payment for daily work done. Where lies the deepest reason for this?

Jesus once declared that "the laborer deserves his wages" (Luke 10:7, R.S.V.). So axiomatic this seems that it is a truism. But why? Jesus is saying, in effect, something like this: "Man as worker benefits man as consumer. Through his daily work an individual provides goods or services which help meet the needs or wants of himself and others." In today's complex industrial society, this equation of daily work with daily need is concealed by the use of money.

The payment of money wages and salaries is the recognition by the community that daily work contributes somewhere, somehow, to the needs of the members of the community, first for simple survival—food, shelter, clothing, health—and beyond these for growth in civilization and well-being. Truth can be seen negatively. When an occupation is no longer regarded as having social value, then doing it is no longer rewarded. For example, blacksmithing used to be a widespread, profitable, and highly respected occupation; now it has all but disappeared because it has forfeited its social usefulness to the auto and the tractor. It can be seen positively, as well. Farming is this nation's way of mobilizing its resources for survival which begins on the land. If for some reason today's farmers should walk off their farms, we would be quick to see that farming was taken over by others, even if we in cities had to do it.

The meaning of daily work, therefore, is rooted in social necessity and grounded in the nature of community. We come upon this same insight into daily work in Paul's advice to the Thessalonians, "If any one will not work, let him not eat" (II Thess. 3:10, R.S.V.). A very severe thought; but is it too severe? Through daily work a man increases, through eating he lessens, the supply of what the community has to eat.

Hence, if a man is to consume what the community has for its needs, let him work—that is, replace what the community needs. Through the daily work of its members, the community —family, tribe, city, nation, and the world of nations—mobilizes its will and its skill to undergird the survival and welfare of its members and their common life.

The purpose that daily work is designed to serve, then, is human need. But understanding *why* the work of men serves the needs of men opens up still further vistas of its meaning. Human survival and well-being are served as men daily apply their strength and skills—physical and mental—to what they discover or come upon in the world of nature. One of our nation's weeklies is running a series on "The World in Which We Live." One way of telling that story, as done by a book I read many years back, is in terms of the changes which the physical environment has undergone as it became growingly capable of sustaining life. Gases, metals, and liquids went through chemical and physical changes by which at long last there appeared properties in the natural world which could nourish life, beginning at its lowest manifestations; and these latter—such as grasses that have metamorphosed into coal— became in turn aids to higher forms of life.

God created the universe; in it he created the earth upon which life could survive and flourish; and upon this earth he created man after his own image. But now we come upon a startling truth about God the Creator. Men can freeze upon mountains in which are imbedded rich veins of coal. For unless men mine coal, they go without warmth from coal. It is purely an academic matter to your and my clothing needs that there is cotton growing on Southern soil or wool growing on sheep on Western plains unless by their daily work men are able and willing to "humanize" that cotton and that wool; that is, transform what is in nature into what is humanly useful. In short, God the Creator, upon whom man depends, has so created this world that he needs man as his co-worker so that his creative process will now cover the daily needs and wants of man.

A story which probably most of you have already heard,

93

in one version or another, is worth repeating here. A man took over a piece of ground that was a mass of tangled under-brush and weeds. Under his care and work it became a garden spot of rare beauty and joy. A friend once said, "How wonderful God is, who has given such beauty to your place."

"Yes," said the gardener, "but you should have seen what it was like before I started working on it."

This need of God for man as co-worker may have been the first divine humiliation. Paul writes that in Jesus, God "humbled himself" (Phil. 2:8). In making man as a necessary participator in the divine creative process, God humbled himself. God the Creator and man his co-worker, while not equal, are now both necessary for the daily ministering to man's needs of God's continuing creative activity. The potential for human survival and well-being that God gave to nature is now changed into what is necessary for man as consumer, through the worker on the land, the worker in the factory, the worker in transportation, the worker in processing and packaging, the worker in merchandizing.

Does Daily Work Differ in Its Worth?

The meaning of work for the Christian, then, is ultimately established in the doctrine of creation. Daily work is ordained by God. Man as worker is both object and subject of the continuing creative activity of God as known to men in Christ Jesus. All useful daily work becomes of equal worth before God. Because men at work are co-workers with God the Creator, their daily work is "co-worthy" before God, who ever seeks the good of those whom he created in his own image.

With the purpose of useful work seen within the purpose of God the Creator, the Christian will see his work as a means of serving God. Dr. John Oliver Nelson has written: "Christian vocation means interpreting your life work, whatever it is, as fulfillment of God's purpose for you." [2] It is therefore central in the mission and responsibility of the churches to inspire and develop in their lay people a compelling sense

[2] *Christian Youth and Christian Vocation* (Chicago: United Christian Youth Movement), p. 21.

of Christian vocation, so that each will work in his occupation as "under God."

There are with us today, however, strongholds of practical denials of this Christian insight into daily work. A British layman who is contributing some solid thinking on "work and vocation" writes:

There is, in fact, a tendency to grade work something as follows:

a) Directly religious work (the Christian ministry, missionary work, organizing religious societies);

b) Work with "human content" (teaching, healing, social work);

c) The professions (research and scientific work, architecture, law, public administration, etc.);

d) Ordinary commerce and business.

He notes that in this prevalent attitude toward daily work is the "implication that a Christian will try to move up the scale if the change occurs." [3]

This grading of the intrinsic worth of daily work is compounded out of two inherited traditions. One is nothing more than social snobbishness. Early in civilization, manual work was equated with menial work and laid upon slaves; this view was carried out in spirit and largely in letter into the feudal age. In our democratic society this lingers on in the intrinsic worth we give to the professions, as over against unskilled to skilled jobs.

This grading is compounded also of the religious view of the medieval church. Daily work meant then, as it does now, involvement in and compromise with the evil in human life, individually and collectively. So it became assumed that if, instead, a man fled into a sheltered physical setting such as a monastery, or into an ecclesiastical setting, such as the priesthood, he automatically took on an occupation to which God

[3] W. G. Symons, *Work and Vocation* (London: Student Christian Movement Press), p. 28.

imparted an intrinsic religious worth that he denied to other types of work. Suffice here simply to conjecture what would have happened to God's loving creative outreach toward the needs of the members of medieval society if there had been only monks and priests and no hewers of wood and drawers of water!

In its central affirmation the Protestant Reformation swept aside this hierarchical structure of the worth of work before God, the Creator and Father of men. It did this not by lowering the so-called sacred down to the level of the so-called secular callings, but by raising the secular level up to that of the sacred. In this view, both a pastor and the members of his congregation who Monday through Saturday are at work in socially useful occupations are one in the worth of their work before God.

This truth is in no wise vitiated by the recognition that the work which men do differs widely in its functions. The lawyer arguing a case on behalf of justice under law has a different function from that of a telephone linesman. But common to both is the provision of services in which we stand in need.

Paul has given striking emphasis to the truth that although parts of the human body differ in their functions, yet each is indispensable. He writes in his first letter to the Corinthians, "The eye cannot say to the hand, 'I have no need of you,' nor again the head to the feet, 'I have no need of you'" (I Cor. 12:21, R.S.V.). Likewise in the body social—or, more profoundly, in the body divine creation—of functions there are many. In helping the members of the community provide for their needs and wants, a musician supplies quite a different function from that of a seasonal vegetable picker. But they stand on the same level in the worth of their work before God.

DEPERSONALIZATION OF MODERN WORK

Without laying a blanket charge that all modern work robs the worker of a sense of its meaningfulness, one cannot be blind to the depersonalization that is so widespread today. Let me point out four characteristics of work today that bear this out.

We speak familiarly, and truthfully, of the "division of labor." Without it mankind would be little above the feudal level in the productivity of his workmanship. But this is looking at what has happened from the sociological point of view; the fragmentation of work and hence the separation of the worker from the result of his work puts it in more intimate, individual terms. Compare the farmer, who participates in the process from the plowing to the harvesting, with the worker who pulls a lever.

Second, there is depersonalization through the machine. The human body has its rhythm; so also does the machine have its tempo, as determined by its inventor and operator. Like a slave master, the machine often sets a tempo that makes no room for the variations of the inwardness of individual workers. The mechanical process seeks from workers a mechanical response, so that men at work often become hardly higher than the parts of the machine itself.

Third, there is depersonalization in organizational structure. It is significant as well as encouraging that industry today is making much of what it calls "communication." This stems out of the recognition that in our highly organized economic life the individual worker is lost in a hierarchical structure. It is strikingly true that thousands work under others and over others and alongside others but have no feeling of working *with* others or *for* others. When a man works for this great steel corporation or for that vast automobile corporation, *whom* does he work for—or is it a case of *what* does he work for? Students of worker psychology today recognize that inadequate work habits frequently are not due to worker laziness but to a lack of worker identification with the enterprise.

A further form of depersonalization is more subtle but not the less serious. The satisfaction of daily work for so many is not personal, in the doing of work itself, but materialistic, in the wage or salary paid after it is done. Money is a reward, to be sure, but it lies outside the work process itself. The worker as a person finds his satisfaction apart from his work itself.

ETHICAL DILEMMAS

Daily work as a living experience and as a challenge to Christian responsibility always comes dressed up as a particular occupation; to some, it is as pinpointed as "my job." "I teach," says one; "I am a steelworker," another declares; "I keep house" is what another will say; "I sell," still another says. These occupational categories break down into subcategories: wage earners in factories work in quite a different pattern of circumstances from those in offices; both a manufacturer and a department-store owner may be described as "in business," but it is "business" with a difference.

The occupations are to the worker what the nations are to the citizen. Of course, all nations are part of the same world of nations; and human nature being what it is, the same broad moral and social problems underlie the responsibilities of citizenship within every set of frontiers. But this gives no ground whatsoever for American Christians to urge dogmatically an analysis of their citizenship responsibilities upon the Christians of Italy or India, or even upon such close cousins as the Canadians.

There is here a close analogy to the occupations. It is true that each occupation is part of the same world of work as are all the others; and human nature being what it is, the same broad moral and social problems underlie the responsibilities of work within all kinds of jobs. But this gives no warrant at all for a Christian drugstore proprietor to assume that the ethical dilemmas which he faces in his occupation are interchangeable with those of a men's tie manufacturer.

Occupations, and their subdivisions, vary in the source and the form of the ethical dilemmas which they create. I have time only to mention these in passing. First, the pattern of relationships with people—clearly, the pattern is different for a salesgirl in a Macy's or Marshall Field's on the one hand,

and a member of a high-school teaching staff on the other hand. Second, the materials or the work situation which determine the skills called for—a real estate agent and a textile worker deal with a quite dissimilar job content. Third, the working arrangements—an assembly-line worker tied to the tempo of the machine, and an insurance agent with his highly individualized clientele, point up the comparison here. And fourth, the dominant tradition, spirit, and philosophy that are attached to an occupation—Ruskin put this matter most bluntly when he wrote that a soldier is expected to take in his stride the occupational hazard of injury or death in the performance of his work, while a businessman is not expected to work unless he feels that it will pay him a profit.

Now these "specifics" of each occupation are in themselves ethically neutral; there is nothing morally better or worse about having the bodies of clients as one's material to work on, as in the case of a doctor, than having to work on the chemicals from which plastics are made; and the same may be said of the relationships inherent in the teaching profession compared with those in coal mining. And even in regard to the spirit or tradition, the picture is ambiguous, for there are positive as well as negative elements in each case. In short, these relationships, materials, arrangements, and so on are the scenery in relation to which the worker has to play his part. To change the metaphor, they are the raw material on which the Christian at work is to exercise his ethical sensitivity and responsibility under God.

This stress on the occupational breakdown of daily work is fundamental to any effective program by the churches. The challenge that God has for the Christian as a worker is not posed by the question, "What is my responsibility as a Christian worker?" but rather, "What is my responsibility as a Christian production manager or as a Christian garage mechanic or as a Christian doctor or as a Christian insurance agent?" If the churches are to help their members grow into committed co-workers under God the Creator, they must stimulate vigorous probing into the unrecognized as well as the prevalent dilemmas of high ethical content that have their source and form in the specific characteristics of each particular occupation.

CHRISTIAN VOCATION AND SOCIAL JUSTICE

We have just been looking at the on-the-job call for bringing Christian principles into one's Monday-through-Saturday daily work. But this work is also done within a social context. The daily work of a man is his community's way of seeing to it that he and his family and the common life of its members have the means of survival and of well-being. For the Christian, *how* society goes at setting up the way its members shall work is a challenge to his sense of Christian vocation. In the rules that govern how men shall work, in the structure through which men are related to one another through their work, and in the criteria by which the collective judgment of the community rewards men at work, every society shows where it stands on the ladder of Christian values.

A prominent sociologist once told his friends that when he set out to study or investigate a social problem, he always began with the question, "Who is being hurt the most?" For those who see each man in a useful occupation as a co-worker with God the Creator, this will always be the pressing question about his own work and that of his fellow workers. For the consequences of daily work are not alone needed goods and services for members of the community; there are inescapable consequences upon the workers themselves—physical and spiritual. The moral development of a community is reflected in what it allows work to do to men as the price for the benefits of work by men.

Every society, ancient and modern, distributes its injustices and its favors through its generally accepted standards and practices of daily work. Slavery showed up the dominant values toward the worth of the individual. The feudalistic pattern and structure of daily work are open windows by which we see both light and shadow. The ruthless exploitation of workers in early industrialism here and in Great Britain shows the antihuman values which then controlled daily work. Until recently we Americans revealed a shocking in-

69029

sensitivity toward children through the accepted patterns of children at work. The way we set up our daily work permitted—indeed, encouraged—young children to work long hours under harsh conditions.

Let us look at some of today's customs, practices, and goals which impinge so sensitively upon a Christian sense of vocation toward daily work.

One area is the distribution of the fruit of men's work. Who is to receive how much of what men at work in our interdependent world produce? Obviously, many who have worked have been hurt by the grossly unjust pattern of distribution of what work has produced; others have been in a very favorable position under the socially sanctioned pattern of distribution.

Since daily work is men participating in God the Creator's outreach to men's needs, then the worker is entitled to the community's maximum consideration of his needs for survival and well-being. The minimum wage, social security, industry-wide pensions, and similar social measures show an intention by our American society to effect greater justice in the distribution of what comes to men from their daily work.

A second area is the relationships in the work process itself. Because 85 per cent of Americans today who work for a wage or salary work for someone else, the pattern of relationship between employer and employee is a major relationship. The values in our American society can be decisively weighed and measured by the spirit of justice and brotherhood in this relationship. Collective bargaining, seniority provisions, profit sharing, the annual guaranteed wage, labor-management committees, voluntary agreements for settling industrial disputes—these have to do primarily not with means and techniques, but with human values in the crucial working relationship in our highly organized work life.

A third area is freedom to work, and to be trained and advanced in one's work, without let or hindrance because of one's race or national origin. Here indeed is where work life today hurts so many. How sensitive should a sense of Christian vocation make one toward the struggle for fair employment practices! Discrimination and segregation have no place where God seeks to enlist men as co-workers in his making what is in nature to serve men's needs for survival and well-being.

A fourth area is incentives for stimulating men to work at their best. If daily work is God the Creator entering into the community's need for goods and services, then for the sake of the community the worker should be stimulated to maximize the product from his time at work. But, just because daily work is a form of co-working with God, the spirit and purpose with which men work are all important. Because this is God's world, of his creating and of his continuous creation with men as co-workers, the motivations as well as the products of daily work need to be in accord with God's purpose for men's work.

The traditional stress has been on "self-interest." Suffice here and now simply to urge that this has been done with too little imagination and understanding of what human nature is and what makes for a healthy community. There are other forms of self-interest than the narrow one; there is another side to human nature than the self-regarding one; there are other drives within the individual than for his own self-contained enhancement. Within the Christian view of human nature there is a place for a quite different kind of self-interest than that upon which Western society has depended so much for eliciting the best from men in their daily work.

A final area is the war-oriented result of daily work today. A stale wind of deep futility seeps through much of daily work today, for much of what men produce is intended to mortally hurt whole armies and entire civilian populations. I have a friend who for years now has chosen what he works at on the basis that it does not contribute any goods or services within the military way of life. Most members of our churches will not agree with this basis of selection of one's daily work; but few will fail to see that our massive military expenses tie daily work to the intention to kill and destroy. The Christian insight into the meaning of work gives added urgency—if that is possible—to the Christian commitment to increase the spirit and to forge the means for a world of nations wherein men at work will turn out pruning hooks instead of spears and plowshares instead of swords.

7

The Organization of Economic Life

Walter G. Muelder

Historical Background

American economic life today is highly organized. The development of economic organizations has been so important that at least one American economist, Professor Kenneth Boulding, has called it the organizational revolution. In attempting to confront businessmen, farmers, workers, and consumers with their social responsibilities, the churches find themselves in a situation quite different from that of any previous period of history. The early days of Christianity found the church recruited from among the lower classes primarily and surrounded by an economic life based on slavery, agriculture, crafts, and trade which were quite modest in organizational scope when measured by modern standards. Christians accepted private property for the most part, though several of the church fathers stressed the communal nature of property; slavery was gradually repudiated; many crafts were "out-of-bounds" for Christians; and they expressed their sense of economic responsibility primarily through philanthropy.

With the collapse of the Roman Empire, town and city life almost disappeared in many parts of the West. For centuries the dominant organizational patterns of economic life were agricultural. Land was the chief form of wealth. The common people attached themselves to powerful landowners, and the feudal system with its class and status structures developed.

The church accepted this economic organization. It became in time a powerful landowner also, in some countries owning finally a third and even a half of all the land. Then came the new development of town life and the appearance of merchant guilds and craft guilds. Within the monasteries the economic organization was communal; within the church the organization was feudal and imperial; outside it continued predominantly feudal, but there were also emerging capitalistic institutions in banking and trading and in the organization of such industries as textiles and weaving. Innumerable regulations and privileges surrounded all economic life. Christian morality stressed status, condemned usury, pleaded for charity, protested the greed and exploitation of the rich and powerful, recognized the place of labor in the new town life, but stressed ideals which were largely medieval.

The modern period is radically different from the medieval. But modern economic life has gone through several stages— mercantilism; the relatively free-trade market; the growth of factories, corporations, and cartels; and the emergence of such phenomena as socialism and communism in response to capitalism, imperialism, and colonialism.

The period just prior to the American Revolution was mercantilist. Great trading and manufacturing companies were chartered and controlled by national governments which conceived of wealth in terms of gold and consequently restricted trading and manufacturing privileges to the mother country and viewed colonies as places of raw-material resources and agricultural life, and as consumers of the products of the motherland. Then came the period of the great inventions and the growth of the factory system. Industrial cities and mill towns grew up. Slums became chronic, as did the exploitation of women and children, destitution, vice, prostitution, and poverty. As the inhabitants of eastern American cities poured west to the receding frontier with its free land and other opportunities, millions of immigrants filled up the old slums and were herded into ever larger, bulging slums, mining camps, and mill towns. The owners built pretentious homes and developed exclusive residential districts.

In England and America the capitalistic philosophy expressed itself in terms of laissez-faire individualism, the ideal of the free market in which consumers and producers confronted each other in unrestricted competition. The general conception was that free individual consumers and producers meet in a market place where the prices of goods respond impersonally to the supply and demand of goods. Consumers register the results of their desires and decisions to buy by purchasing or promising to purchase specified quantities of specific goods and services in a competitive market. Scores of independent, unrelated decisions by businessmen operating for profit are made as they observe the reactions of consumers reflected in the market place through the price system. The profit motive was regarded as the keystone, while free enterprise, private property, free competition, and free contract were the other basic principles of the price system. One of the chief functions of government was conceived to be to prevent monopolies from interfering with the rights of others to engage freely in enterprise.

The businessmen of the young American republic did not, however, adhere to the ideal of free trade. On the other hand, they sought governmental protection of industries through protective tariffs. The government intervened in the free market in other ways also: through favorable patent laws; through programs of internal improvements; through the virtually free gift of western lands; through liberal disposition of vast natural resources; through subsidies to railroad companies; through the abolition of slavery; through immigration policies; through the public-school system, whereby a nation's chief economic resource, its manpower, was prepared for participation in an industrial and urban age; and through many other types of lavish assistance.

The rapid industrialization and urbanization of the United States following the Civil War found the churches largely unprepared to formulate a social morality of responsibility in terms of the grave new problems that had arisen. It became quite apparent, however, that the economic ethics of the ancient, medieval, early modern, and frontier periods had to be reformulated. Some wished to cling to a purely private or individual expression of the gospel, while the profounder leaders saw that a new formulation of social Christianity was needed. In the face of the organization of economic life in the late nineteenth century the great social-gospel writers made the following points as summarized by Howard Hopkins: [1] they insisted that the workers obtain justice, not charity; they refuted classical economic dogmas, insisting that labor is not a commodity and criticizing laissez-faire as an excuse for exploiting the poor; they expressed interest in trade unions, strikes, and mutual aid; they were critical of labor violence and other excesses; and they advocated arbitration and such forms of co-operation as profit-sharing. Before the century was past, some interpreted the kingdom of God in terms which condemned monopoly and approved Christian socialism.

In this chapter we are primarily concerned to note the nature of economic organization in the current American scene. It is well to keep in mind, however, that the church's concern for social responsibility is world wide and that the church's own institutional life is imbedded in a variety of economic systems all over the world. The economic life in which British Christians are involved is a mixed economy with a strong socialist emphasis; the same is true of western Germany; Christians in Russia live in a communistic order; in India the village system predominates, but there are also capitalistic, colonial, and socialistic elements; in China a vast rural and urban revolution is in process; in Africa colonialism and imperialism are still rife; and in South America a mixture of feudalism and authoritarian capitalism is dominant. There is no principle in Christian ethics which requires a Christian to hold that any one economic system is to be identified with the kingdom of God. On the contrary, Christianity must not be identified with any system of economic organization. All systems stand under the judgment of God's righteousness and love and are answerable to the principles of the dignity of man, of brotherhood, and of the motive of service.

[1] *The Rise of the Social Gospel in American Protestantism* (New Haven: Yale University Press, 1940).

The Organization of American Business Life

American business life is highly organized. This fact stands in sharp contrast to a prevailing popular opinion that small business and industry operating in a free market with keen competition among individual persons is the characteristic pattern. Industry is highly organized; as also are the labor unions and the farmers. Then there are the organized consumers. Beyond these is government itself with its myriad operations. Among these operations military life is playing an important part and influencing economic activities in many ways. Then, too, there are the highly organized professions like medicine which make a profound impact on the economy. Supporting all these from various perspectives are special associations exerting pressures on public opinion and on government.

The American economy has been called a capitalist system, though more recently the slogan "free enterprise" has been used by its chief proponents. There is a great deal of freedom of enterprise in the United States as compared with the economies of some nations, especially of the Soviet Union. Actually, however, there are several types of economic order operative, so that it could be more accurate to say that the United States has a "mixed" economy. For example, (1) there are still millions of people involved in small independent businesses. Many Americans are self-employed. But (2) there are also powerful industrial corporations which dominate production. Then (3) there are giant financial corporations, banks, and holding companies. Besides these are (4) the great nonprofit economic activities of the municipal, state, and federal governments. And then there are (5) innumerable voluntary associations which range all the way from consumers' co-operatives to churches, schools, social agencies, hospitals, and other philanthropies. Each of these not only has a distinctive economic organization of its own, but exerts significant pressure on every other.

To understand the corporate organization of industry, it is instructive to note, on the one hand, who owns our corporate wealth, and on the other hand, how the wealth is controlled—i.e., how economic power is concentrated. Shareholdings in publicly owned stock issues in the United States are estimated to aggregate 30,000,000—a "shareholding" being defined as possession of one issue by one owner, no matter how many shares are held. The total number of shares is estimated to be 4,900,000,000, of which 13,650 issues are common stocks and 3,005 are preferred stocks. These shares are owned by 6,490,-000 individuals and represent 4,750,000 family spending units. This means that about one in every sixteen adults owns shares in one or more stock issues, and there are one or more share owners in one tenth of all families.[2] Nine tenths of all families in the United States do not have any participation in the ownership of corporate wealth.

Devices of control are many. There is concentration into a limited number of companies. Then there is "price leadership," whereby the most powerful company in an industry announces its price schedules and the others fall in line. Other devices include holding companies, patent pools, basing points, apportionment of market among competitors, open-price understanding, "gentlemen's agreements," tying-clause arrangements, and certain kinds of trade associations. The organizational revolution is apparent in all these areas, but the growth in trade associations has been phenomenal. In the decade from 1865 to 1875, during which the social gospel was born, there were six associations formed. By 1900 there were about a hundred, by 1920 there were a thousand, and by 1941, according to the Department of Commerce, there were nineteen hundred listed in the directory of *Trade and Professional Associations of the United States*. Eleven hundred were associations of manufacturers. Kenneth Boulding states that there are today at least sixteen hundred trade associations alone. Not all of these exist for the purpose of price fixing or output control, but many of them do perform these functions in one way or another, directly or indirectly. In addition their members tend to belong to the powerful Chamber of Commerce

[2] See Lewis H. Kimmel, *Share Ownership in the United States* (Washington, D.C.: Brookings Institution, 1952).

and some to the even more powerful National Association of Manufacturers.

In the "mixed" economy of the United States we may profitably note also the nature of the dominant organization of manufacturing corporations. "Oligopoly" is the name which economists assign to the concentration of output among relatively few sellers. This is the dominant pattern. In 1947 "the 113 largest manufacturing corporations owned 46 per cent of the property, plant, and equipment employed in manufacturing." [3]

As long ago as 1937 there were 121 manufactured products valued at more than $10,000,000 in which more than 75 per cent of the output was manufactured by four firms. For manufacturing as a whole about one third of the total value of products was produced under conditions where the four largest producers of each individual product turned out from 75 to 100 per cent of these products. Concentration of organization may be measured not only (1) by the value of manufactured products, but also (2) by employment by establishments, (3) by employment by firms, and (4) by sales handled by giant corporations. If we use these four criteria for measuring the concentration in major manufacturing industries and range these industries in order from the highest to the least concentration, we must list them as follows: (1) automobiles, (2) tobacco manufacturers, (3) rubber products, (4) transportation equipment, (5) electrical machinery, (6) products of petroleum and coal, (7) iron, steel, and their products, (8) nonferrous metals and their products, (9) machinery, except electrical, (10) chemicals, (11) textile-mill products, (12) stone, clay, and glass, (13) food and kindred products, (14) furniture and finished lumber, (15) printing and publishing, (16) lumber and basic products, (17) apparel and other finished products. [4]

---

[3] See John K. Galbraith, *American Capitalism* (Boston: Houghton, Mifflin Co., 1952). Quoted in *Information Service* (Oct. 4, 1952).

[4] *United States versus Economic Concentration and Monopoly:* A staff report to the Monopoly Subcommittee on Small Business of the House of Representatives (U. S. Government Printing Office, 1949), pp. 99-104.

The organization of industrial life must be understood not only in terms of the above pattern but also in terms of financial control. In the modern large corporation, management runs the business, with the advice of the directors; the owners do not. Berle and Means point out that these officers and directors may or may not have any considerable share in the ownership of the corporation. According to their study 65 per cent of the two hundred largest nonfinancial corporations and 80 per cent of their combined wealth are controlled either by management or by a legal device involving a small proportion of ownership, and only 11 per cent of the companies and 6 per cent of their wealth are controlled by a group of individuals owning half or more of the stock interest outstanding.[5] It is characteristic of American capitalism today that the bulk of the money used in capital formation comes from corporate earnings or from internal sources such as depreciation. Industry now plows back 60 per cent of its profits, as against 30 per cent in the 1920's.

In the capitalist world the corporation has in many cases become collectivist in type and runs into many of the internal problems, such as the conscious co-ordination of specialists, which present difficulties in the theory of the bureaucratic collectivist state. It has been said that General Motors' internal political and group problems, for example, are as vast and complex as those of a whole country the size of Yugoslavia. One of these problems is that of bureaucracy. Though this problem is editorially associated in much propaganda with government, it is basically an aspect of all complex institutional life, ecclesiastical and academic as well as political and economic. Business in America is becoming increasingly bureaucratic. Robert A. Brady notes that in business organization it grows in a sort of geometric ratio with each passing decade as efforts are made to increase the size of the business unit or extend the scope of control. With bureaucratic organization come such problems as red tape, "passing the buck," cliquism, undue differentiation of function, the tendency to expand staff

---

[5] Adolf A. Berle and Gardiner C. Means, *The Modern Corporation and Private Property* (New York: The Macmillan Co., 1948).

regardless of function or after functions have atrophied, lack of individual initiative, and the tendencies promoting identification of occupational level with invidious social status.[6] These are problems which have a profound bearing on the Christian doctrines of the dignity of the person, Christian vocation, freedom, creativity, and responsibility. Collectivism within "private enterprise" raises many of the same issues as collectivism within political life.

The church, as it faces this organization of business life, raises a number of questions. Are the proper goals of economic life being realized, or are they being overshadowed by power, wealth, profit, and acquisitiveness? Why do business enterprises and labor unions (see below) at times limit their production even when there is need and demand for their goods? How can a just organization of economic power be developed so that all who participate have a responsible share in decisions affecting their welfare and that of the community? In the face of this dominant concentration of power how can freedom and security, productivity and distribution, democratic control and the service motive, be best developed? Can the social conscience of the church ignore the warning issued in 1947 by the Federal Trade Commission in its *Report on the Present Trend of Corporate Mergers and Acquisitions?*

No great stretch of the imagination is required to foresee that if nothing is done to check the growth in concentration, either the giant corporations will ultimately take over the country, or the government will be impelled to step in and impose some form of direct regulation in the public interest. In either event collectivism will have triumphed over free enterprise, and the theory of competition will have been relegated to the limits of well intentioned but ineffectual ideals. This is a warning which the Commission has repeated time and again, and one which some of those who have the most to gain by the preservation of competition seem determined to ignore.

[6] Robert A. Brady, "Bureaucracy in Business," *The Journal of Social Issues*, December, 1945.

ORGANIZATIONAL REVOLUTION IN AMERICAN LABOR

If oligopoly is the dominant pattern in manufacturing, it is not the sole example of concentration of power. New constellations of countervailing power have arisen. Distributors have also become enormous units in the market. There are the giant mail-order houses, the chain stores, the mammoth department stores, the independent retailing organizations, and the farm-supply co-operatives. But quite as important as these organizational giants are the labor unions, the farm marketing co-operatives, and the like. Big labor has risen as a response to big business.

Historically, some of the labor unions such as in the building trades, bituminous coal, and clothing industries emerged to correct an intolerable market situation and to take advantage of the comparatively weak market position of the builders, operators, and manufacturers in these respective industries. On the whole, however, the development of powerful unions has been in response to the development of the concentrated power of the buyers of labor. Today about 15,000,000 workers are organized into unions. This constitutes hardly more than a fourth of all the gainfully employed persons in the nation's labor force.

At the beginning of the Roosevelt administration organized labor numbered about 3,500,000 members. These were members of craft unions belonging to the A.F. of L., to railway brotherhoods, or to independent unions. Then came the C.I.O. In 1937 membership had climbed to almost 7,500,000. At that time the unions successfully entered the mass-production industries such as steel, automobiles, rubber, and electric products industries. During World War II there was a tremendous growth in union activity and in participation in co-operative undertakings in production promotion alongside government and management. By 1945 labor-union membership passed the 14,000,000 mark, about 7,000,000 belonging to A.F. of L. unions, about 5,000,000 to C.I.O. unions, and 1,-750,000 to independent international unions.

The significance of the strategic power of unions can be partly grasped from the fact that while in 1945 they totaled considerably less than half the wage earners of the nation, almost all the workers in some trades and industries were organized, so that they were and continue to be in a position to influence directly the whole economy of the United States, as, for example, in coal and iron mining; transportation; commercial building construction; newspaper printing and publishing; aircraft and automobile manufacturing; shipbuilding; and clothing; steel; machinery; glass; rubber; meat packing; and metal industries. Size is of itself not so important as the militant spirit and the political and social potentialities of a highly organized minority. We have noted above the high concentration of productive power and control in manufacturing. It is in those very industrial concentrations that the countervailing power of organized labor is largely to be found.[7] The average worker today finds himself employed in plants where several hundred other workers are to be found. Half the industrial employers work in plants with over 500 employees.

Thus "big business" and "big labor" are giant power groups covering many of the principal products of industry. The extent to which they act responsibly and the extent to which they maintain industrial peace is a concern of the whole national and even international community. When the General Motors Coporation and the C.I.O. United Automobile Workers of America signed their five-year agreement in 1950, a union with over a million workers (470,000 in General Motors plants) contracted for industrial peace with a company which shares with Chrysler and Ford about 90 per cent of the production of passenger automobiles.

The churches have a great concern over the social role of these power groups because righteousness is not to be defined by superior might. In 1907 and 1908 when the churches first formulated their social creeds, they defended the right of collective bargaining, of voluntary association of workers into unions of their own choosing. Unions were then still in their childhood years. They have not completed their work in many parts of America today, notably in the South. The

[7] See Florence Peterson, *American Labor Unions* (New York: Harper & Bros., 1945), Chap. XII.

Protestant churches have an obligation to support the rightful claim of workers and not to stand with reactionary resistance to this form of democratic power. The churches have also much to gain by friendly influence of religion in industrial life. Yet the churches have also the duty to represent the cause of community-wide righteousness, the rights of individual workers, public interest in industrial relations, the rights of consumers and of innocent bystanders, the claim of interracial justice, and the larger democratic goals of the general economic welfare. The churches must examine themselves as to their own class biases and as to the recurrent demands of social justice. If the church is to be prophetic, it must transcend the culture which surrounds it.

Organized Farmers

The United States began as an agricultural nation. In 1790, 4 per cent of the population lived in cities of eight thousand or over. In 1940, 56 per cent of the American people lived in cities and towns, and some 43 per cent were classified as rural. Only half of the latter really lived on farms. In 1949, 59 per cent of the total lived in cities and towns. Less than 20 per cent lived on farms.

Many of the same factors at work in urban industrial life have influenced agricultural life, producing here too an organizational revolution. Mechanization, better seed, improved methods of cultivation, extension of communication systems, educational opportunities, population pressures—all have played a part. In 1930, according to the U. S. Census of Agriculture there were 6,289,000 farms and 10,472,000 persons ten years old and over engaged in agriculture. The greatest part of the labor on farms was performed by the farmer and his family. In 1940 the number of farms stood at 6,097,000 and the persons engaged in agriculture at 11,226,000. In 1945 there were 5,859,169 farms, and in 1950 there were 10,351,000 persons being employed on farms. The number of farms is decreasing, while the acreage is increasing. American agriculture is varied. In 1945, 30 per cent of American farms accounted for 70 per cent of our production of food and fiber. These farms averaged nearly four hundred acres and had an average capital investment of about $40,000. At the other end of the scale are over half a million holdings of under ten acres, with production mostly for home use. In between are over 3,000,000 farmers who are 70 per cent of those producing for the market but responsible for only 30 per cent of the food and fiber. Their holdings average eighty-one acres, their investment less than $10,000, their gross income $2,400, barely a fifth of the more than $11,000 of the first group.

There has been much mobility in agricultural life, some of it by migratory workers, some of it by tenant farmers and sharecroppers, and some of it from farm to nonfarm areas. The President's Commission on Migratory Labor reported in 1951 that the migrant labor force in American agriculture numbers approximately one million persons, a large percentage of whom work as families. The evil effect on family life of this situation is a challenge to the church and to the nation. Between 1925 and 1929 over 3,000,000 persons, and between 1930 and 1949 over 20,000,000 persons, moved from farms to nonfarm areas.

The forces responsible for the rapid changes in rural life represented by these figures have elicited efforts at mutual help, at self-help through co-operation, and of outside aid from government. Farmers have historically been in a weak market-exchange position. The farmer not only sells to the city, but also buys from it. About 60 per cent of his living and business expenses are consumed in purchasing commodities and services from urban agencies. Moreover, farm wages have lagged behind urban wages. It has been estimated that in 1920 (using 1914 as a base of 100) the percentage that the farm-labor rate bore to manufacturing hourly earnings was 97.2; in 1929, 62.0; in 1939, 38.4; and in 1948, 61.8.[8]

Farmers competed vigorously with one another in a national market dominated by urban industrial and financial giants. Little by little the farmers developed forms of co-operative buying and marketing. These associations reduced competition. Loss of individual freedom was compensated for by

[8] *Annual Report*, The National Bureau of Economic Research, May, 1949.

higher monetary income. In 1946-47 there were 10,125 marketing and purchasing associations with 5,436,000 members doing $7,116,000,000 of business transactions, of which $1,-452,000,000 was purchasing and $5,664,000,000 was marketing. In 1949-50, 10,035 associations, with 6,854,000 members, did a business of $8,726,000,000. The tendency, it may be added, is for consolidations in associations to take place, thus reducing the total number, and for membership to increase. Agriculture is becoming centralized in control.

The government has encouraged co-operative associations among farmers, including what are commonly referred to as consumers' co-operatives. Their activities extend not only to ordinary consumers' goods but also to life insurance, telephone service, and electrification. With these included, rural America has well over 20,000 co-operative associations. Federal laws have also given special permission to the marketing of their products in interstate or foreign commerce.

Perhaps the most spectacular aspect of agricultural economic life has been the recent power of the farm bloc in politics and the parity programs involving market prices. "Imperfect competition" and the managed market are now characteristics of what was once the most individualistic and freely competitive aspect of American enterprise. Relative surplus production in the late twenties and early thirties almost ruined American agriculture. The government gave assistance through programs of acreage retrenchment, through soil conservation, through credit and many other plans. It helped seek new markets and to expand the domestic market. The government made direct purchases of surplus products from farmers, handlers, and processors. Food-stamp plans and cotton-stamp plans were initiated. Tariff protection was enacted.

The over-all national policy in agriculture has as a key concept that of parity. Parity means conserving the ratio of the purchasing power of farm products in relation to other prices. Since 1941 farm prices have been above parity. From 1945 to 1949 they averaged from 17 to 21 per cent above the standard pegged to 1909-14. In March, 1949, the figure was 106. In this and many other ways farmers as a class are "married to government, and there is no possibility of divorce or separation." A Washington correspondent remarked in 1940: "Once the farm organization stand united, they can get anything out of Congress short of good growing weather." [9] When the organizations in the "farm bloc" stand together, they control at least fifteen million votes. The phrase "farm bloc" loosely covers three kinds of members: the Congressmen especially amenable to farm legislation, farm organizations of a general kind and their Washingon lobbies, and special crop organization—as, for example, the American Livestock Association. The general organizations include the Grange, which has 800,000 members; the Farmers Union, with 92,000 members; and the Farm Bureau Federation, which claims 690,000 members. This latter organization is to agriculture what the National Association of Manufacturers is to the field of manufacturing. One of its major goals was parity, which, as we have seen, is a price-fixing program.

The American farmer today is more prosperous than ever before in history. When we view his rising organized power, the same ethics need to be applied to his situation as to others, for nonfarmers are deeply affected by agricultural policies. In the struggle of group with group for a preferred place in the economy, the general welfare is often forgotten. The Christian church is challenged to develop concepts of social justice which can effectively relate Christian ethics to the organizational revolution in all phases of American life. The church has a stake in an over-all policy regarding the farm family, tenancy, conservation, education, mobility, understanding among farm and urban workers, production for domestic and world consumption, the rural community, and the integration of all agencies serving agriculture so as to enhance freedom, personal dignity, and responsibility.

Government as Big Business

Government is deeply involved in business life because government defines and largely creates property. The functions of government from the establishment of the Constitu-

---

[9] Quoted in Stuart Chase, *Democracy Under Pressure* (New York: Twentieth Century Fund, 1945), p. 94.

tion onward were tied closely to the manfacturing and business interest. Internal improvement, funding of state debts, protective tariffs, patent laws, opening the West for settlement, homestead laws, and innumerable other acts have assisted the growth of all phases of economic activity. Government itself is a major part of economic organization. Economic organization of government has grown tremendously. In 1913 the per-capita cost of all government, federal, state, and local, was $33.31. In 1941 it was $217.09. In 1913 there were 1,879,-000 government employees at the three levels; in 1941 more than 6,000,000—including the growing army. When in 1941 the total of expenditures was $24,100,000,000, it represented almost a fourth of the net national income. In 1951 the total federal expenditures for a year were $44,632,821,908. In 1948 there were 1,859,807 employees in the Civil Service of the United States. In 1951 there were 2,489,531 such employees.

Government expenditures go generally for (1) national defense, (2) relief and welfare, (3) schools and libraries, (4) highways and transport, (5) social security, (6) agriculture and conservation, (7) administration and legislation, (8) health, (9) police, (10) recreation, (11) interest and debt retirement, and (12) miscellaneous. It is well to keep in mind that these expenditures originate in over 165,000 units of government. Besides the federal government and the 48 states, there are 3,050 counties; 16,000 incorporated places—mostly cities; 19,000 townships; 118,000 school districts; and more than 8,000 special districts like water, irrigation, and conservation.[10]

Big government arises partly as a compensating force to other titanic groups in the economic order. It arises partly to take care of emergencies. It expands rapidly in wartime. The military aspects of the federal budget assume enormous proportions. When from July 1, 1949, to June 30, 1950, the expenditures reached $40,200,000,000 75 per cent were war-related, and only 25 per cent were for all other federal expenditures and services. In 1939 the war-related portion of the budget took only 29 per cent. In that year the normal

[10] *Ibid.*, pp. 111-12.

civilian services took an amount equal to 9 per cent of the national income; in 1950 they dropped to 4 per cent.

The non-war-related expenditures went in substantial amounts to the following: aids to agriculture developing natural resources and general government administration (F.B.I., flood control, Treasury Department, etc); and business aids (R.F.C. loans to industry; shipbuilding subsidies; aids to aviation industry; aids to trucking, rivers and harbors, "pork," Commerce Department, etc.). The smallest share of the budget's non-war-related 25 per cent went for items usually designated under "the welfare state." This was only $1,800,000,000 of the $40,200,000,000 budget.

Because the matter is so much under discussion, a comment by a C.I.O. analyst points up the moot question of whether the nation is being dominated by a "welfare state."

In 1950 the richest nation of the world spent less than five cents of each Federal tax dollar for public assistance for widows, orphans, the aged and the blind, help educate the nation's youth, rehabilitate the handicapped, eradicate slums, erect low-rent public housing, improve the people's health, meet the cost of all national parks, museums and libraries, and support the national school lunch program. These (plus Labor Department costs) are all of the much derided "welfare" and "social" services. To pay for them Uncle Sam collected less than 1 per cent of the National Income in fiscal 1950. For the nation as a whole, our use of public funds—local, state *and* federal—for health, education, and assistance to the needy, amounts to two-thirds of our spending on liquor and tobacco.[11]

The military-related aspects of governmental business affect all national business. When *Time* on December 1, 1952, commented on the appointment of Mr. Charles E. Wilson of General Motors as President Eisenhower's Secretary of Defense, it pointed out that he would preside over the nation's largest industry. Large sections of the economy are dependent on military contracts. Speculation is naturally rife regarding the effect on the economy when defense spending is radically curtailed.

[11] Quoted in *Social Questions Bulletin*, 41 (January, 1951), 1.

We have already noted, in connection with business organization, some of the problems of bureaucracy. In governmental organization these are matters of broad social concern for the churches. The problem is not primarily one of intelligence or expertness or motivation. There is much social idealism among the members of the bureaucracy. Moreover, they have a good record in courtesy. Goodwin Watson says, "It is a superstition of private enterprise that clerks in a department store just yearn to be of service while government employees show no consideration for the public." [12] But bureaucracy does breed power seeking, usually as an inevitable accompaniment of effort to do the work of an agency well, the "expansive tendency common to most complex business or engineering undertakings." The real problem is in impersonality, the tendency to reduce persons to mere parts of a vast systematic mechanism. This is a challenge for Christians. It challenges social inventiveness for correctives. Then there is the problem of red tape, of inaction in the face of innumerable regulations. There is the pressure to stay in line. Here a certain deterioration of character may set in. Accommodation to compromise is a chronic temptation. Then, too, there is little opportunity for intellectual growth in a vast routine organization. There are correctives for these problems, but they must be faced by any group dedicated to human dignity under God, to brotherhood, and to the motive of service. We have noted that bureaucracy is a function of complex institutions of whatever character. In its quest for social justice the church should educate its people for a full appreciation of this fact. In its positive appreciation of government it may rightly teach that "government of the people and by the people is also best for the people."

This chapter has barely touched upon the vast organizational interdependence of American economic life. We have only noted its broadest outlines. It is clear, however, that the church's concern for social responsibility must take into serious consideration not simply the private and personal problems

---

[12] "Bureaucracy in the Federal Government," *The Journal of Social Issues, December,* 1945, p. 18.

of individual church members and nonchurch people. The church must seek to understand the organization of economic life. Individualistic conceptions of business and industry do not correspond to social realities. In the midst of a "mixed economy" the church must be a social conscience, and it must have a broad and deep social strategy. It must understand the idolatries of power in all major economic groups. It must fearlessly confront and challenge the militarization of the economy. It must understand the dynamics of industrial democracy. It must be able to transcend all self-interested group efforts to mold church opinion to support special interests and the *status quo*. It must understand the forces that give rise to countervailing power groups. In short, the church must bring the whole economic order under the judgment of God and see it, as it were, "under the cross." There can be no simple identification of the kingdom of God with any economic system.

8

The Production and Distribution of Goods

George Hedley

"The earth is the lord's and the fulness thereof" (ps. 24:1). from this poetic but explicit declaration of the psalmist it was a fully natural step to Jesus' "Seek ye first the kingdom of God, and his righteousness; and all these things shall be added unto you" (Matt. 6:33). The uniform view of the Hebrew-Christian tradition is that this is indeed our Father's world, and that our tenancy within it is at his good pleasure.

The unhappy contrast, with this, of much current sub-Christian thinking and behavior was oddly pointed up by a student reader in a recent Thanksgiving service at a well-known college. "Take no thought," she read, "saying, What shall we eat? or, What shall we drink? or, Wherewithal shall we be clothed? (For after all these things do the *genteels* seek.)" (Matt. 6:31-32.) The "genteels" in fact have sought these things for themselves, and as ends, forgetting all too often that these are but instruments to a larger purpose. True Christian gentility sees rather the material good in its basic character as means, and thanks God not for the thing in itself but for the goal which the thing may help us to attain.

There is of course a subtle paradox involved. To use "Seek ye first the kingdom of God" to argue that a Christian should be indifferent to economic justice is completely to misinterpret the Gospel position. The point is not that man should live without bread, but that he cannot live truly by bread alone (Matt. 4:4-Luke 4:4, quoting Deu. 8:3). Bread then is given us that we shall be free to live the life of the spirit; and they who live in the spirit not only will use bread aright, but also will do their best to see that others have a fair chance to use bread too.

Bread and God's word alike are his gifts to us. Neither of them is to be monopolized, to be clutched to oneself for one's private advantage. He "who giveth us richly all things to enjoy" (I Tim. 6:17) expects of us that our "us" shall include all men and women everywhere. We who have been granted these gifts in full measure thus are appointed to be stewards both of the materials and of the mysteries (I Cor. 4:1); and both material and mystery are of God and not of ourselves.

Biblical Perspectives on Property

The religion of early Israel was a matter of Israel's total life. It was communal in its outreach, and controlling as to every detail. The primitive desert community knew almost nothing of personal property as such. Perhaps it was by an early contagion from Canaanite attitudes that Achan pre-empted for himself some of the loot of Ai. In any event the record in the book of Joshua (Chap. 7) indicates that it was not so much for looting Canaanite possessions, as for trying to withhold the loot from the Israelite community as a whole, that Achan and his household were condemned: "And they have put it even among their own stuff." We cannot share the ethnocentrism of ancient Israel. But we should note that Israel seems from the earliest days to have repudiated self-centeredness and even family-centeredness.

It was to the desert tradition, contrasted with the develop-ing personal wealth and poverty of settled agricultural life, that Amos appealed in his bitter assault on those who "sold the righteous for silver, and the poor for a pair of shoes" (Amos 2:6). Temperamentally at least Amos seems to be at one with the Rechabites, whose devotion to desert freedom and equity was symbolized by their refusal to use the products of the grape, and by their stubbornly living in tents instead of in the newly fashionable stone houses (Jer. 35:6 ff). Furiously the Tekoan prophet condemns the privileged women of Israel as "kine of Bashan," that is to say, "fat cows," "which oppress the poor, which crush the needy" (Amos 4:1).

In a later and different cultural setting, but with the same passion for justice to the weak, Micah the small farmer cries out his protest against urban finance and metropolitan domination.

They covet fields, and take them by violence; and houses, and take them away. . . . They build up Zion with blood, and Jerusalem with iniquity. The heads thereof judge for reward, and the priests thereof teach for hire, and the prophets thereof divine for money. . . . Therefore shall Zion for your sake be plowed as a field, and Jerusalem shall become heaps, and the mountain of the house as the high places of the forest. (Mic. 2:2; 3:10-12.)

If Amos and Micah may be discounted because each of them spoke for his own interests, the one as a desert herdsman and the other as the despairing holder of a mortgaged acreage, no such charge can be levied against Isaiah and Jeremiah. Isaiah, closely related to the king, clearly is a "traitor to his class": "Cease to do evil; learn to do well; seek judgment, relieve the oppressed, judge the fatherless, plead for the widow" (Isa. 1:16-17). Jeremiah, entitled by birth to a clerical living, abandons it to cry in the very temple gate, "If ye thoroughly execute judgment between a man and his neighbour; if ye oppress not the stranger, the fatherless, and the widow, . . . then will I cause you to dwell in this place, in the land that I gave to your fathers, for ever and ever" (Jer. 7:5-7).

The "second giving of the Law," in the book of Deuteronomy, probably is almost exactly contemporary with the beginning of Jeremiah's work. Here we find the rationale of the Sabbath commandment stated as "that thy manservant and thy maidservant may rest as well as thou. And remember that thou wast a servant in the land of Egypt" (Deut. 5:14-15). Even later, in the priestly code of Leviticus, the farmer is enjoined, "Thou shalt not wholly reap the corners of thy field, neither shalt thou gather the gleanings of thy harvest.

And thou shalt not glean thy vineyard . . . ; thou shalt leave them for the poor and stranger" (Lev. 19:9-10). In almost the same breath the law requires, "Thou shalt not defraud thy neighbour, neither rob him: the wages of him that is hired shall not abide with thee all night until the morning" (Lev. 19:13). The sabbatical year for land and people also is provided for in this system, and the year of jubilee, in which Israel was to "proclaim liberty throughout all the land unto all the inhabitants thereof . . . ; and ye shall return every man unto his possession, and ye shall return every man unto his family (Lev. 25:10).

The early Christians were in no position thus to legislate for a whole community. Their treatment of questions of property therefore was of a more immediate and personal kind. It is a grave misreading of the New Testament, however, to suppose that its authors rejected the communal and humanitarian emphasis which throughout had marked authentic Judaism. Jesus and Paul could not set up laws for a nation. They did call emphatically not only for justice, but also for generosity beyond the claims of justice. "If any man will . . . take away thy coat, let him have thy cloke also. . . . Give to him that asketh thee, and from him that would borrow of thee turn not thou away" (Matt. 5:40, 42). And the one saying of the Master which Paul (through the editor of the Acts) adds to the Gospel record is, "Remember the words of the Lord Jesus, how he said, It is more blessed to give than to receive" (Acts 20:35).

It was not formal Communism, but a vital communion in love, that produced the sharing of goods among the first Christians in Jerusalem.

Neither said any of them that ought of the things which he possessed was his own; but they had all things common. . . . Neither was there any among them that lacked: for as many as were possessors of lands or houses sold them, and brought the prices of the things that were sold, and laid them down at the apostles' feet: and distribution was made unto every man according as he had need." (Acts 4:32, 34-35.)

126

TYPES OF PROPERTY IN RELATION TO PRODUCTION

That last clause of course is quoted in the familiar Socialist slogan: "From each according to his ability; to each according to his need." But much has happened since the days of the spontaneous sharing among the Jerusalem Christians. Quite evidently the familiar patterns of personal ownership in the Greco-Roman world were not overturned by the Christian church. Rather the church accepted the prevailing modes, softening them here and there but by no means attacking them with revolutionary intent.

The medieval community, allowing for very definite advantages held by the feudal nobles, was in a real sense still a community of sharing. Even lord and peasant shared, in that the peasant gave service in return for security; and the peasants shared among themselves in a wholly literal way, plowing their assigned strips of the manor and turning their animals into the common pasture. Theoretically, as nationalisms developed, the king was understood to own all the lands of the realm. The barons held their properties under him, and the people theirs under the barons.[1]

This worked reasonably well as long as the only significant productive property was the land itself. In the Renaissance, however, capital as monetary wealth began to complicate the picture. Early in the eighteenth century we find, in *The Spectator*, Sir Roger de Coverley as landlord, arguing violently with the aptly named Sir Andrew Freeport, who is the spokesman of the new world of commercial enterprise.[2]

The next step, itself produced by a wealth which greatly increased public purchasing power, was the invention of machines to enlarge and speed the production of goods. Capital now began to express itself as "capital goods"; and in England in particular the principal means of production became factories rather than fields. This involved serious displace-

---

[1] An excellent description of medieval agricultural economy will be found in Shepard B. Clough and Charles W. Cole, *Economic History of Europe* (Boston: D. C. Heath & Co., 1941), Chap. I, "A Society Based on Manors."

[2] Richard Steele, *The Spectator*, No. 174 (September 19, 1711).

ments of population. The trading cities, themselves a recent creation, now were turned into manufacturing centers. The landowners saw increased possibility of profit in enclosing the "common lands" and reserving them for their personal enterprises, notably the production of wool for the factories to spin and weave.[3] The peasantry, thus divorced from the soil, became the labor supply for the factories.

Land and capital were identified as the two kinds of productive property. The land mostly was retained by the families that so long had held it. Capital belonged to those whose energy had made them leaders in the new kind of enterprise, and whose luck in the very risky commerce of those days had been good rather than bad. Scarcely anyone thought yet of productive property in labor, save as an abundant and cheap labor supply itself was regarded as a kind of property of the capitalist.

Types of Property in Relation to Distribution

At the point of distributing the income of economic production, labor did come into the picture as the early "political economists" saw it. The owner of the land received rent; the owner of capital (money or goods) hoped for profit; the worker was paid in wages. Still, however, rent and profit were regarded as the proper ends of economic production, while wages were considered to be a necessary evil. Thus the wage factor, conceived as a drag upon economic enterprise, was thought best held to the lowest practicable minimum.

"Classical" economic wage theories were rationalizations of this position. The "subsistence" theory assumed labor to be on a par with any other capital goods, therefore to be secured at the least possible cost and used to the greatest possible advantage. The "wage fund" theory was a refinement of this,

[3] In addition to the standard economic histories, see the first part of Sir Thomas More's *Utopia* (1516); e.g., "one covetous and insatiable cormorant and very plague of his native country may compass many thousand acres of ground together within one pale or hedge, the husbandmen be thrust out of their own. . . . Away they trudge . . . out of their known and accustomed houses, finding no places to rest in."

assigning to the enterpriser a bookkeeping task in holding his wage costs to a fixed, predetermined amount. The "marginal productivity" theory still regarded labor as means only, with the advantage of the capitalist as the only significant end.[4]

In violent contrast to all this came the explosive theorizing of Karl Marx.[5] He held land and capital to be things dead and useless in themselves, and labor to be the only real creator of value. Labor therefore, he argued, merited the full return of all production; and rent and profit were to be rejected as completely improper drains upon labor's rightful possession of all the fruits of industry.

Our modern world is one of dispute between these two conflicting positions, with the Soviet Union speaking for Marxist conclusions, and the West for the historic views which grew up in its growing economic society. Actually of course the increments of rent and profit have by no means been eliminated in the Communist lands. The common ownership of the means of production, whether administered democratically as the Socialists hope or autocratically as the Soviets practice, still demands that a large part of productive income shall be put back into the land for fertility, and into the factories to cover depreciation of old equipment and creation of new. Under no system can labor secure immediately and without exception the total price received for the goods to which labor has given the utility of form.

Problems of Justice in Relation to the Production of Goods

A wholly different approach, antedating that of Marx by three quarters of a century, was that of Adam Smith. The

---

[4] For a brief and clarifying statement of historic wage theories see Richard A. Lester, *Economics of Labor* (New York: The Macmillan Co., 1941), Chap. 7, "Wages: A Parade of Theories."

[5] The Marxist classic, of course, is *Das Kapital* (1867), conveniently available in a Modern Library "Giant." An earlier and somewhat more readable work is his *Critique of Political Economy* (1859). *The Communist Manifesto* (1848) is a revolutionary, but scarcely an economic, document. An excellent and dispassionate treatment of Marx and his thinking is Otto Rühle's *Karl Marx: His Life and Work* (New York: New Home Library, 1943).

foundation of Smith's whole argument was that wealth consisted not in possession, but precisely in production.[6] Thus he anticipated Marx in denying to both land and capital the character of self-validating assets. "The annual wealth of a nation," as Smith spoke of it, was the value of the goods actually produced within a given year. Land which lay fallow, and factories which lay idle, had created no wealth and therefore had earned no return.

Effective production, Smith's argument went on, depended upon the greatest possible division of labor; for only by specialization, whether among nations as to specific products or among workmen as to specific jobs, could efficient and therefore abundant production be achieved. But such a division of labor, Smith continued, hinged inevitably upon the existence of a large and demanding market for the goods to be produced: and so upon the purchasing power that was available.

It was for these wholly logical reasons, not in any devotion to the selfish interests of industrial and commercial enterprisers, that Smith opposed all governmental interference in restraint of trade.[7] We must remember that "mercantilism," representing the dominant business attitudes of Smith's time, stood not at all for business freedom but rather for all sorts of tariffs, subsidies, and quotas. To a very large extent both those who worship Smith today and those who execrate him have misunderstood his whole position. What he sought was the fullest possible production; and to that end he pleaded for the greatest possible freedom.

Though Smith had been a professor of moral philosophy, he rested his argument chiefly on practical rather than moral grounds. It is important to notice here, however, that ethics and economics come together in a very striking way at the

[6] *The Wealth of Nations* (1776) is much more lucid than is *Das Kapital;* no one who cares for clear economic thinking is to be excused from reading it through. Again the Modern Library provides a useful and inexpensive edition (New York: 1937).

[7] To learn what Adam Smith really thought of most "merchants and master manufacturers," see the conclusion of Book I of *The Wealth of Nations* (Modern Library edition, pp. 249 ff.).

point of genuine economic productivity. The history of the automobile industry provides a noteworthy specimen case.

In its early days the automobile was strictly a luxury product, and its appeal was to the limited number who possessed an important share of this world's goods. "The ——— Company of America," said a nationally circulated advertisement in the autumn of 1917, "offers to the wealthy men of America an expensive car: a car that will cost you money to buy, and money to maintain." That company, charging snob-appeal prices and paying its workers some $2.00 a day, long ago went bankrupt.

Meanwhile a mechanic in Detroit had a wholy different idea. He offered to the common people of America an inexpensive car, a car that cost nothing in particular to buy and a few feet of baling wire to maintain. At the same time he did the unprecedented thing of paying the workers in the Ford plant a minimum of $5.00 a day, which meant that even they could afford to buy for themselves the car they were building.

It is not necessary to approve all Henry Ford's personal peculiarities as Harry Bennett recently has recounted them.[8] It is impossible to deny that Ford's policies of low prices and high wages revolutionized all of American industry. This was the efficient production of wealth, in truth; and a production achieved largely by that division of labor which was the assembly line. It produced great wealth indeed for the Ford family, and for the few other original stockholders. But it produced untold wealth also for the whole nation, including those millions of workmen whose standard of living now automatically includes not only a car, but also a house complete with electric refrigerator and television.

When in 1908 the Methodist Episcopal Church in its first "Bill of Rights," and the newly organized Federal Council of Churches in its derivative "Social Creed," declared for "the highest wage that each industry can afford to pay,"[9] they

[8] *We Never Called Him Henry* (New York: Gold Medal Books, 1951).
[9] It will be instructive to trace the successive revisions of the "Social Creed" in the quadrennial editions of *Doctrines and Discipline of the Meth-*

131

were stating the case not only for economic justice but also for economic good sense. Productive efficiency, as Smith so clearly saw, rests upon an effective division of labor. Such a division of labor is possible only in a widely extended market. The extent of the market, which is nothing other than broadened purchasing power, is best guaranteed by seeing that everyone, including the production worker himself, is in a position to buy what farm and industry produce.

PROBLEMS OF JUSTICE IN RELATION
TO THE DISTRIBUTION OF GOODS

Thus it becomes evident that production itself rests upon distribution. Our mistake in the Coolidge era, which led to the crash of 1929, was not in our producing too much. It was rather in our having distributed inaccurately, which was the same as having distributed inequitably. We had held too much of the product of industry out as rent, too much as profit. When the common man had exhausted not only his cash but his credit as well, the end of the halcyon days had come.

Gallantly enough President Hoover pleaded with employers to maintain their payrolls. But no one could do that without continuing income; and few enterprisers moved soon enough to cut prices in an effort to stimulate renewed buying. Rather (exactly like the much-condemned A.A.A.) they cut production in the hope of maintaining prices. Thereby they wiped out wholly the buying power of the workers who were laid off; and thus they spun the spiral of deflation ever faster and deeper.

There are signs that both the public and the business world have learned something from the 1929 collapse and the long depression which followed it. Nobody talks favorably now of "subsistence wages," and industry resists wage demands only on the ground of alleged inability to pay more. That the laborer is worthy of his hire is not denied, at least in words; and the genuinely advantaged position of the American work-

odist (Episcopal) Church. Note also the economic pronouncements made by the World Council of Churches at Amsterdam in 1948.

man, as compared with those of other lands, attests his success in gaining a large and increasing share in the products of his work.

Within industry there remains the question of proportioning wages aright in terms of productivity. Organized labor here seems often to be working against its own long-run interests, when it sets maximum quotas of output or demands the hiring of needless hands. This does not create wealth, and so ultimately it does no one any economic good.

On the other hand, it is no easy matter to determine just how much hire each individual worker has merited. Much has been done by personnel departments to devise tables showing necessary preparation and experience; inevitable, even if hidden, costs of working at the given job; and relative inconvenience, discomfort, or danger; as well as actual productive output.[10] There is manifest fairness in trying to use such factors in wage determination; but there is no possibility that any such table ever will guarantee to each worker a pay check exactly reflecting his personal economic usefulness.

Nor does this type of procedure help at all to solve the problem of economic distribution to those who contribute nothing in economic productivity. What about relative wages for the same job when it is held by a bachelor and when it is assigned to a man with a large family to support? What about the unemployables, whether mentally or physically incompetent, the orphans, or the aged? A simple neighborhood society took care of such cases in an informal but fairly effective way. A complex urban society has to work out much more complicated answers.

Recently in a California community there was discovered a Mexican laborer with twelve children, who under the existing rules received much more from the combined product of unemployment compensation and county relief than he could possibly earn if he took a job. This manifestly makes no sense; but just what would be the sensible answer? In another Cali-

---

[10] The reader is advised to visit personnel departments of business and industrial establishments in his own vicinity to learn what is being done in job analysis.

fornia town the local shopkeepers, free enterprisers to a man, vigorously supported striking miners because they knew that the local wage scale was directly reflected in their own business success. Where does justice lie here, and where sound economic judgment? [11]

The theory behind the W.P.A. was not that men and women should be kept alive for humanitarian reasons, but that they should have enough buying power to stimulate a business revival.[12] A similar theory apears in the more thoughtful promotions of old-age pension plans, in the argument that larger pensions would create better business for everybody. Most economists would say that the W.P.A. was usefully inflationary, but that some pension plans are dangerously so. Where, however, shall we draw the line?

No economic issue of today is trickier than that of provision for the aged. Our traditional attitudes lead us to hold that younger members of the family ought to take care of their elders; and no doubt most of them are willing to do so. But at what point does the reduction of both the elder and the younger to a subsistence standard of living endanger the healthy flow of trade, and so the economic well-being of the entire community? How far does justice require, how far does practicality suggest, that the community itself should distribute this burden among all its members?

ETHICAL PROBLEMS OF CONSUMPTION

It used to be argued that great individual fortunes were justified because of great individual expenditures, and so in the filtering down of wealth into all the levels of society. The fallacy here is that no really great wealth ever can be ex-

---

[11] These two cases were reported to me by students in my classes at Mills College. I can supply the names of the towns, and further details, to anyone who is curious enough to ask.

[12] The underlying position, of course, is that made famous by John Maynard Keynes. Lord Keynes's own classic statement is his *General Theory of Employment, Interest and Money* (New York: Harcourt, Brace & Co., 1936). For an analytical summary of Keynesian views see H. Gordon Hayes on "Keynesism and Public Policy," Chap. VI in Glenn E. Hoover, *Twentieth Century Economic Thought* (New York: Philosophical Library, 1950).

pended altogether upon consumers' goods. It tends rather to pile up as investment, and so to build reserve capital rather than to increase general buying power.

At somewhat lower levels of income, however, the problem of expenditure remains a serious one. Obviously it is wise, for one's own advantage, to spend when everyone else is trying to save, and to save when everyone else is spending; that is, to buy in depression and to sell in prosperity. But if everyone gets the same idea at the same time, the result is either inflation as the result of too enthusiastic spending, or depression as the product of too careful saving. The ethical question for the individual thus involves not only the welfare of his immediate family, but also his family's effect upon our whole economy.

Again it is manifestly unwise, and it is not economically useful, to indulge in "conspicuous waste." [13] But just as it is unfair to deprive the laborer of his hire, so it is dubiously Christian to seek to cut the seller's profit beyond the point where he can keep going. Admittedly this is a somewhat theoretical point, for those who get cut prices the most readily seem to be those who best could afford to pay in full. Yet every buyer does have a moral obligation to the seller's well-being, even as has the employer to the employee's. Both are buying what they want, and from persons who must be regarded always as ends in themselves.

The ethical aspects of commercial advertising also require careful examination. Fair Trade laws and Better Business Bureaus represent efforts to hold the wilder kinds of selling under some measure of control. The individual can do something here, by careful scrutiny of magniloquent claims and by refusing to buy under intensive pressures. He will be well advised, too, to investigate such services as those of Consumers' Research and Consumers' Union, which promote business ethics by advice as to sensible buying.

Perhaps we need some reconsideration of the ancient medieval concept of the "just price." We shall not establish

[13] See Thorstein Veblen, *The Theory of the Leisure Class* (New York: The Macmillan Company, 1899 and after).

such a price, however, merely by pleading for good will on the part of buyer and seller. Individually we have to be clear as to the nature and the validity of our own wants, and we have to be informed about qualities and costs. Nationally we scarcely shall attain the end without some legal restraint of those who seek consciously to profit by misrepresentation and so by injustice.

SUGGESTED AREAS FOR SOCIAL ACTION

The church as an institution will find it difficult to affect at all directly the economic structures and procedures of our nation and of the world; but the individual Christian can do much to develop sanity and decency in his own economic life and in that of his immediate milieu. The first requisite is that he shall know whereof he tries to think, and speak, and act. The suggestions here offered are therefore mainly for investigation; and they are phrased in the form of questions.

1. What relevance if any have the social ethics of the Hebrew prophets, and the ethical teachings of Jesus, in the very different social settings of our own time?

2. What is the scale of agricultural land ownership in your own region? Does it appear to you to be a healthy one? What effect has corporation farming had upon the workers? Upon the communities in which they live and buy?

3. Is yours a one-industry or a multiple-industry community? What are the effects of layoffs, whether seasonal or due to labor disputes? Do your local businessmen depend for their income chiefly upon management or upon employees? Does the answer to this suggest any revision of their standard ways of thinking?

4. What are the aims and methods of your local employers' associations? Do they enforce a "closed shop" among enterprisers in their respective fields? Does their activity serve the interests of the community as a whole?

5. How strong is organized labor in your vicinity? What useful services has it contributed, to its members and to the community at large? What unwise procedures does it advocate in industry? What improper methods has it used in disputes?

What would be the effect upon the community of the total dissolution of the unions?

6. Who has benefited most from the "protective" tariff? Is support of tariffs consistent with demanding the freedom of business from governmental interference? Are farm price supports comparable to tariffs? What would be Adam Smith's opinion of such devices?

7. Who owns, technically, the farms and industries in your region? How much influence does the average stockholder exert upon management policies? What have been the effects of the recent divorcement of stock ownership from managerial responsibility? What is being done by business itself to change this situation? Do you approve the measures taken or proposed? [14]

8. How far are the farmers and business enterprisers in your local church interested in the ethical aspects of their functions in the economic world? Are they fair to their employees? To their consumers? To their competitors?

9. Do the employed persons in your church work in establishments where unions are organized? Do they belong? Do they take part in union activities? Do they offer constructive criticism as to union policies?

10. What does your community do about unemployables? Is it aware of their existence? Can their condition be improved, either by private or by public action?

11. What proportion of your local population is beyond working age? How do these people get a living? What sort of life do they have? How serious a burden are they upon their families? What are the state and the local community doing to meet their needs? Could they do more, and more wisely?

12. What do your people buy? Do they have adequate information about commodities and market trends? What is their basis for decision between satisfying immediate wants and saving for the future? What have been the effects of recent inflation upon the stability of their thinking and action?

The seeking of factual replies to such questions as these sure-

[14] For recent changes in corporation attitudes and policies see *Fortune* for February, 1951, an issue devoted to "The Permanent Revolution." The text of this number was published as a book in the same year.

ly will result in the finding of practical answers. One's conclusions about the production and distribution of goods should lead him to align himself with that political party which most nearly shares his considered position; to join the economic group—Chamber of Commerce, trade association, union, club, society—which is most likely to serve his chosen ends; and to plan the economy of his own life in a fuller realization of its ultimate meanings and effects, both economic and human. The intelligent Christian will do all these things. First, however, he will seek the kingdom of God, and God's righteousness; and as he does, he will find all these things falling rightly into place for him.

9

World Economic Problems

Eddy Asirvatham

IN THEIR SEARCH FOR A STABLE AND JUST WORLD ORDER, FEW EVEN WELL-MEANING PEOPLE SEEM TO REALIZE THE IMPORT-ance of a proper understanding of economic problems. Political problems push themselves to the forefront everywhere and attract attention chiefly because of considerations of national patriotism, while economic problems are often tucked away in the background. Even the man in the street understands the meaning of political order and security and the broad differences between democracy and communism as political systems. But he does not have a firm grasp of the economic factors which underlie democracy and nationalism, as well as war and peace.

If this situation is to be set right, as much attention should be paid to a study of the economic bases of peace and order as to the political. This was well understood by the framers of the United Nations Charter when they set up on a par with the Security Council, which is mainly responsible for order and security, the Economic and Social Council together with its various commissions and subcommissions and the related specialized agencies.

Poverty in the Midst of Plenty

It is ironical that in a world of plenty there is abject poverty. Outside of the United States, Canada, western Europe and

Great Britain, Australia, New Zealand, and a few other countries, grinding poverty seems to be the fate of the common man. The resources of the world are plentiful, and modern Western man has made an unprecedented advance in science and technology. Yet over a great part of the world the earning capacity is unbelievably low and the standard of living depressed. The income per capita averages $80 a year in the economically underdeveloped areas. While the per-capita income for the United States is about $1,675 a year, for India it is as low as $54. The average diet in underdeveloped areas is 20 per cent below minimum health standards. While the United States consumes on an average of 3,100 calories per person per day, the average for the underdeveloped areas is 2,000. Several countries, including India, do not even reach this low figure. Malnutrition is concentrated in underdeveloped areas.

World War II has meant further decline in the standard of living for the economically underdeveloped countries of the world. Between 1937 and 1950 the cost of living of all items in India went up by 300 per cent, and the cost of food went up still higher, without anything like a corresponding rise in wages and salaries. In the United States, on the contrary, the cost of food for the same period went up by a little over 100 per cent. Under long years of British rule more people in India were driven to the land to eke out a miserable livelihood. While the total wealth of the country may have steadily increased, the common man's lot in 1952 was worse than it was a generation ago. Liberia, one of the few free areas in Africa, entirely dominated by American capital, had in 1949 one of the lowest per-capita incomes in the world—$38.

For this state of affairs the blame rests much more with man than with nature. Asia is rich in natural resources; and yet the people in general are unbelievably poor. The countries of south and southeast Asia and the Far East produce large quantities of one or more of the following items: rice, tea, sugar, tobacco, rubber, and tin. They have a virtual monopoly of some of the commodities required for an expanding economy. India and Pakistan produce practically the whole of the world's jute crop. In 1937 China produced 67 per cent of the world's antimony ore. China and India are rich in bauxite. China and Burma produce practically the whole of the world's tungsten. India is the second largest producer of manganese in the world. Asia has a vast amount of tin and iron ore. Burma and the Middle Eastern countries of Iraq and Iran have considerable resources of oil and allied mineral products. Japan produces nearly 80 per cent of the world's raw silk. Nearly all the rice that is grown in the world is produced in South and East Asia. Considerable quantities of wheat, millets, and pulses (lentils) also are grown in several parts of Asia to supplement rice. As regards oil seeds, copra, tea, and tobacco, according to Ghate, Asia has either a world monopoly or at least a controlling influence on world supplies.[1]

In the words of President Truman, in a speech delivered on March 6, 1952, "Four fifths or more of the manganese, the tin, and the chrome in a United States destroyer or jet fighter comes from outside the Western hemisphere." The underdeveloped areas within the so-called free world produce 93 per cent of the world's manganese, 100 per cent of the rubber, 55 per cent of the lead, 100 per cent of the chromite, 42 per cent of the copper, 100 per cent of the industrial diamonds, 100 per cent of the graphite, 100 per cent of the sisal, 40 per cent of the zinc, 92 per cent of the mercury, 99 per cent of the nickel, and 93 per cent of the cobalt; also large quantities of the uranium ore and mica.

REMEDIES FOR MASS POVERTY

In spite of all these natural advantages, a majority of the people of Asia are chronically hungry owing to a variety of reasons. One of them is undoubtedly their backward state of industrialization. For the most part they are still raw-material producing countries and are unduly dependent upon the West for the sale of their products. When the demand for rubber and tin, for example, is high, countries like Indochina, Indonesia, and Malaya have a relatively prosperous time. But when there is a slump, they are hit hard. Countries

[1] Most of the facts in this paragraph are taken from B. G. Ghate, *Asia's Trade* (New Delhi: Indian Council of World Affairs, 1947).

which are dependent on a few raw materials and do not produce their own food are the first to feel the effects of a depression and the last ones to recover. The moral of this seems to be that these countries should develop a more diversified economy, process their raw materials before shipping them abroad, and thereby assure themselves of a better price; and regulate their supply and prices through some such organization as an Inter-Asian commodity organization. Ghate, who makes a powerful plea for such an organization, believes that it will help to co-ordinate policy and effort. At present Asia has very little effect on world policies or prices; and until now European consumers have dominated international policies. Such domination is bound to continue as long as imperialism continues. It may be that a free Asia in time will devise something of a Schuman Plan for different regions of that continent.

Asia's trade at present does not exceed 15 per cent of the total world trade. If Asia is to capture more of that trade, she needs not only a rational system of industrialization, but also improved communications and transportation, capital, and technical assistance. It is at this point that the United Nations Technical Assistance program, Point IV of the United States, and the Colombo Plan of the British Commonwealth countries can be of maximum service.

Economic and Technical Assistance

Primarily because of the exigencies of the cold and limited war of today the United States is vitally interested in the economic improvement of the underdeveloped countries. Unfortunately what aid is given is meant to win political friends and military allies in the combat with Communism. Considerations of expediency are often back of the aid on the part of the giver as well as the receiver. From any religious and truly moral point of view, however, the gift should bless and ennoble the giver as well as the receiver. Because of the continued opposition to the military provisions of the Mutual Security program of the United States on the part of some Asian countries, India, Pakistan, Burma, and others are receiving American economic and technical assistance without any explicit military commitments. India is not willing to lease bases or sell strategic materials to any world power, and here she is right.

In this general context the story of Horace Holmes, the Point IV administrator of the United States in India, sounds almost like a miracle. There are others equally qualified as he, if not better, in his own field. But he has brought to his work a spirit of humility, thorough understanding of local conditions and the psychology of the people, and dedication which are difficult to match anywhere. Through befriending the peasants and working with them, he has helped to raise food production in the area where he works by an average of 46 per cent. He has introduced better-yielding wheat, potatoes, tomatoes, and mustard in the Etawah district in North India. Farmers are now using steel plows, a simplified type of harrows, improved threshers, five-tooth cultivators, and the like. Peasants are taught the use of legumes, the making of compost, the filling of mud holes, the elimination of mosquitoes by the use of DDT, and the making of soakage pits for disposal of waste water. Special attention is paid to animal husbandry. Peasants are persuaded to raise Egyptian clover for feeding milch cows and to innoculate their cattle against hemorrhagic septicemia and rinderpest. Co-operatives are encouraged, and community wells are dug. Adult education is promoted through schools, libraries, local dramas, and audio-visual aids. High-caste people are persuaded to admit Harijans (former Outcastes or Untouchables) into the Hindu temple and to give them equality of opportunity. Indian voluntary workers are trained in different parts of the country under the leadership of Horace Holmes with the financial aid received from the Ford Foundation.

It is work of this kind that can best promote peace and understanding and stave off national and international fear and suspicion, which not infrequently lead to war. It is no wonder that recently Nehru said that if the United States could spare six hundred Horace Holmeses, he could use every one of them. All that India insists upon is that no military strings should be attached to economic and technical assistance. It is regrettable that American public opinion places its faith much more in arms and ammunitions than in economic and technical assistance. The amount voted by Congress for this latter type of aid for the current year is only 10 per cent of the total voted under defense support. Point IV should become Point I.

As important as the pilot projects conducted by the United States is the over-all social and economic planning work undertaken by the technical assistance program of the United Nations. Agencies such as the FAO, WHO, UNESCO, and World Bank are doing much to make up-to-date knowledge, expert help, and some financial assistance available to many countries in the world. This kind of help is comparatively free from the suspicions which go with American aid. Unfortunately the United Nations does not have the funds to render more practical assistance. Some of its excellent schemes languish for lack of funds. Yet efforts are being made through the pooling of scientific and other resources to enable countries to wipe out epidemic, to improve food production, to increase literacy, and to expand transportation and communication facilities.

INDIA'S FIVE YEAR PLAN

Valuable as economic and technical assistance from outside may be, the most that it can do is to point the way. Pilot projects can serve as models and stimulate interest. But self-help is the best kind of help. This alone can eventually solve the economic and social ills of the economically backward countries of the world. Realizing the truth of this, India launched a Five Year Plan in 1951 at a cost of $3,800,000,000. The major emphasis is placed upon agriculture, irrigation, rural electrification, and prevention of erosion; 135 river valley projects, comparable to the TVA, have been prepared, and work has been started on some of them. By 1955-56, when the work on the latter will be completed, it is expected that 8,800,000 acres will be brought under irrigation. When all the schemes are completed, 16,500,000 acres will have the benefit of irrigation. Four million acres of land will be restored to cultivation. One and a half million acres will be reclaimed with the aid of tractors.

According to a survey made by the FAO, food production in India can be raised by 20 per cent in ten years, her present shortage being 10 per cent or five million tons a year; 10 per cent can be added by using fertilizers, 5 per cent by introducing new varieties, and 5 per cent through protection from insects and diseases.

The Five Year Plan has an industrial sector too, which aims at pushing the existing production up to 1,315,000 tons of steel, 4,600,000 tons of cement, 200,000 tons of aluminum, and 165,000 tons of paper and paper board. Provision is made for supplementing private enterprise by state enterprise. India already has the largest textile industry in the world and the largest steel industry in Asia. India welcomes foreign capital and even foreign plants like motor-car assemblage plants and oil refineries, provided they do not throttle India's economic life.

In the opinion of many Asian observers, scientific agriculture and national industrialization with adequate wages and protection for the worker need to be supplemented by a well-thought-out and carefully worked system of cottage industries or rural handicrafts. B. G. Ghate, quoted above, writes: "The country-side has probably become the poorer for the disruption of handicrafts which unbalanced industrialization has brought about [as well as] the migration of its most productive and progressive sections to urban slums." [2]

J. C. Kumarappa, an ardent follower of Gandhian economy, is opposed to both capitalism and communism, and claims that both involve violence and exploitation. He advocates a decentralized village economy planned and executed democratically, nationalization of the principal heavy industries of the country, elimination of the middleman, and use of electricity and power on a small scale to supplement manual labor and labor of draft animals. Public utilities are to be run under collective or co-operative control. Kumarappa's ideals are production for use rather than for profit, reduction of large-

[2] *Op. cit.*, p. 159.

145

scale manufacture to a size sufficient to meet local needs, and economic self-sufficiency as far as possible. These methods, Kumarappa believes, are most conducive to the development of human personality. Some of the personal vows which an adherent of this type of economy undertakes are nonviolence, truth, nonstealing, continence, nonamassing, physcial labor, control of the palate, fearlessness, and *swadeshi* (patronage of homemade goods). Whatever the shortcomings of this scheme may be, it rests solidly on sound moral and social principles. It is doubtful whether such an economy can solve mass poverty within a measurable length of time, or that a majority will adopt it as their way of life without the moral force of a person like Mahatma Gandhi.

OTHER FACTORS RESPONSIBLE FOR ABJECT POVERTY

Capital, technical assistance, and national and rational planning including rural industries alone cannot solve the economic ills of the day. Over a great part of Asia landlordism has been a fruitful cause of mass poverty. This has been and still is a major factor to contend with in Japan, Korea, China, southeast Asia, India, Pakistan, and the Near and Middle East. Under American occupation valuable land reforms were brought about in Japan. Through well-timed and far-reaching land reforms the Communists in North Korea and China stole the thunder from the nationalists and democrats. The Huk rebellion in the Philippines had landlordism as one of its justifiable grievances. A vexing problem in Indonesia is the problem of the landless rubber tapper and rice cultivator. Until recently 64 per cent of the cultivated land of India belonged to landlords. India today is manfully tackling this problem. Seven thousand square miles of cultivated land have been taken away from the Nizam of Hyderabad for distribution among the peasants. Several state legislatures have enacted measures for a fair distribution of land among the peasants after making some compensation to the present owners. Following the Gandhian tradition of moral suasion and nonviolence, Vinoba Bhave has secured 100,000 acres of land from the rich for distribution among the poor. Justice Douglas of the U.S. Supreme Court, who understands Asian conditions better than many Americans, writes: "When we go with the Point IV program, let's be prepared to make up our minds whom we are for. Are we for the people, or are we for the landlords?"

As guilty as landlords are irresponsible businessmen. The East is passing through some of the stages through which the West passed when it began to industrialize itself. Cheap and abundant labor, scarcity of consumer goods, weakness of trade unions, lack of unity among laboring people because of caste, linguistic and provincial differences and jealousies, and mass illiteracy give an enormous advantage to capital and management over labor. The average businessman in the East has not yet learned that contented labor means better and more abundant production. Frequently he finds legal loopholes through which he can escape in meeting his legitimate obligations under various forms of social security. He still has to learn simple lessons in business honesty and the scrupulous fulfillment of the terms of a contract. Without learning such lessons he cannot successfully compete with the Western world.

Other factors which need to be tackled immediately are the general inertia and listlessness of the people induced by chronic hunger and disease and a fatalistic outlook on life which rests content with things as they are. The East abounds in ideologies which frown upon a multiplication of creature comforts. While nobody wants the East to give up its age-long traditions of nonattachment or nonpossession and self-renunciation, yet it is necesssary to remember the words of Augustus Comte that the noble things of life rest on the less noble. Even for the erecting of a lofty spiritual structure some material basis is necessary. Material goods are not an evil in themselves. They become an evil when they are sought after for their own sake. The East needs to be shaken out of its pathetic contentment with conditions as they are.

Mass ill health is a problem which needs to be tackled immediately and in a concerted fashion. The Netherlands, Sweden, the United Kingdom, Australia, and the United States all have high life expectancy. The expectancy of life for the United States between 1939 and 1941 was 61.60 for males and 65.89 for females. It has gone up since. The shortest life expectancy at birth is found in India, where it is less than 27 years for both sexes. Taking the world as a whole, the life span is on the increase.

Infant mortality is on the decline everywhere. A bulletin of the United Nations says that whereas in 1930 five countries had an infant mortality rate of over 200 for every 1,000, the highest rate shown for 1949 was 169. In the former British Indian provinces in 1949 it was 122.8 as against 167.1 for 1938.

It is needless to point out the urgent need there is in the East for more hospitals and dispensaries and for more doctors, nurses, midwives, health visitors, and the like. The government of India is setting up more medical colleges, more maternity and child welfare centers, and more clinics. Already some concerted efforts are being made through the clinics to restrict population. Under present-day conditions in the East subsidized hospital care and medical attention seem inevitable. People cannot afford to have their own family doctors. Because socialized medicine is generally anathema in the United States, it does not follow that it should be so everywhere.

The widespread use of contraceptives is out of the question in countries where poverty stalks the land and where illiteracy reigns supreme. Simple and inexpensive methods of birth control, coupled with full employment, higher wages, a higher standard of living, literacy, and greater ambition for oneself, one's family, and one's country can all help to put a check upon mounting population. Many of the followers of Gandhi look upon the use of contraceptives as a form of violence. Gandhi himself strongly recommended and practiced continence as against the use of contraceptives. This is likely to be too much of a strain on the average person. Yet there is no justification for prolonging or abusing the sex instinct by subtle appeal to it through various forms of advertisement, commercialized recreation, questionable magazine and newspaper articles and novels, and convenient social compromises in the relation between the sexes.

It is possible to argue that underproduction rather than overpopulation is the problem of underdeveloped areas. While England and Wales have a density per square mile of 750,

Belgium 708, pre-war Germany 382, Italy 389, and Japan 426, that of India is 246. It may surprise some to know that India's rate of increase is not the highest in the world. For the period 1940-50 the United States registered a net increase of 14:5 per cent, while that of India for the period 1941-51 was 13.4 per cent.

The real trouble is too little productivity—agricultural and industrial. There may be considerable truth in the contention of Jasue Le Castro, an FAO top expert on nutrition, that it is hunger and undernourishment which are the causes of fertility rather than the reverse. An indirect advantage of large population in the East has been the impossibility of the West permanently to subdue or kill off the East. It may still be done through the new weapons of mass destruction which an amoral society will have fewer and fewer scruples to use.

Even if productivity can be stepped up all over the world, something needs to be done to regulate overpopulation. Every year the population of the world is increasing by 12 per cent, whereas the increase of food is only 9 per cent. India alone is increasing its population by four to five million a year. Planned parenthood is an urgent need. Nehru even suggests compulsory sterilization in the case of the careless and improvident. Abolition of early marriage and polygamy can also be of great help. Provision of varied activities for both men and women, full employment, abolition of the *purdah* (seclusion of women), widespread practice of adoption instead of marrying a second or third wife in case of the barrenness of the first wife, change in diet, more outdoor recreation, and healthy social intercourse between men and women can all be conducive to the limitation of population.

IMPERIALISM AND COLONIAL EXPLOITATION

Imperialism and colonial exploitation have been and still are the direct causes of poverty in many areas in Asia and Africa. Under British rule, according to modest calculations, four shillings out of every pound belonging to the British person came from India. In South Africa 2,500,000 whites have crowded 9,000,000 blacks out of all the desirable land and are driving them into ghettos, treating them as subhuman beings.

Although Iran was not a colony or dependency of Britain, the oil resources of that country were exploited primarily in the interest of Britain, under a one-sided contract which sacrificed the interests of the people of Iran to those of the Anglo-Iranian Company, in which the British government owned 53 per cent of the shares. An annual lump sum which fell far below the demands of justice was paid to the government of Iran.

According to a writer in *The Nation*, September 6, 1952, the Anglo-Iranian Company linked with the Royal Dutch Shell and American oil interests forms a monster combine which draws in all the important oil operations of the Middle East. The same writer says that some of the international cartels have more political and economic power than national governments. Oil men occupy strategic diplomatic and administrative posts. At times they are members of legislatures and control committees and commissions. The writer quoted in this article claims that five American and two foreign companies have acquired virtually exclusive rights to the major oil fields of the world outside of the United States, Russia, and Mexico. The methods of control are "interlocking directorates and/or joint ownerships through which the cartel controls exploration, production, transport, and marketing organizations in many parts of the world."

For five years France has been carrying on a relentless war in Indochina, using one set of Indochinese to kill another set. The plea is that France is defending the free world against the inroads of Communism. It is obvious that this is too naïve an explanation. The conflict is between suppressed nationalism making common cause with Communism on the one hand and a feeble form of democracy hiding imperialist designs behind it on the other. The financial and military aid poured into this country by the United States is not helping to bring about justice. America cannot hope to win the sympathy of most Asians as long as she continues this indirect form of imperialism. Even if the United States is convinced of the necessity of stopping Communism by force, the outside world expects her to put pressure upon the French to prepare a timetable for the political freedom of Indochina and execute it.

Great Britain, like France, claims that she is defending Malaya against the Communists. This is only a half-truth. The fact of the matter is that she wants to hold on to the natural resources of Malaya—viz., rubber and tin—and prevent them from falling into the hands of Americans. In bringing about order in this disturbed area, as well as in Kenya, Britain is inflicting vicarious suffering on the innocent. Punitive fines are imposed on whole villages, and food supplies are reduced to the starvation point. Both the innocent and the guilty are made to suffer.

The Point IV Program is so administered in the Belgian Congo as to bring primary benefit to Belgians and Americans. The United States draws the bulk of its uranium from this country and possesses 90 per cent of the stock of the Beneguela Railway, which carries all the Congo uranium and many other Congo minerals. "Tanks" is the biggest financial holding corporation in tribal Africa; and huge stocks are held by Anglo-Belgian and American groups. The last few years have witnessed a new and powerful alignment of monopolistic mining capital in East and Central Africa. About half a dozen Englishmen control today the economic destiny of these territories. In the Rhodesias and Nyasaland the white settlers are agitating for a federation free from British control so as to intensify the exploitation of the natives. In this area American, Belgian, and South African interests are the beneficaries. As Basil Davidson says, if the federation comes about in this area, "it will not be a federation of free men, but of vested interests." [3] To quote him again: "We are faced with a well-prepared plan to saddle the whole of British Central Africa with a financial oligarchy designed to carry imperialist venture into a new phase." [4] British mining interests are wanting to transfer their headquarters from London to the Rhodesias so as to escape high British taxation and to oblige American investors.

[3] *The Statesman and Nation*, August 9, 1952.
[4] *Ibid.*

Capitalism, Communism, and War

Free enterprise or private enterprise undoubtedly has given full scope for individual initiative and leadership. In recent years it has meant full employment, high wages, and abundance of production for the industrial countries of the world, especially for the United States. But it has also meant the ruthless exploitation of raw-material areas, unequal trade, enormous waste, periods of slump following periods of prosperity, and the commercialization and vulgarization of values. At present it looks as though war and preparation for war mean full employment and high wages for countries like the United States with a great industrial potential. While in industrially advanced countries capitalism has improved economic conditions and more or less has kept its abuses under check, elsewhere it has whetted the appetite for private gain and acquisition and has meant the exploitation of the many by the few. Even in industrially advanced countries, long-range programs meant for the welfare of future generations have frequently been sacrificed for short-range programs calculated to bring immediate benefits to the fortunate few. Also, free enterprise has not always been "free" or "enterprising," especially as regards heavy industries. It is nothing unusual for huge concerns to buy up patents and lock them up in order that nobody else may have them. Improved methods of production and distribution are purposely kept off the market in order to favor certain interested groups.

Realizing all this, most countries have made serious inroads into the private-enterprise system, and there is no simon-pure capitalism anywhere. National ownership and national control, on the other hand, which look rosy from a distance, have their serious limitations in actual practice. They show clearly that no human system, however well conceived, can work satisfactorily until it has behind it honest officials and an equally honest public.

Communism, as it is practiced today, is totalitarian and dictatorial and crushes individual liberty. In its actual operation it is a form of state capitalism. The communist motto, "From each according to his ability, and to each according to his need," is in keeping with the Christian spirit. Only it has to be brought about by redeemed men in a redeemed society and not by means of brute force. If communism is, as Toynbee says, a Christian heresy, the Christian part of it should be recovered.

Capitalism, socialism, and even communism are only experiments in social living. Being experimental, none of them is final. Every one of them is man-made and therefore open to all the weaknesses which attend human institutions. The part of wisdom is not to uphold any one system as the best for all times and for all places but "to prove all things [systems]; hold fast that which is good" (I Thess. 5:21). An ancient country like China or India should explore the possibilities of all rival economic systems and choose the one which is best suited to its needs and adapt it to its own tradition and genius.

For the present it appears that mature people with unsolved economic problems will do well to experiment with mixed economies. The Scandinavian countries have made a success of co-operatives and mixed economies. What they have done splendidly, other countries too might well do. In his *Blue Print for India*, Nehru puts forward a scheme which includes national ownership and control of heavy industries, of armament manufacture, and the major forms of transportation and communication, private enterprise in such well-established industries as textiles, private enterprise modified by state control without state ownership, peasant proprietorship of land, and rural industries. Of late Nehru has been advocating co-operative farming as an experiment in limited areas, and gradual socialization of key industries.

When China is allowed to work out her own salvation, it is possible that, in keeping with her past tradition and genius, she can work out an economic system which will be part-time capitalist, part-time communist, and full-time Chinese. China may well be able to combine private enterprise and peasant proprietorship at the village level with joint enterprise at the state or national level. On his return from a good-will mission to China in 1951, Professor V. K. R. V. Rao of Delhi University wrote that China today has (1) multistructure economy for two thirds of heavy industry and one fourth of light industry; (2) co-operative economy; (3) unorganized or individualistic sector; (4) private capitalists; and (5) state-*cum*-capitalist economy, where the state and private capitalists co-operate. The goal, according to Premier Chou-en-Lai, is the establishment of a socialistic society to be achieved only when the people are prepared for it.

What the Church Can Do

It is not the business of the church to canvass for any particular economic system, since every one of them has in it its own seeds of decay. The business of the church is to apply the mind and spirit of Jesus Christ to all economic systems. It should make it crystal-clear to all who will heed its word that moral and spiritual values are of much greater consequence than the material, that wealth is a trust, that man is a born trustee, and that a sense of this trusteeship can be promoted by institutional changes. The ancient Roman formula, "private property small, common property large," is a good Christian goal to strive toward; but it should be brought about largely by voluntary methods and free group action.

In the missionary field which happens to be in the underdeveloped areas of the world, the church should initiate and direct useful pilot projects—do such things as improve agricultural conditions, promote village handicrafts, pay more attention to vocational and technical education as well as to art and craft education, help to liquidate illiteracy, and organize community projects, such as recreation centers, health centers, rural banks, community housing, and the like. In all that it does the church should work *with* the people and not simply *for* the people. It should aim at enduring results and not make the work unduly dependent upon an energetic foreign missionary or foreign funds. It should be integrated into the life of the community.

As people in the underdeveloped areas gradually adjust themselves to a changing world, care should be taken to see that they do not surrender moral and spiritual values and become robots, machine-made men and women fashioned according to the needs and interests of a totalitarian state or the vested interests in a democratic state. They should be taught not to hanker after luxuries and the senseless multiplication of creature comforts. The church has a duty to help people to overcome injurious social customs which hold back economic progress and retard the free development of human personality. Some of these customs are irresponsible parenthood, contempt for manual labor, the dowry system, graft, and prejudice against the employment of women in gainful occupations doing equal work with men and receiving equal emoluments. The church can also help in the orderly production and distribution of the raw materials of underdeveloped areas and see that foreign investments are regulated in the interests of both the lender and the borrower.

On the moral side the church should make it plain that no mere man-made economic system can succeed unless it has sound character behind it. It is generally accepted today that Protestant ethic helped to develop capitalism, with its by-products of hard work, thrift, family limitation, productivity, and frugality. These values today have to operate in a different environment. It is the duty of the church, especially in underdeveloped countries, to cultivate traditions of public and business honesty and induce people to place the service motive above the profit motive. There is some truth in the statement, "If one area is rich and another poor, it is not because of anything inherent in the natural resources or in the genetic make-up of the people, but because of the cumulative effect of certain familial, educational, and religious practices."[5]

The church in the United States should take the initiative in urging people to accept the Christian philosophy of life. It is time that the rank and file realized that if Communism makes its seductive appeal to many in the underdeveloped areas, it is largely because of abject poverty, the continuance of imperialism and colonial exploitation, of war, racialism,

[5] *Public Affairs*, Vol. XIV, No. 4 (Summer, 1952).

and unbridled forms of capitalism. As Dr. Charles Malik of Lebanon says: "Communism cannot be met by a mere nay. It requires a mighty yea." If Communism is to be effectively checked, the church should take the initiative in combating idea by idea, plan by plan, and program by program; and not idea by emotion, plan by platitude, and program by a vision in the sky.

If anything like the Point IV Program is to succeed, it should be free from military strings and extend over a number of years. As a mere political expediency, it will do more harm than good. This program should be dovetailed into the United Nations program. The church should further give its active support to the strengthening of the peacemaking functions of the United Nations as conducted by the FAO, WHO, ILO, UNESCO, World Bank, World Court, and the Economic and Social Council.

As long as the church supports war and believes in the casting out of Satan by Satan, it will betray its trust. Many oriental countries were pushed off the narrow economic margin on which they were living by World War II. World War III will push them into an abyss out of which even a Hercules will not be able to lift them. It is primarily for this reason that a country like India has set its face resolutely against war as a solution to the present impasse in world affairs. War is a luxury which a rich country like the United States can afford, but it will mean utter ruination to the underdeveloped countries which are learning to stand on their feet. Should a World War III come about, military victory may go to the free world, but practical victory may belong to Communism and forces of disorder. Coercive militarism is no answer to a coercive Communism. The sale of arms and armaments, so long as that continues, should be taken out of private hands and national control and regulated by a suitable international agency.

It is the duty of the church in the United States to make its people understand that mere charity is no permanent solution to the economic ills. More opportunity should be provided for the rest of the world to trade with the United States, which means a reduction of tariffs and a possible lowering of the standard of living for a while. The world cannot go on indefinitely with one Dives and many Lazaruses all around.

Toynbee says that civilizations are not murdered, but commit suicide. It is the sacred duty of the church to prevent such calamity.

PART IV

The Church
and
The Political Order

10

The Christian and Citizenship

ROBERT E. FITCH

IN THIS CHAPTER WE SEEK THE ANSWERS TO CERTAIN BASIC
QUESTIONS CONCERNING THE ROLE OF THE CHRISTIAN AS A
citizen of a state. What is the basis of the authority of the
state? What are the connections, if any, between our Hebrew-
Christian-Protestant heritage and specific forms of government? What are the social conditions under which we may
preserve our freedom? What should be the scope of political
power in a democracy? Just how does the Christian conscience
make a decision in politics? And, finally, what can the church
do about Christian citizenship?

THE MORAL BASIS OF POLITICAL AUTHORITY

There are two theories concerning the basis of political
authority. One theory says that basis is moral in character.
This was the view of the Hebrew prophets, who believed
that the state is subject to the justice and the righteousness
required by the will of God. It was the view of the great
Greek philosophers Plato and Aristotle, who held that the
state must serve the ends of wisdom and of intelligence. It
is the view of political democracy, which makes the state an
instrument of certain values like life, liberty, property, fraternity, and the pursuit of happiness. The other theory says
that the only basis of political authority is power. It is might
that makes right. The only vice is weakness; the only virtue
is strength.

In modern times this second theory has made two great attacks on the doctrine of the moral basis of political authority. First there was the frontal attack of the Nazis. Adolf Hitler was quite honest about his principles. His politics was as old as Machiavelli, and his ethics as recent as Nietzsche. In effect he said to the world: "You delight in peace; I glorify war. You believe in brotherhood; I believe in the rule of a race of supermen. You praise democracy; I praise dictatorship. You extol morality; I worship power."

The second attack, delivered by the Communists, has been more subtle, more indirect, in character. It has kept all the grand old phrases but has perverted them so that, in practice, they have turned out to mean exactly the opposite of what they originally meant. Thus the ideal of a classless society simply means the enshrinement of a new ruling caste—the Party. A peoples' democracy means a dictatorship. The peoples' courts mean a repudiation of all due process of law. A peace offensive is a maneuver in a cold war. And the liberation of a nation is, in effect, its enslavement. This strategy has the advantage of using the words that may delude idealists, while practicing the deeds that satisfy the brutal realist.

The first point about which we have to make up our minds is whether we do believe that, in fact, might makes right. The Greek philosophers and the Hebrew prophets believed otherwise. Plato and Aristotle knew that might must be exercised with wisdom; and Amos, Micah, and Isaiah knew that might must be exercised with justice and with righteousness. According to their brand of realism, which should be ours, only the might which is accompanied by wisdom and by right can continue to be might.

We have also to realize that no state will be absolutely pure in devotion to its principles. Both the power state and the ethical state may be guilty of the same kind of hypocrisy—pretending to serve noble ideals when the real ends are selfish and predatory. Nevertheless, the basic cleavage in the world today lies between those forms of government which ruthlessly pursue their own aggrandizement in cynical contempt for all moral standards, and those forms of government which, however imperfectly, acknowledge their subordination to a higher moral law. This is the line that divides the friend from the enemy.

THE CHRISTIAN ROOTS OF DEMOCRACY

More specifically, now, the ethical theory of the state rests upon three great ideals. First there is the great ideal of social justice given us by the Hebrew prophets. This is an ideal of justice which always tips the scales in favor of the poor and the oppressed. Next there is the great New Testament ideal of the sacredness of the person. He is not sacred because of his reason, or because of his talents, or because of his personality, but quite simply because he is a child of God and because Christ died for him as for all other sinners. Finally, there is the distinctively Protestant emphasis on liberty—a liberty which is spiritual in its roots, but which branches out into secular liberties that are personal, political, civil, and economic.

It is simply a matter of record that the great stable democracies of the world are those which had their institutions rooted in the Hebrew-Christian-Protestant tradition. One thinks of Great Britain, Canada, the United States, Norway, Sweden, Denmark, Holland, and Switzerland. The two notorious exceptions we must confess are German Lutheranism under the Nazis, and the Dutch Reformed Church in South Africa today. There are three other exceptions which really confirm my original observation—three Roman Catholic democracies which borrowed their form of government from the Protestant power which once ruled over them: Belgium from Holland, Ireland from Great Britain, and the Philippines from the United States.

Suppose we eliminate the ideal of liberty from this trinity of political principles and see what we get. What we get is the Roman Catholic state. The Roman Catholic Church certainly cherishes the Old Testament ideal of social justice and the New Testament ideal of the sacredness of the person, but it does not accept the distinctively Protestant beliefs about liberty. It happens, then, that the majority of Roman Catholic countries have a form of government which is feudal or fascist in character, and is often shaped up in a dictatorship. To be sure, one thinks of France and of Mexico as democracies. But they are anticlerical democracies. They had to establish democracy against the opposition of the church, rather than drawing their strength from the church. As a consequence, their democratic institutions are relatively *un*stable compared with the *stable* Protestant democracies.

Let us discount still another one of the three ideals—the sacredness of the person. This leaves us with nothing but justice. In effect, this was originally the great ideal of Marxian communism. It is the devotion to this ideal that makes some passages from Marx read like a paraphrase of the great Hebrew prophets. But what sort of ideal of justice is it which respects neither liberty nor the sacredness of the person? This sort of justice becomes a devouring Moloch, which in the end consumes itself and turns justice into injustice.

The sacredness of the person, made real in justice and in liberty: here lies the heart of the matter. Of course the institutions which express these ideals may vary greatly from one country to another—may give us an American pattern, or a Swiss federation, or a constitutional monarchy, or temporarily, as in India today, a benevolent oligarchy. Nevertheless, these three ideals are central, and, what is more, as a complex they are unique to the Hebrew-Christian-Protestant tradition. In any case, they are not secular in origin. They are rooted in the deepest religious faith, and they will not flourish when they are cut off from those roots. Whether or not, or to what degree, other great religious traditions—Islam, Hinduism, Buddhism—may help or hinder these ideals is an important practical question, into which, however, we cannot inquire here.

Freedom and the Forms of Human Association

Of the three ideals indicated, the one that seems to be most imperiled today is liberty. How do we preserve our freedom in the modern state? The important thing to remember is that the state is only one of several forms of human association. Men come together in groupings that are political, professional, familial, economic, religious, recreational, cultural, and communal. Some of these forms of association, such as the professional, usually reach beyond geographic and political barriers. Another form, the church, may transcend not merely political barriers but even the barriers of time, and reach into a fellowship with noble souls both in the past and in the future. Another one, the community, may cut across and partially embrace the other forms of association. The effective freedom we enjoy in society is defined by the way in which these forms of association are related to one another.

The simplest and oldest device of all is tyranny. What we call totalitarianism is merely the name for tyranny when it is organized with scientific thoroughness. The gist of totalitarianism is that some one form of association—it does not matter which—should claim absolute authority over all the rest. In the time of Abraham there was a sort of benevolent, patriarchal totalitarianism. In the Middle Ages in Europe there was an ecclesiastical totalitarianism. In the latter part of the nineteenth century in the United States it could be argued that there was a sort of economc totalitarianism. Today it is the political variety of totalitarianism that concerns us most. This means that the state, as the supreme form of human association, is in a position to dictate to all the others—to prescribe not only our politics, but our religion, our recreation, our occupations, our family life, our literature and art, and in effect the whole meaning of existence for us.

Another device, at the other extreme, is anarchy. Actually there can be no society in a condition of total anarchy. Nevertheless human beings have made some heroic efforts to approximate this goal. When every nation in the world insists upon its own absolute sovereignty and acknowledges no law higher than itself, that is anarchy in politics. When every religious denomination insists that it alone is the one true church with a monopoly on salvation, that is anarchy in religion. When each business corporation and each labor union acts as though it were a law unto itself, that is anarchy in economics. But since men cannot long endure anarchy, they tend to heal it by turning to some form of monopoly. So it is, as Plato remarked long ago, that anarchy is only a prelude to tyranny.

A free society stands somewhere between these two extremes. It rests on the fact of the great variety of the forms of human association. These several forms—the family, the state, the church, the economic order—are related in ways that are partly overlapping and partly independent. On the one hand we shun anarchy: no family, no church, no nation may be completely isolated from the other forms of human association. On the other hand we shun tyranny: no state, no church, no economic association may claim absolute authority over all other human activities. Furthermore, these relationships that are partly overlapping and partly independent will be constantly shifting according to the needs of the day. It is a part of our perpetual problem to define and to redefine these relationships. The important thing is to avoid the two extremes, to preserve a certain freedom and flexibility, and so to maintain the conditions for a dynamic and creative society.

As long as we maintain this condition in a political democracy, we have an effective freedom. If the government is a good one at the moment, let us remember that it is not the sole agency of social salvation. If the government is a bad one at the moment, let us remember that there are other sources of evil than the political. In any case, whether for good or for evil, we are free to do our work not only through the government, but also through the other forms of association, which are the family, the church, the school, the economic order, and our cultural and recreational groups.

The Scope of Political Power

Let us concede, then, that in a free society the government is only one of several forms of human association, only one of several ways of doing our business. But just what part of our business is it the business of the government to do?

The problem we face is exemplified by two contradictory uses of the expression "police state." In an older political theory it was customary to speak of the state as a *passive* policemen. Here it was believed that the government should be restricted to a *minimum* of functions—maintaining internal order, protecting the nation against a foreign enemy, and perhaps building roads and establishing a few tariff barriers. Today when we speak of the police state, we are thinking of an *active* policeman, and of a state which has expanded its functions to the *maximum*. This is the totalitarian state.

If it be asked how the democratic theory defines the functions of the state, I think the answer must be that it defines them as being *anywhere between* these two extremes.

Let us make an analogy from Christian missions. About a generation ago the functions of the Protestant foreign missionary were defined at a maximum. He was an evangelist, to be sure, but he might also be an educator, a doctor, a public-health authority, an agriculturalist, and a respected mediator between local warring factions. Under either one of two conditions, however, the function of the missionary may shrink. Under persecution he may have to limit himself to a purely personal witness to the gospel. But also, under prosperity, he may elect to turn over to secular agencies some of the projects which he has done so well to pioneer.

In a democracy we need a similarly flexible theory of the function of the state. In a time of emergency, such as war, the state will expand its powers; in other times, when there is real peace, those powers should be contracted. The federal government may initiate something which it will later turn over to other interests—as in the case of great power projects. Again, the federal government may take over something that was started by private initiative—as in the case of the post office. In a time of crisis the government may decide to nationalize certain properties—as it did to the railroads in World War I; and upon the next occurrence of a similar crisis—World War II—it may decide not to nationalize those same properties, because that device proved to be inefficient the first time. It is likewise conceivable that what at one period in our history is rigorously left to private enterprise may at a later time, with public consent, be turned over to federal control. All of this illustrates what John Dewey meant when he spoke of the experimental logic which is inherent in the processes of political democracy.

Here it may be alleged that this is a dreadfully vague theory of the functions of government, and that it seems to allow for almost anything. The answer is, in part, that the only cut and dried theories of the functions of government are to be found in the anarchist or the totalitarian doctrines. Meanwhile, it must be insisted that there are definite, limiting factors in democratic theory. First of all, every development is to be judged in the light of the three great ideals of the sacredness of the person, social justice, and liberty. In the second place, we dare never get too close to either of the extremes of tyranny and anarchy. When we see ourselves moving too far in one direction, it is time to move in the other. Finally, there are practical questions to be kept in mind. Just what is demanded by the needs and made possible by the resources of the moment? As we solve the immediate and pressing problem, are we keeping the way open for the democratic solution of the unanticipated problems of the future?

In brief, it takes character and intelligence to operate a democracy. It takes a perpetual exercise of good judgment, and a constant discipline in self-control, in human sensitivity and charity, and in loyalty to the highest principle. This is another way of saying that political democracy rests upon the foundations of the school and of the church.

THE CHRISTIAN CONSCIENCE AND POLITICAL DECISION

And now just how does the Christian conscience make a decision when it is choosing among political candidates, parties, policies, and programs? At he risk of a little pedantry, I shall propose a formula: The Christian decision is a comparative choice, among possible alternatives, in the light of an ideal, on the basis of a probability calculus.

It is a *comparative* choice. We often hear of the relativities of politics. I prefer to speak of the comparative rather than of the relative, because the comparative is a reminder that there really is a standard—the superlatively best—in terms of which we make our judgment. Theoretically we have a double scale of alternatives: good, better, best; and bad, worse, worst. In this imperfect world we are not likely to come upon the absolutely best and the absolutely worst in politics. When we are fortunate, we are privileged to choose the better in preference to the merely good. When times are dark, we may be compelled to accept the bad in order to avoid what is worse. But choose we must if we are to remain responsible in our Christian citizenship.

It is a choice among *possible* alternatives. Some people like to exercise their idealism by choosing what is manifestly impossible. They will have the best, or nothing. As a consequence, they get nothing—or, more probably, the worst. The fact is that, at any given point of decision, there is just a certain range of possibilities. Sometimes when the Christian citizen goes into the voting booth, he may feel as though he is being called upon to elect either Charlie McCarthy or Mortimer Snerd to the United States Congress. In an ideal sense he may regard both alternatives as "impossible," and the decision as most painful. He must still choose. And if he doesn't like the alternatives this time, he has a responsibility to go out and, with more creative energy as a citizen, see to it that next time the alternatives come closer to the Christian ideal of the "possible."

It is a choice *in the light of an ideal.* Let us be clear that there are two things we are not doing. We are not choosing without any ideal at all. The comparative has meaning only in relationship to the superlative. We are not choosing, either, the ideal itself. Indeed, there are two realms where perfectionism is out of place—matrimony and politics. For one thing, the ideal simply does not exist. But, more to the point, we don't deserve it, anyway. To be a perfectionist in either area is to be, finally, a total abstainer. Nevertheless, we do choose in the light of an ideal. The ideal is the clue to the tendency of an activity, to the direction of an effort. We may not presume to believe that we are going to leap into the heavenly city with one sweep of our angel wings. But we want to be sure that we are headed for the heavenly city rather than for the city of destruction.

It is a choice based on a *probability* calculus. This means two things. First there is the exercise of good judgment—the effort to get at the relevant facts, and to make an intelligent choice in the light of them. But there is also the act of faith in which we make our commitment—the element of taking a chance. This is because we can never know all the relevant factors, and because we can never judge of them with a perfect wisdom anyway. If the leap of faith results in a step ahead, then we are fortunate. If it results only in a fall, then we can rise and try again the next time. In any case, if our political faith is subordinate to our Christian faith, then the higher commitment will enable us to face the hazards, to accept the hurts, and to reap the rewards of the lesser commitment, without cynicism in failure and without idolatry in success.

What Can the Church Do About It?

There are several things that the church can do about this Christian citizenship. First of all the preacher can saturate himself with the political lore and history of his people, and let that lore become a part of the illustrative material in his sermons. This means more than the usual perfunctory attention to George Washington, Abraham Lincoln, and Robert E. Lee. It means a closer acquaintance, developed by systematic reading, with the heroes and some of the rascals of American history, so that the preaching in the pulpit will accustom the people to the notion of the intimate relationship between religious and political ideals in the history of the nation.

Another thing that can be done is to establish a study group in this field. There are some excellent books to challenge the adult mind. For a survey of historical material that will jolt anyone to alert attention, try H. Richard Niebuhr's *Social Sources of Denominationalism* and James H. Nichols' *Democracy and the Churches*. For a sketch of the main outlines of Christian strategy, try Richard Niebuhr's *Christ and Culture* and John Bennett's *Christian Ethics and Social Policy*. For good examples of the Christian faith in political action over a considerable period of time, follow both the careers and the writings of the late Archbishop Temple in England and of Reinhold Niebuhr in this country. There are other good authors and good books that could be mentioned.

Another device is that of the church forum. Many things can be discussed here with a detail of contemporary application that is not always appropriate in the pulpit. When partisan matters are under discussion, it is important that there be a regard for both sides of a question. Also a church group should distinguish between what can be done in an open session, where the church appears to sponsor the speaker, and what can be done in a private and closed session where there may be free discussion without any implication of sponsorship. The Christian church, moreover, has no utter impartiality about all issues. It dare not betray the three principles of the sacredness of the person, of social justice, and of human liberty.

There are some churches that make a point of seeing to it that all their members do their duty at the polls. This, of course, is done without any regard for party alignment. First there is a check of the register of voters, with a phone call to prompt those who have been delinquent in registering. Then facilities for transportation and for baby-sitting are provided on election day, to make sure that all can go to the polls. Sometimes, toward the latter part of election day, there is even a telephone check on those who have not yet cast their ballot.

Finally, every church should have its social-action committee, which is concerned with political issues as well as with other issues. The function of this committee should be informative, but at times it should be prophetic. And if the rest of the church community feels that the prophet at times is arrogant and self-righteous in his idealism, it may remember that the prophet is also there to check its own smugness and complacency with the challenge of a more difficult ideal.

171

In conclusion, it is true that our citizenship in the state is not the ultimate citizenship. But it is unlikely that we can be prepared for citizenship in the heavenly city if we show contempt for our duties as citizens of the earthly city.

11

The Church and the State

ANSON PHELPS STOKES

THE PRESENT INSISTENCE OF THE CHURCH-STATE PROBLEM
IS SHOWN BY SEVERAL FACTS, SUCH AS: THE LARGE NUMBER OF
cases involving religious freedom which have come before the
Supreme Court, many of them at the instance of Jehovah's
Witnesses; the acute discussions on state financial aid to parochial schools as urged by the Roman Catholic Church; the
question of bus transportation to parochial and private schools;
and the problem of religious education for public school
students.

CONTEMPORARY PATTERNS OF CHURCH-STATE RELATIONS

There are, in general, four major contemporary patterns of
church-state relations. These are: (1) *the rigid church-state
plan* in force in many Latin countries, of which Spain is an
example; (2) *the tolerant constitutional church-state plan*,
such as is in existence in England, where one communion—in
this case the Anglican Church—has a special "established" relationship to the state, but where all churches and religious
bodies are given complete religious freedom; (3) *the constitutional religious freedom plan*, such as is in existence in
the United States, where there is virtually complete separation
between church and state and no church is in a favored position; and (4) *the opposition-to-religion plan*, which we find
in Russia and her satellites, in which although freedom of
religious *faith* is generally provided for, any *activities* of the

churches are virtually limited to worship, and everything ecclesiastical is subject to complete state control.

HISTORICAL BACKGROUND OF THE AMERICAN PLAN

To understand religious freedom in the United States, we must go back to the period of the Revolution. At that time there were three major church traditions in the colonies developing into the United States: those of Puritan New England; those of Anglican Virginia and other southern colonies; and those of the proprietary middle and southern provinces where Presbyterianism was strong. A large percentage of the original colonists had come to this country for the purpose of seeking religious freedom. The New England Congregationalists had suffered from a bishop-controlled state church in England and were determined to have none here. The majority of people in most southern provinces would have been satisfied with episcopacy, but this was ruled out by opposition from strong minorities within and by other sections of the country. The middle states contained a very large number of religious denominations, especially of German origin. Under these circumstances, it was quite impossible for the founders of the country to establish a state church. They were opposed to it in principle, and knew that it was not workable in practice. A church-state would be as impossible today as it was when the founders established church-state separation. They had approximately the same percentage of denominations in proportion to their population as we have —according to the 1951 figures we have 265 religious bodies in our forty-eight states.

SEPARATION OF CHURCH AND STATE IN THE UNITED STATES

This has three constitutional foundations:

1. The Constitution (1787-89). This provides for the separation of church and state. The Constitution contains at the close of the Sixth Article the following statement, for which Charles Pinckney (1757-1824) was mainly responsible: "No religious Test shall ever be required as a Qualification to any Office or public Trust under the United States."

Attention must be called to the fact that the word "under" and not "in" was employed. This limited the original requirement to officeholders under the federal government and did not at the time necessarily apply to the states. But it was almost inevitable that if all federal legislators and officeholders were to be chosen without any religious test, complete religious freedom would follow.

2. The Bill of Rights, which dates back to 1789-91. This begins as follows: "Congress shall make no law respecting an establishment of religion, or prohibiting the free exercise thereof; or abridging the freedom of speech, or of the press; or the right of the people peaceably to assemble, and to petition the Government for a redress of grievances."

This clause probably represents the most significant action regarding religious freedom ever taken in any country if one considers both its scope and its influence. It is significant that religious freedom is the first of the different freedoms mentioned. There are two major points in this amendment. The first, using the broadly inclusive word "respecting," prevents the "establishment" or aid by law of any church; while the second guarantees religious freedom—that is, every person or group can worship God as he or she or it pleases without any state interference so long as the usual requirement of law and order and the rights of others are observed.

3. The Fourteenth Amendment (1766-68).

All persons born or naturalized in the United States, and subject to the jurisdiction thereof, are citizens of the United States and of the State wherein they reside. No State shall make or enforce any law which shall abridge the privileges or immunities of citizens of the United States; nor shall any State deprive any person of life, liberty, or property, without due process of law; nor deny to any person within its jurisdiction the equal protection of the laws.

This amendment was undoubtedly designed primarily to prevent slavery in the United States, but it has been interpreted by our courts since 1923 in a series of important decisions as also protecting religious freedom. In the case of Meyer versus Nebraska in 1923 the Supreme Court stated, with only two dissenting votes, that the Fourteenth Amendment denotes, among other things, the right of the individual to "worship God according to the dictates of his own conscience." It has been this extension of the Fourteenth Amendment to cover constitutional religious freedom that has been largely responsible for most of the Supreme Court decisions on the subject in recent years, and it has now become firmly established as part of the law of the land.

In dealing with these three foundation stones of religious freedom which have given us our self-supporting and self-governing churches, it should not be forgotten that they all, in a way, go back to the opening words of the Declaration of Independence of 1776: "We hold these truths to be self-evident, that all men are created equal, that they are endowed by their Creator with certain *unalienable Rights*, that among these are Life, Liberty and the pursuit of Happiness."

There were many other early national acts contributing to our firm establishment of religious freedom, among which two at least should be mentioned: the Ordinance of 1787 for the government of the Northwest Territory, which referred to "extending the fundamental principles of civil and religious liberty," and stated that "no person, demeaning himself in a peaceable and orderly manner, shall ever be molested on account of his mode of worship or religious sentiments, in the said territory"; and the provision of the Constitution for "one supreme Court" with the definite statement—also reiterated in the Judiciary Act of 1789—that

The interpretation of the laws is the proper and peculiar province of the courts. A constitution is, in fact, and must be regarded by the judges, as a fundamental law. It therefore belongs to them to ascertain its meaning, as well as the meaning of any particular act proceeding from the legislative body. If there should happen to be an irreconcilable variance between the two, . . . the Constitution ought to be preferred to the statute, the intention of the people to the intention of their agent.

Founders of American Religious Freedom

In considering the persons mostly responsible for religious freedom, we should mention particularly five men: Roger Williams, an Independent and Baptist (*ca.* 1603-83), who first developed the idea in his colony of Rhode Island; William Penn (1644-1718), a Quaker, who brought about in some respects the best conditions regarding religious freedom in Colonial times; George Mason (1725-92), an Episcopalian, who drafted the Declaration of Rights of Virginia, which preceded and underlay our national constitutional religious freedom guarantee; [1] James Madison (1751-1836), who—realizing that mere "toleration" was inadequate—secured the substitution in Mason's draft of the words "All men are equally entitled to the free exercise of religion, according to the dictates of conscience," instead of the words "enjoy the fullest toleration in the exercise of religion," and who, with the help of Judge Samuel Livermore, was mainly responsible for the First Amendment; and Thomas Jefferson (1743-1826), Unitarian in belief, who was responsible for the Declaration of Independence and did more than anyone else, except Madison, to advance the general cause of religious freedom in the forming republic. Madison also wrote the famous "Memorial and Remonstrance Against Religious Assessments," which killed the plan for state financial aid to churches in Virginia, then (1784-85) the most influential state.

These men were all equally interested in the cause of religion and religious freedom, and they saw the connection between them.

[1] This clause, as it was finally adopted, read:

That religion, or the duty which we owe to our Creator, and the manner of discharging it, can be directed only by reason and conviction, not by force or violence, and therefore all men are equally entitled to the free exercise of religion, according to the dictates of conscience; and that it is the mutual duty of all to practice Christian forbearance, love, and charity towards each other.

RECOGNITIONS OF RELIGION WITHOUT REFERENCE TO DENOMINATIONS

In addition to the main constitutional references to religion there are certain notable institutions, customs, and laws which show the high regard in which religion was held by the founders and has been held by their successors in this country. Among these attention may be called to the following:

1. The calendar. This legally provides for Sunday, and by common consent for Thanksgiving (with its religious emphasis in presidential and gubernatorial proclamations), and Christmas Day. The provision in the Constitution excludes Sunday, considered a day of rest, from the days to be counted in the period when the President must veto a message to prevent its becoming law. Sunday laws in all the states are evidences of the same character. Sometimes they go to an extreme and are thought unfair to some religious bodies, but on the whole they are the recognition of a day to be treated somewhat differently from other days in accordance with religious tradition.

2. Chaplaincies—in which all denominations are treated alike. Chaplaincies are accepted by the overwhelming majority of our people as right and proper in connection with the Senate and House of Representatives, state legislatures, state prisons, and certain other public institutions, the Army, the Navy, etc.

3. Exemption from taxation of church property. This is universal as far as church edifices are concerned throughout the United States. It is also generally customary in connection with buildings used for parish houses, rectories, church schools, cemeteries, etc.

4. Mottoes. The motto "In God we trust" on our coins represents the deliberate action of Congress. In 1865 it authorized, but did not require, the director of the mint at Philadelphia, with the approval of the Secretary of the Treasury, "to cause the motto 'In God we trust' to be placed upon such coins hereafter to be issued as shall admit of such legend thereon," and later, after the procedure was questioned,

adopted an act (May 18, 1908) which read: "That the motto 'In God we trust,' heretofore inscribed on certain denominations of the gold and silver coins of the United States of America, shall hereafter be inscribed upon all such gold and silver coins of said denominations as heretofore."

5. Judicial oaths. The government requires oaths in connection with certain judicial documents and certain acts before the courts. It is thought that added reverence is given to statements of fact when they are in this way certified before God.

6. State constitutions. These all recognize religion and religious rights.

Many other recognitions could be mentioned. These are enough to show how completely different the attitude of the United States toward belief in God and the church is from that, for instance, in Soviet Russia. No one of the recognitions mentioned would be possible there.

HISTORICAL EVENTS INVOLVING CHURCH-STATE RELATIONS

Such events and incidents are much more common in this country than is generally realized. Sometimes they involve co-operation between church and state in such matters as the care of the poor; sometimes conflicts, as in the case where the churches did all in their power to oppose the government over the removal of the Cherokee Indians from their homes. Three historical events may be taken as illustrative of these relations.

1. The settlement of the West. There has been no movement in American history where the churches played a more constructive part and more definitely aided the state. Each of the great religious bodies had a home-missionary society or something corresponding which saw to it that the settlers were accompanied or closely followed by ministers of the gospel to establish churches, hold camp meetings, advance education and temperance, aid in maintaining ethical standards, and in general provide factors for law, order, and culture. It would be almost impossible to overemphasize the important part played, for instance, by Bishop Francis Asbury (1745-

1816) and other circuit riders who were pioneers under rough frontier conditions in laying the foundations of Christian civilization. Roman Catholics, of whom Father Pierre De Smet (1801-72) was a noble example, also did a highly constructive work, especially among the Indians, greatly facilitating the work of government. Congregationalists and Presbyterians were perhaps particularly active in establishing educational institutions, many of which became state universities, while the Methodists rendered an almost unique service in evangelism.

The Great Awakening of 1740-90 and the Revival of 1799-1803 left their special mark on the frontier. As Professor Gabriel, in his *Course of American Democratic Thought*, says: "The frontier was great, turbulent, and godless. Evangelical Protestantism, more than any other single force, tamed it."

2. The slavery contest, which inevitably involved the churches. In the early days of the Republic, public-spirited citizens, and especially church leaders, were almost unanimous, in both the North and the South, in holding that slavery was an evil which should be gradually superseded. But three factors changed the outlook in the South in the late thirties. These were: the slave rebellions; the extremes of northern abolitionism under William Lloyd Garrison and others; and the believed dependence of the financial prosperity of the South, stimulated by the cotton gin, on slave labor. The battle was long and bitter. One can see the change in a striking way in the Methodist Episcopal Church. In its Discipline of 1784 it gave an elaborate plan to "extirpate this abomination of slavery." Question forty-three was important:

Question: What shall be done with those who buy or sell slaves, or give them away?
Answer: They are immediately to be expelled, unless they buy them on purpose to free them.

The contrast between this and the action of 1844 when northern and southern Methodists separated over the slavery issue, is striking. The southern Methodists became supporters of slavery as an economic institution, although urging their members to treat slaves with Christian consideration. The northern Methodists, on the other hand, although divided on the subject of the abolitionist program, were opponents of the institution of slavery and strong supporters of emancipation.

3. Social welfare. Social Christianity in the United States had a slow growth. An important landmark was made in 1819, when William Ellery Channing, main founder of American Unitarianism, preached his famous Baltimore sermon on the dignity and divine possibilities of man, the eminence of God, and the importance of life in this world. The movement was helped by Ralph Waldo Emerson, some English writers such as Charles Kingsley, and many preachers and sociologists in the United States such as Henry Ward Beecher, and later, Washington Gladden, Walter Rauschenbusch, and others. It came to a head in the adoption by the Methodist Episcopal Church of its social creed in 1908. This had seventeen features, of which the first was: "Practical application of the Christian principle of social well-being to the acquisition and use of wealth, subordination of speculation and the profit motive to the creative and co-operative spirit."

Little by little and with some modifications this program for applied Christianity to meet the social needs of the day met with the approval of most of the churches. The general purpose was to transform the "kingdom of this world into the kingdom of God."

Of course this creed and similar statements of church policy were bitterly fought by a conservative minority who felt that religion organically had little to do with social ethics. But certain agencies, such as the Federal Council of Churches—now the National Council of Churches (Protestant), the National Catholic Welfare Conference, especially under the leadership of the late Monsignor James Hugh Ryan, and the Central Conference of American Rabbis, helped mightily. In 1942 the National Conference of Christians and Jews published a study entitled *Religion and the Good Society*. President Clinchy in his introductory note said:

Formulating their convictions in almost every instance independently, without mutual consultation, we discover what will be a surprise to many, that these three religious bodies, thinking separately, have been guided by the same aspirations and have reached the same general conclusions as to how men must live together if human society is to be happy, harmonious and just.

It is probably in the fields of race relations, international peace, and support of labor in its demand for decent standards of wages and living, as a quarter of a century ago in the steel industry, that the churches have rendered their most important social contributions.

What the State Should Give the Church

The Oxford Conference on Church, Society and State (1937) in its report showed that the duties of the state to the church should be primarily threefold: (1) to assure every religious body *freedom* of thought, worship, utterance, and action as long as its *practices* are not inconsistent with fundamental moral standards and the safety of the state; (2) to provide protection of its property and protection of its ministers and other agents in the carrying out of their lawful activities; and (3) to adopt laws and practices which show a sympathetic attitude toward the churches in proclaiming their faith in a universal God of love and in the carrying out of their purpose to develop character and high social ideals for the individual, the nation and its constituent groups, and the family of nations.

Most religious leaders in the United States would interpret the third statement to include exemption from taxation, at least for buildings used for religious worship, the general theory being that through its religious and ethical teachings the church renders a tremendous contribution to the state in preventing crime and aiding the cause of law, order, morality, and progress. The church is very dependent upon the state through the courts for protecting its constitutional rights. In this connection the statement of Luigi Luzzati (1841-1927), a Jew by birth and an honored premier of Italy, is highly significant: "The character of politico-ecclesiastical legislation in the United States is one of religious freedom in *favor* of the churches and not *against* them."

WHAT THE CHURCH SHOULD GIVE THE STATE

The Oxford Conference stated its duties to be: (1) that of praying for the state, its people and its government; (2) that of loyalty and obedience to the state, disobedience becoming a duty only if obedience would be clearly contrary to the command of God; (3) that of co-operation with the state in promoting the welfare of the citizens, and of lending moral support to the state when it upholds the standards of justice set forth in the Word of God; in general the church should aid the state by training God-fearing citizens fitted to lead it in the way of justice, righteousness, and peace, with conduct based on Christ's summary of the law and the Golden Rule.

THE POINTS OF CONTACT AND DIVERGENCE BETWEEN CHURCH AND STATE

It will be seen that the church and the state have different spheres, the one having to do primarily with man's relationship to God, the other primarily with his relationship to his fellow men. This division has its classic expression in Christ's words "Render to Caesar the things that are Caesar's, and to God the things that are God's." It is mainly in the spheres of the family and education that conflicting rights and duties emerge. Here the rigid but sincerely held point of view of the Roman Catholic Church sometimes makes it difficult to adjust matters locally in a mutually satisfactory way. This church, through its hierarchy and councils, promoted the idea that parochial schools in which the Catholic religion is taught should be the norm for all members of the church. As a matter of fact about half the Catholic children are for one reason or another permitted to attend public schools, but there is a tendency to look upon these as "Godless" because of the lack of definite religious instruction. The parochial-school issue has been acute lately and was brought to a head in 1949 by the controversy between Cardinal Spellman and

Mrs. Eleanor Roosevelt. The spark plug which brought about the public discussion was the attitude of the church toward the Barden Bill, which provided for educational appropriations to public schools but not to parochial schools. Fortunately, the pressure of public opinion and the arguments of constitutional lawyers were such that Cardinal Spellman modified his position and finally issued a statement which considerably cleared the air. It said, among other things:

> We are not asking for general public support of religious schools. In the State of New York, as in practically every other state, the State constitution prohibits the use of public funds for the support of sectarian schools. The Supreme Court of the United States has interpreted the Federal Constitution in the same sense. . . .
>
> Under the Constitution we do not ask nor can we expect public funds to pay for the construction or repair of parochial school buildings or for the support of teachers, or for other maintenance costs. . . .
>
> There are, however, other incidental expenses involved in education, expenses for such purposes as the transportation of children to and from school, the purchase of non-religious textbooks, and the provision of health aids. These are called "auxiliary services." The Supreme Court of the United States has upheld these practices as constitutional. . . .
>
> It is also quite clear that public schools cannot teach denominational doctrine of any kind, although the courts have decided that there is nothing to prevent a State permitting, under suitable provisions, the giving of released or dismissed time for religious instruction to public school students outside of school buildings.[2]

The cases involving marriage, divorce, and birth control are often acute, for the Catholic Church feels that it has a right to determine what is ethical for its members and what is not, and it thereby often comes in conflict with non-Catholic public opinion and public authorities.

[2] T. Ernest Johnson, *American Education and Religion*, pp. 188-90. Contrast Zorach vs. Clauson with Everson and McCollum cases.

The General Basis of Church-State Relations in the United States

In spite of our state system, which provides for much differentiation of policy, the federal constitutional provisions, as interpreted by the Supreme Court, and the general American tradition are so strong that there is substantial legal agreement on all major matters of church-state policy throughout the country. Here are the outstanding facts:

1. No state permits the establishment of any form of state religion.

2. No state permits required attendance upon religious worship in public schools, though some permit simple undenominational opening exercises.

3. No state permits the support of denominational worship or instruction through taxation or other sources of state income. (There are some slight, unconstitutional exceptions to this.)

4. No state permits interference with the dictates of conscience in matters of religious faith.

5. No state permits any restraint on the expression of religious belief as long as this does not interfere with the public peace or welfare.

6. No state permits a religious test for any civil or political office, or for exercising the rights of citizenship.[3]

The Problem of Social Action by the Churches

There is much difference of opinion as to the extent to which the church should enter the field of legislative action. General agreement exists that it should do all in its power to uphold patriotism, constitutional provisions, and ethical standards. There is equal agreement that it should not play any part in ordinary partisan politics. There is, however, a middle ground which has to do particularly with the marriage life, education, and social welfare where both state and church may act within certain limits. It is considered right and proper that the church should emphasize the ideals of the kingdom

[3] Anson Phelps Stokes, *Church and State in the United States*, III, 447-48.
[4] (London: Macdonald & Co., 1951), pp. 46.

of God in the world as well as in the life of the individual. There can be no question that its main task is spiritual—the regeneration of the individual and of society through the gospel of Christ, of which religion, communion between God and man, is the center. But the church recognizes that it must take account of the needs of the whole man—body, mind, and spirit. It cannot merely preach purity, improvement of housing conditions and of recreational opportunities. Elsewhere I have written:

The Church must not adopt the method of the politician, namely, that the end justifies the means; Let the Church keep its vision with the goal of the Kingdom ever before it, but let it never descend to the methods of the agitator, the unscrupulous lobbyist, or the political party, while it tries to accomplish the regeneration of society. In other words, the Church must "be the Church," trying to make its definite contribution toward the higher welfare of the State, but remembering always that it must represent in thought and action the mind and spirit of the Master.[4]

How Can the Church Aid in Maintaining Religious Freedom and Church-State Separation?

Here are a few things that the church should do:

1. It should urge the careful study of American history, especially the Constitution and Bill of Rights, and other charters of freedom.

2. All efforts should be encouraged which aid different churches to know and understand each other.

3. The public should be alert to oppose all forms of intolerance such as anti-Semitism, nativism, and narrow denominationalism.

4. Constructive efforts for the churches to unite in social welfare projects should be encouraged for their own sake, for the breaking down of prejudice, and for the benefit of society.

5. The Sunday school and the home are places where Christians should emphasize religion and religious toleration,

[4] *Ibid.*, III, p. 678.

and the differing responsibilities of the church and the state in spite of their need of co-operation.

6. The church should be scrupulously careful to avoid asking of the state any favors that are not clearly permitted by the Constitution.

After ten years devoted largely to the question of church-state relations in this country I have some twenty-one conclusions which may be studied by those interested, in my book *Church and State*, Volume III, pp. 721-723. The gist of the matter is that our American history, as well as the history of other countries, proves that democracy cannot well exist without religion, and that the cause of religion is advanced when church and state are separated under the friendly traditions which have held here.

Constitutional religious freedom has been a real success in the United States from the standpoint of the federal government, the states, the churches, and the public. It has met all reasonable demands except that no satisfactory and adequate constitutional plan has yet been found by which religious illiteracy among public-school pupils, about which Protestant and Catholic leaders are equally concerned, can be prevented. However, the general plan of released-time instruction such as is in force in the state of New York, has been found constitutional, and this, or its dismissed-time alternative, may prove to be a partial solution of the problem. The schools may also give, without any propaganda, the major facts *about* religion and the churches—Protestant, Catholic, Jewish, and other—as these occur inevitably in high-school courses in history, literature, and the social sciences. But church and home must assume the full responsibility for promoting religious faith and activity.

12

The Church in the Prevention and Treatment of Crime

L. Harold DeWolf

IF ANY PEOPLE IN THE WORLD OUGHT TO BE INTERESTED IN CRIMINALS, THEN CHRISTIANS SHOULD HAVE SUCH AN INTEREST. As Christians we are the disciples of One who was convicted, sentenced, and executed for crime. Although the crucifixion of Jesus was a monumental miscarriage of justice, that fact should itself incite our interest in convicted prisoners. For it is beyond doubt that in modern times too, many men have been sentenced for crimes of which they were not guilty, and several books have been written which tell of men executed for murders of which they were later proved innocent.

Moreover, it was not for the righteous but for sinners that Christ died. If we are too proud and self-righteous to identify ourselves in sympathetic understanding with the men and women who are convicted of crime by the courts, then we have not yet learned what it means to stand in need of God's forgiveness, and we do not belong to "the Body of Christ." His gospel is a gospel for sinners. Most sinners are not in jail, and many of the worst are not, but no other person is so conspicuously marked as sinner as is the convicted criminal. If we have a gospel for anyone, it is for him.

While he was enduring the agonies of the cross, Jesus found strength to give his love, comfort, and hope to a convicted thief who was suffering the death penalty beside him. He thus went beyond his own warning that in the last judgment those who visited prisoners in their loneliness would go to his right, into eternal life, and those who did not visit the imprisoned would be condemned of God.

Among Christians, Methodists have special reasons for being concerned with criminals. The founder of Methodism, John Wesley, began regular ministrations to the prisoners in nearby jails while he was still a student at Oxford. He never lost interest in convicted criminals nor ceased urging his followers to be concerned for their welfare. The particular mission of early Methodism was to outcasts regarded as beneath the concern of respectable people. If we have now become too respectable for serious work with delinquents and criminals, we have become unworthy to be called Christians.

Indeed, we should also be quite stupid citizens of the United States if we were not seriously concerned with the criminal members of our population. A vast number of crimes, including many serious ones, go unreported. But in 1947 the major crimes reported in the United States totaled about 1,-665,110. This number included 13,500 murders and manslaughters by negligence, 17,200 rapes, 58,000 robberies, 75,-000 aggravated assaults, 373,000 burglaries, 940,000 larcenies, and 185,000 automobile thefts.[1] These figures are regarded by competent authorities as a gross understatement of the actual serious crimes committed.

The economic cost of crime to the American people cannot be accurately computed, but it runs into many billions annually. This economic cost is not, however, the major concern of the church. Indeed, it might cost more in dollars to eliminate the causes of crime than to suffer the present losses. But the change in the quality of life that would result from spending these sums on schools, housing, playgrounds, and properly equipped churches, instead of on the crime that results from the lack of these, would be immeasurably great. Our concern as Christians is with the awful toll in human life which crime entails. Leaving out of account the much greater number of minor crimes, but including major crimes not reported, what do two million or more serious crimes

[1] Donald R. Taft, *Criminology; A Cultural Interpretation* (New York: The Macmillan Co., 1950), p. 33.

committed in our country in one year actually mean in terms of human life? Consider the death, grief, poverty, hatred, and bitterness caused in the lives and homes of the victims. Think of the guilt, humiliation, fear, broken families, and un-relieved sorrow which fall upon the criminals and their homes. Finally, take into account the fears, suspicions, and hatreds which often take possession of whole neighborhoods where crimes have occurred. Every person who grows up in America is to some degree injured in body or soul by crime, and literally millions have their lives crushed by it into desperate grief or hopelessness.

Let no one suppose that this is an evil in which his own region is not very deeply involved. As a Nebraska boy, I grew up under the common illusion that crime was mainly an affair of the great wicked cities in the East. Actually, that was and is now a radically false notion. If we consider murders alone, for example, we find that in 1951 the lowest rate of murders was in New England, which had less than half as many murders per 100,000 population as the next best region, and that the middle Atlantic states of New York, New Jersey, and Pennsylvania have the second best record. As compared with the Massachusetts rate, murder is two and a half times as common in my native Nebraska or on the Pacific Coast, three and a half times as common in Ohio or Indiana, seven times as frequent in Texas, nine times as frequent in Kentucky, and fifteen times as prevalent in Georgia.[2] Some crimes, like larceny and auto stealing, occur most in large cities. But others, such as burglary, murder, and rape, are more frequent in small towns and in rural areas.[3] Let no one suppose that because he is located in the West or the South, in small town or country, that the crimes which are so conspicuous in city newspapers do not affect his community. A closer view will

[2] George B. Vold, "Extent and Trend of Capital Crimes in the United States," *The Annals of the American Academy of Political Science*, Vol. 284 (Nov., 1952), pp. 3-5.

[3] Austin L. Porterfield and Robert H. Talbert, with assistance of Herbert R. Mundhenke, *Crime, Suicide and Social Well-Being in Your State and City* (Fort Worth: Texas Christian University, 1948); and Hans von Hentig, *The Criminal and His Victim* (New Haven: Yale University Press, 1948), p. 237.

probably show a quite scandalous quantity of crime very close at hand.

THE CHURCH IN THE PREVENTION OF CRIME

Now, what are the churches doing about the prevention of crime?

First of all, the churches are helping to produce many citizens who do not commit crime. It is true that where studies of this matter have been made, there is about the same proportion of inmates in prisons who have reported church affiliations as in the general population outside, and this is just as true of Protestants as of Catholics. However, closer inquiry reveals that many prisoners claim church affiliation in order to make a good impression on the parole board, and many of the claims have little or no ground in fact. On the other hand, the number of church members genuinely active in church attendance who are convicted of serious crimes is sufficient to show that we have not always succeeded in making our gospel message so gripping and practically relevant in the lives of our own people as we should like to believe.[4]

Secondly, the churches and their people are helping to combat crime-breeding conditions and to establish conditions favorable to law-abiding citizenship.

In the personal background of juvenile delinquents and young adult criminals the most common condition differing from the experience of the majority in the general population is the seriously abnormal home. Sheldon and Eleanor Glueck found that of one thousand juvenile delinquents in Boston, nearly half came from homes broken either by the death of one parent or by the desertion, separation, or divorce of the parents. Only 2.5 per cent of the delinquents had mothers who provided sound oversight. In most cases the parents subjected the children to erratic and emotional control, varying unpredictably from overindulgent laxity to unreasonable repression and domination.[5] It is apparent that whatever we

[4] Taft, *op. cit.*, pp. 215-21.
[5] Sheldon Glueck, *Crime and Justice* (Boston: Little, Brown and Co., 1936), pp. 184-88.

can do to prepare young people for faithful marriage and wise, understanding parenthood will be important in combatting crime. Some churches are now providing such preparation through instruction and counseling, not only for their own members, but also for the surrounding communities, and are thus raising the whole level of family life in their vicinity. All ought to do so.

Another important factor in the causing of crime is alcohol. The Gluecks found that two fifths (39.4 per cent) of the five hundred young male criminals they studied had been making "excessive" use of liquor, while a quarter (25.4 per cent) of the five hundred delinquent women were given to drunkenness in adolescence. William Healy and Augusta F. Bronner found that from one fourth to nearly half of delinquent children had alcoholic parents.[6] In a large proportion of the cases studied the alcohol was apparently a major contributing cause, while in many instances it was the *only* evident cause of crime.

There is an urgent need to educate our people more adequately, from the adults to the children, concerning the evils of alcohol. Until this is better done, laws against its sale, even when passed, will not be enforced. Another clear challenge to action is afforded by the advertising campaigns to increase demand for alcoholic beverages. There are plausible arguments against banning legal sales of alcohol when half the adult population seeks to purchase strong drink and will try to break down any "dry" laws which may be passed. But there is no argument whatever to defend efforts deliberately to foster a craving for alcohol through advertising. No sane person can believe that the public welfare is served by efforts to increase alcohol consumption. There is no reason why the public advertising of strong drink should be tolerated. If brand names must be made known, then let this be done only where alcohol is actually sold. Why not require that for every dollar of money spent by the liquor producers in such restricted advertising of brand names they must put another dollar into a great public advertising campaign under

---

[6] Taft, *op. cit.*, pp. 252-53, and works there cited.

state control, teaching the perils of beverage alcohol and the advantages of abstinence?

A third condition characteristic of criminals is poor education. In approximately one third of all case histories of delinquents and adult criminals studied by the Gluecks, one or both parents were found to be illiterate. Three fourths of the adult criminals studied had at least one parent with no formal schooling.[7] There is no deadlier foe of crime than good, well-equipped, well-directed public schools. Individual cases of well-educated criminals must not blind us to this fact, which is supported by overwhelming evidence. The public schools of America are fighting for their lives these days under the best organized efforts to destroy them which they have ever had to withstand. They need our wholeheared support to secure adequate equipment, a better salary scale for their teachers, and a better public appreciation of their particular function in our national life. Assistance to the public school is a particularly effective way of preventing crime.

A fourth characteristic of criminal case histories is poor economic conditions, particularly poor housing. Of all the delinquents studied by the Gluecks only 13 per cent came from homes with adequate room, light, ventilation, and cleanliness. Sixty-eight per cent came from homes which were physically detrimental to a serious degree.[8] The battle for slum clearance, decent housing, and a fair distribution of our national prosperity has only begun.

A fifth factor of great importance in the incubation of crime is the lack of adequate recreational facilities for youth. Where boys and girls must play on crowded sidewalks and streets and adolescents have no better place to meet and court than street corners and dark alleys, a heavy incidence of crime is to be expected. Many people in small towns would be surprised to find how acute are the needs for better recreational and social facilities in their own communities. In one small town where I lived for several years, the people became greatly exercised about the scandalous number of juvenile offenses reported by the police. But after we organized an active

[7] Glueck, *op. cit.,* p. 185.
[8] *Ibid.,* pp. 190-91.

Parent-Teacher Association and through it instituted a supervised-playground program, not a single juvenile offense was reported in an entire year.

A sixth condition tending to produce crime is individual isolation. When any person, young or old, finds himself alone in a situation where it seems as if no one cares how he fares or what he does, he is likely to resort to methods of diversion or escape which are personally and often socially destructive. It is the special mission of the church to leave the crowded fold and seek the lonely, wandering sheep, bringing them in where they can share in a fellowship of Christian love and faith. Especially needing such services are young men in military service wandering in strange places looking for relief from the deadly routine of the training camp. Thousands who have never considered such activities before, turn, from sheer loneliness and boredom, to drunkenness and vice. Many continue the road down into lives of crime. The churches must work with other agencies to help provide wholesome alternatives. Among civilians, aged people living in lonely widowhood and young people attracted to strange cities for employment and finding themselves isolated from all the familiar, friendly associations are classes requiring especially resourceful help from our churches. One of the most alarming present trends in American Protestantism is the tendency to withdraw our churches from the rooming-house areas of our cities, where these needs are most acute, and to concentrate in the more prosperous and stable suburbs. To maintain an effective church in a rooming-house district requires interdenominational co-operation and help from people in more stable areas. But it is just such services that we must maintain if we are to enter seriously the battle against crime or to accept in earnest the discipleship of the Good Shepherd.

A seventh condition which breeds crime is racial segregation and discrimination. In all parts of the United States, Negroes are convicted of far more crimes of violence than are white people. Even when it is recognized that Negroes are more likely to be caught, convicted, sentenced, and punished than are white offenders, it is still apparent that they commit from two to eight times as many murders and other crimes of violence as do white people in the same communities.

This is *not* due to racial inheritance. As evidence it must be observed that within the South it is not the states with most Negroes which have the worst rates of crime. It must also be observed that Negroes in Connecticut commit fewer murders per hundred thousand than do white people in Kentucky. It *is* due in part to the inferior opportunities for profitable employment and sound education. It is also due to the bitterness and irresponsibility engendered by political race-baiting and segregation from full participation in community life. When Mayor Hartsfield put just eight Negroes on the police force of Atlanta, Georgia, the rate of crime and misdemeanors in the Negro community dropped 50 per cent. Other cities have had similar experiences.

Yet there is no city in the United States where Negroes are welcomed into full participation in the total economic, social, political, and religious community. The wonder is not that so many colored people show so little sense of obligation to preserve the order in which they are not permitted fully to share. The wonder is that so many show such a high sense of social responsibility, with so much patient self-discipline.

If we want our land to be free from its burden of crime, we shall have to free it also from the monstrous evil of white arrogance. In establishing real interracial brotherhood, the church ought to lead all other institutions. But in North and South alike, we must say to our shame, the church lags far behind many secular institutions.

The Church in the Treatment of Crime

Not alone in preventing people from falling into crime, but also in the treatment of those who are convicted of criminal behavior, the church has a real responsibility, as was pointed out at the beginning. If we do not accept it, we dare not call ourselves followers of Him who came to save sinners. But what can we do?

First of all, we can see to it that prisons are provided with capable chaplains. Where church services are held in prisons by devout and able ministers, they are usually attended better

THE CHURCH AND SOCIAL RESPONSIBILITY

than are services among the population outside. This is partly because there is so little else to do in a prison and partly because some prisoners hope to make an impression on parole and pardon boards. But it is also due to the fact that many prisoners, in their loneliness, humiliation, and deep sense of guilt, feel a great need for God. The prison chaplain who not only holds services but also is available for personal counsel will find unusual opportunities for significant spiritual ministry. Protestants do not generally give nearly so much attention to these opportunities as do Roman Catholics. This is part of our whole tendency to become churches of the respectable suburbs, out of touch with laboring people and the outcast. Among Protestants the Episcopal and Lutheran churches are said to render much more service in prison chaplaincies than do many other churches. It is time that we returned to the concern of the Wesleys and ministered to the people who are most acutely in need of friendly visitation and the gospel of divine forgiveness.

Second, in most communities many criminal offenders, especially youthful ones, are given suspended sentences and saved from attending the schools of crime which most prisons are, when it is known that a minister or respected church layman will assume responsibility for guiding and helping them toward a better life. Every year countless thousands of young people are turned from lives of crime to lives of real usefulness through such arrangements. Many such attempts lead to repeated failures. But the proportion of failures is surely much lower than when prison sentences are served. Many brilliant successes are scored. There are excellent ministers in our churches who were thus snatched from the very gates of jail and led into God's redeeming grace, and many of our finest laymen have had similar experiences, often known only to themselves, a little circle of police and court officials, and a kind Christian friend. Some ministers have made a specialty of such service. According to newspaper reports, a Methodist minister, the Rev. L. M. Stevenson of Oklahoma City, has an especially impressive record of such service. It began five years ago in his church in a low-income neighborhood. Since that time, reports the Associated Press, he has reclaimed over one hundred boys who had been convicted of crime. Some of the most incorrigible repeaters are now among the best citizens. Hundreds of others have been guided out of delinquency and crime before being arrested. Only seven of all this number have broken faith with their minister friend. He has enlisted the help of fifteen hundred laymen who provide jobs, homes, recreational events, and an annual budget of more than $5,000 for this work of human reclamation.[9] May God raise up other leaders for this superb form of Christian ministry.

Again, after criminals have completed their prison terms, the church can be of great assistance in finding for them new employment, lodging, and a new place in the total life of the community. When a released convict finds himself without a job in a suspicious community, he is likely to see every avenue of life closed to him except the way that leads back to crime. At Boston University School of Theology, recently, the seminar on "changing social attitudes," taught by Dr. Allan K. Chalmers, made a study and demonstration of reclaiming young adult criminals. As a result, under the leadership of Dr. Myron W. Fowell, sixty-eight Congregational churches in Massachusetts now have committees of lay men and lay women organized for this work. Bishop John Wesley Lord has recommended such a program to the Methodists of the Boston Area.

THE CHURCH AND PENAL JUSTICE

The church has yet another sphere of responsibility in relation to crime. The laws and court procedures of our country have been deeply influenced by the teaching and practice of the church. The famous dean of Harvard Law School, Roscoe Pound, has clearly shown this influence in his 1939 Jubilee Law Lectures, entitled "The Church in Legal History," at the Catholic University of America.[10] Both in these

[9] *Boston Daily Globe*, Dec. 16, 1952. Cf. Robert L. Carl, "A Prison Without Bars," and John B. Oman, "Juvenile Delinquency," in *The Christian Advocate*, Sept. 4, 1952, and Nov. 13, 1952.

[10] Roscoe Pound et al., *Jubilee Law Lectures* (Washington, D. C.: The Catholic University of America Press, 1939).

lectures and on other occasions he has called upon Christian thinkers to give guidance to the legal profession in reformulating a basic philosophy of law.

The present confusion is so great that it is one basic cause of the widespread disrespect for law. Law is not an instrument of naked power. It is an expression of ideas. When the ideas are contradictory, confused, and poorly understood, both by lawyers and by the public, the system of law enforcement is bound to be hesitant, unpredictable, and relatively ineffective. This is precisely the situation today. The responsibility for it does not rest upon the legal profession alone. Legislatures and courts do not create the moral convictions upon which the whole structure of law must finally rest. The task of reformulating an adequate philosophy of law is a task which requires the best co-operative efforts of leaders in the law, in criminology, and in the church.

The dominant idea in present criminal law is that the criminal must "pay" for his offense by a punishment somehow equivalent to the moral depravity of his offense. This idea has caused increasing difficulty as the Christian protest against retaliation has gained favor, as the difficulties of determining the limits of an individual's moral responsiblity have been made more impressive by modern psychology and theoretical ethics, and as the tragic results of putting the *lex talionis* into practice have become increasingly evident.

Another idea underlying the actions of our courts in criminal cases is the "making an example" of convicted criminals so that others will be deterred from crime by fear of suffering similar consequences. There seems little doubt that there is some deterrent effect of some kinds of punishment, particularly in relation to coldly calculated crimes of economic motivation. However, there is much evidence that the deterrent effect of punishment on serious crime is popularly overrated. For example, although criminals generally prefer any other punishment to execution, capital punishment appears, by every approach we are able to make, to have no effect in diminishing the number of murders. There are now a number of widely distributed states which provide for no capital punishment; and yet, as compared with states of similar population, economic status, and cultural pattern, they have no more—in fact they have slightly fewer—murders. The ineffectiveness of capital punishment as a deterrent seems quite decisively established by the series of articles appearing in the *Annals of the American Academy of Political Science* for November, 1952, devoted exclusively to the subject, "Murder and the Penalty of Death."

A third idea underlying our penal system is that of protecting society by keeping dangerous people confined. Certainly this is an important value. But it is obvious that a man who is too dangerous to be at large for nine and one-half years is not likely to become safe just because he has completed a tenth year behind bars. Determining when a man will be dangerous and when safe is hardly to be done accurately in advance, according to a legal formula.

The teachings of the churches have had a great part in the modern trend toward emphasizing reform as a main objective in the treatment accorded criminals. Whatever the ideas of revenge which may prevail in the press and sometimes in the courtrooms, once a prisoner is behind bars, all decent prison officials will be concerned with his reform. Some criminologists have brilliant records in the moral rehabilitation of prisoners under their charge. But most prisons are not adequately equipped or staffed for this purpose, and often a vindictively minded public puts every obstacle in the way of those who seek the reformation of offenders. Little do most people seem to realize that unless all criminals are to be executed or imprisoned for life, reform is the only way of safeguarding the public from further depredations by them.

There are serious unsolved problems concerning the proper basic idea of penal law implied by Christian teaching. It is a problem worthy of long and serious study by the best theological and legal minds in the church. The World Council of Churches sponsored a European conference of Christian lawyers and theologians held in Treysa, Germany, in 1950 on the subject "The Biblical Doctrine of Law and Justice." [11]

[11] Reported in *The Treysa Conference on "The Biblical Doctrine of Law and Justice"* (Geneva, Switzerland: The Study Department of the World Council of Churches, 1951).

It might well happen here. More prolonged work also must be done across the years. Law without a conscience would be only violence and in the true sense itself lawlessness. If law is to have a proper conscience, the church, above all other institutions, must provide that conscience or abandon hope of making this a Christian nation.

13

War and the Christian Ethic

Roland H. Bainton

War is an ugly business about which Christians have never felt easy save in the age of the crusades, when the bellicosity of the upsurgent northern peoples fused with Christian zeal against the infidel. The church receded from Jesus to Joshua and justified wading in the blood of the unbelievers by comparing the slaughter to the extermination of the Amorites. In succeeding ages the crusading mood has recurred whenever some holy cause, such as making the world safe for democracy, was deemed to be at stake. Yet never have there been lacking critical voices who found the precepts of Jesus on the love of enemies and the turning of the other cheek difficult to square with ripping up the bowels of the Turks or the dictators.

A complete repudiation of war has been recurrently espoused, if not by the whole church, then at times by a dominant majority, and at other times by a far from contemptible minority. The early church down to the time of Constantine was pacifist in the sense that no Christian writer whose work is extant condoned Christian participation in warfare prior to that time, and many vigorously disapproved. At the same time, we have increasing evidence of the presence of Christians in the army, and they were not on that account excluded from communion. The complete repudiation of warfare appears also to have flourished in the peaceful center of the empire rather than on the frontiers threatened by barbarian attacks. A distinction seems also to have been made between military service in peacetime, which was allowed, and in wartime, which was rejected, because in peacetime the soldiers were engaged in police work—there was in fact no separate police force, and a soldier might thus be in service for one, two, or three decades without ever having to shed blood.

The pacifism of the early church exhibits types which have proved persistent. All stressed the incompatibility of killing with Christian love. The accessory arguments were varied. Some, though they were really outside the Christian stream, objected to war as defiling to personal holiness. The body was considered to be unclean and the shedding of blood as rendering one unfit to partake of the sacred mysteries. To a degree this view has fastened itself upon Christian thinking, and the main reason why the Catholic Church demands the exemption of the clergy is that by bloodshed they are disqualified for the celebration of the Mass. The church does not make an absolute of this point, however, and if priests are drafted, they are not forbidden to serve.

The second type of pacifism was literalistic, legalistic, eschatological. The gospel was interpreted as a new law including, of course, the old law which says, "Thou shalt not kill." To this was added the injunction when struck on one cheek to turn the other. The command to Peter, "Put up thy sword," was believed to have been addressed to every Christian and to disarm every soldier. The disciple must obey no matter what might be the social consequences. He might rest assured, however, that God's will cannot be defeated. Christ would soon return to smite the ungodly and to set up his kingdom. If, in the meantime, the wicked should crush the righteous, their turn would eventually come. Until then, however, the church must expect to suffer, and without the hope that such suffering would have any affect on the course of historical events. Pacifism was a testimony and not a device for ending war. Such is the view of many of the Mennonites in our own time.

A third variety of pacifism might be called almost pragmatic, because it believes that prayer and love are more effective than legions of soldiers as a method of establishing social order. Early Christian writers believed that the prayers of the faithful were more efficacious with God and served better to restrain the demonic powers than all the armies of Rome. The winsomeness of the Lord Jesus, which had already taken men captive with a power far exceeding that of any of the ancient philosophers, would continue to subdue the rude wills of men's wild behavior until the very barbarians would bow the knee and the dreaded invaders would become friends. Underlying this position was plainly an optimism as to the persuasiveness of the Christian gospel to enlist the masses of mankind. In modern times this position has been given a somewhat different turn by stressing the redemptive quality of suffering voluntarily assumed. The Cross has been looked upon not simply as a witness, but almost as a strategy, the assumption being that if enough persons with power to do otherwise should of their own accord submit to the brutality of the invader, in time the very oppressor would be ashamed and tamed and converted from an enemy to an ally.

After Constantine's accession, pacifism of whatever variety receded. The church rejoiced that Constantine, having placed the monogram of Christ upon his military standards, had been victorious over all the persecutors and had by arms achieved peace for the church. They were ready to uphold this anointed of the Lord in his endeavors to resist the invader from without or the conspirator from within. By the end of the fourth century the orthodox emperor, Theodosius I, had decreed that only Christians might serve in the army. No lively repercussions occurred for the moment among the spokesmen for the church. The reason may in part have been that the monastic movement was in full swing, and the more rigoristic spirits had withdrawn, not only from military service, but from all participation in the common life. Those who, before Constantine, would have been the martyrs were now the monks, and their critique of life in the world was much more drastic than an objection merely to military service. Here and there, to be sure, one finds some wrestling with the ethical problems involved for the Christian in warfare. The first systematic confrontation with the whole question was that of Augustine. He it was who formulated for the church the doctrine of the just war.

In so doing, he was not for the most part an originator, because the concept of the just war had already been evolved by the Greeks and the Romans. The formulation of Cicero received, at the hands of Augustine, Christian baptism. The just war entailed three cardinal points: It must be just as to its intent, just as to its auspices, and just as to its conduct.

The just intent involved in turn three points. The objects of the war must be to restore peace, vindicative justice, and benefit the enemy. That peace is the object of war had long since been declared by Plato. Wars of adventure he would not condone. The lust of battle manifest in some of the Homeric poems, he stoutly discountenanced. He was thinking in terms of the society of Greek states associated in friendly federation. If one encroached upon another, that state might be repelled but not exterminated. Plato's idea was not devoid of actuality, and even Sparta, the most militant of the Greek states, after a victory over Athens, refused to extinguish the glory of Greece, contenting herself with demolishing the walls without massacring or enslaving the inhabitants. The theory of the just war thus originated in terms of the balance of power among states united in a cultural federation. The heir of this classical tradition was Augustine, who wrote to a Roman general,

Peace should be the object of your desire. War should be waged only as a necessity, and waged only that through it God may deliver men from that necessity and preserve them in peace, for peace is not to be sought in order to kindle war, but war is to be waged in order to obtain peace. Therefore, even in the course of war, you should cherish the spirit of a peacemaker.[1]

But peace cannot be properly restored until justice has been vindicated. Precisely what this meant for Augustine was not altogether clear, though wrongs to nationals and the invasion of territory were deemed injustices to be rectified. The just war was defensive only in the sense that justice was being defended, not that the lands of the vindicator must first have been invaded. The initiative as to hostilities might be

---

[1] Epistle 188, § 6.

taken by the champion of justice. To this classical theory Augustine added a clarification. To his mind a just war implied of necessity an unjust war. Justice should be on one side only. Consequently, if one side were to be just, the other had to be unjust. Augustine was thus responsible for the importance ever since attached in the West to the determination of war guilt.

The point that the object of the war must be to benefit the enemy, that it must have in mind his ultimate good, that the disposition of the warrior must be that of love, was a Christian addition to the classical theory which never went beyond the restriction that the object should not be annihilation. Augustine insisted that Christianity demands not a particular mode of behavior, but a disposition of the heart. The precept to turn the other cheek, to resist not evil, is fulfilled provided the taking of life is directed toward the saving of souls. This is entirely possible because the destruction of the body does not extinguish the soul, and he who by physical death is restrained from crime will actually have been benefited by such an exercise of force. The injunction to love one's enemies admits of no attenuation, but it does not preclude killing their bodies.

The second basic article of the just-war theory was that arms may be taken only at the behest and under the auspices of government. Cicero foresaw that otherwise chaos would ensue. Augustine formulated the distinction even more sharply when he laid down that a private citizen may not take arms even in his own defense. In such a case he must suffer himself to be killed rather than resist. In this instance the precept of the Sermon on the Mount applies literally, and the reason is that no one will be able, when his own interests are involved, to maintain the proper dispositions. Anger, passion, and vindictiveness are bound to enter in. They can be excluded only by one who is not a party to the dispute. Hence, if an individual is wronged, he may invite the intervention of the state, but he may not take justice into his own hands.

A further restriction on the individual is that he is not to determine the justice of the war, but must leave this to his prince. Even though the prince be a pagan, he is to be given unqualified obedience in the political domain. One wonders why Augustine did not impose more checks upon the prince, why he did not face up to the question whether the state could be impartial if defending itself. The reason probably is that he was thinking in terms of the orderly Roman Empire defending itself against the disorderly barbarian invaders. This situation appeared to him so clearly that he did not envisage a congeries of sovereign Christian states, each vindicating its rights by war against the other. His whole thinking about war was set in the framework of government under law. The warrior for him was a magistrate. He did not perceive that among states no genuine analogy to government had been achieved, and we may add, despite the medieval papacy, the League of Nations, and the United Nations, that such a situation remains only in the realm of aspiration.

The conduct of the just war must be just. The conditions were prescribed in a set of rules. Good faith must be kept with the enemy. There should be no wanton violence, no profanation of temples, no looting, conflagration, or massacre. Vengeance, atrocities, and reprisals were excluded. Hostages and prisoners should be respected and noncombatants spared. Among the noncombatants Augustine woud include monks and ministers: the monks because they are dedicated to the practice of the councils of perfection—hence, they must have no wives, no wares, and no weapons; the clergy because they must be undefiled for their ministry at the altar.

Thus was formulated the Catholic ethic of the just war which with slight modifications remains in force to this day. Some changes have subsequently been introduced. In the agrarian society of the Middle Ages the church tended increasingly to think of justice in terms of the maintenance of property relations. The Peace of God tried to enlarge the class of noncombatants by including not only women, children, the aged, the monks, and the ministers, but also pilgrims, travelers, merchants, peasants, and their animals. Thomas Aquinas, by implication at least, allowed for conscientious objection to military service, for he recognized that the individual must follow his own convictions even though they be against church and state; and Thomas, in connection with

the right of revolution, introduced a very important consideration—namely, that the justice of an undertaking depends in
part upon whether the foreseeable outcome promises more
good than ill. Thus, justice was made dependent upon a fal-
lible forecast of the results. The Augustinian rejection of the
right of self-defense to an individual was dropped, and after
a number of independent states had emerged in Europe, to
each of them was conceded the right of self-defense against
the others.

Protestants, who espoused Christian participation in warfare, have in the main appropriated this code with slight al-
terations. The monk for them is, of course, out of the picture.
That is why it is hard for Catholics to understand Protestant
conscientious objectors. If the Protestant objector says that
he must follow the command of Christ to put up his sword,
the Catholic replies, "Very well, but you must also sell all
and forsake father and mother, wife and child." Protestants
commonly agree with Catholics in asking for the exemption of
the clergy, though less on sacramental than on vocational
grounds. The reasons for conscientious objection on the part
of the Catholic are less broad than for the Protestant because
for the Catholic, war, as such, can never be wholly excluded.
The question is rather whether a particular war is a just war.
Some Catholics say that no modern war can be just, because
in view of the intricacy of the relationships of states, guilt
can never be completely localized on one side; because apart
from world government, war cannot properly be said to be
waged under the auspices of government; and because the
indiscriminate character of modern weapons precludes any
sparing of noncombatants. In addition to these considerations,
Protestants may adduce others which revive in modern dress
the varieties of pacifism evident in the early church.

Inasmuch as all Catholics and all warring Protestants think
in terms of the just-war theory, it is not amiss to raise the
question whether as a matter of fact wars, and in particular the
Korean War, can be squared with the requisite conditions.

Take the point that justice must be on one side only. At the
outset in the Korean conflict this seemed abundantly clear.
The thirty-eighth parallel had been set up first for military

convenience, then had been continued as a device for implementing the peace under the auspices of the United Nations. The violation of this boundary line by the North Koreans was a flagrant defiance of the authority of the United Nations, and if tolerated, would in the minds of many have spelled the collapse of the second great effort in our time to achieve world government. But then, the victorious forces of the United Nations, having reached the thirty-eighth parallel, resolved on the unification of the country and pushed beyond. Thereupon the Communist bloc became meticulously devoted to the prior covenant, and the Chinese Communists accused the United Nations of violating the agreement. They were branded as the aggressors, and the Chinese then threw their weight to the aid of the North Koreans. Both sides now claimed that a violation had been committed by the other.

If one views the question not in the light of the immediate outbreak of hostilities, but from the perspective of the last century, the case becomes more involved. Since the United States is the prime mover in the United Nations, it comes to be a question of relations of the United States to the Orient. A chief place was taken by the United States in compelling Japan to receive the Western world, and the United States had a share in forcing upon China the open door, though without exacting any territorial concessions. And now, though the United States has been of all great powers the least implicated in colonial imperialism, yet in the eyes of Asia she is regarded as the legatee of the imperialists. This picture is rendered the more plausible by American aid to the French in Indochina. Strange irony that we who have eschewed imperialism, we who have liberated the Philippines, should now find ourselves bearing the onus of all the white man's depredation in Asia, so that whereas we conceive of ourselves as the upholders of world government, the Orientals picture us as the latest among the vultures! The reply may be that their picture is wrong, and that actually our hands are clean, but we cannot quite so easily disclaim the past of which we have become the custodians.

The intent of the just war must be to restore peace. There is much to indicate that the United Nations and the United

States have no other intent than this. The stalling appears to come from the other side. But while one can discern nobility in the refusal to repatriate unwilling prisoners, one can but query whether a genuine concern for the right of asylum or a desire to prolong the conflict is causing postponement. Proof in this area is impossible, but we may engage in searching of heart.

Love for the enemy is one of the Christian ingredients in the attitude of the just war. In a measure this may be operating. The leaders of our nation do not desire any permanent impairment of North Korea or of China. The conscripted soldiers commonly take their task as a grim assignment to be gotten over with, and when it is finished, they can meet those who are on the other side and talk about the conflict as if it had been a football game. This is particularly true when the enemies are Europeans, and our own men have not found it difficult to establish such a rapport with the Germans. But when Orientals are the foes, the arrogance of the white man asserts itself. The enemy is called a "Gook," and his death is taken no more seriously than the squashing of a melon.

The just-war theory requires that war be conducted under the auspices of government. This is the weakest spot in the entire concept because if all the elements in the theory are to be realized, the government must be a supergovernment, not a party to the conflict and operating impartially under law after the manner of civil government. In the Korean situation some felt that this condition had been realized because the order to fire came from the United Nations, a world government. So clear did this appear that certain pacifists indorsed the intervention on the ground that it was not war but only police action. If, however, one examines more closely the structure of the United Nations, this is not so evident, for Communist China was not permitted to be a member. The United Nations, in consequence, can be construed as something of a cross between a world government and an anti-Communist power bloc. John Foster Dulles, writing in 1950, recognized that here is a genuine defect in the structure of the United Nations. He wrote,

I have now come to believe that the United Nations will best serve the cause of peace if its Assembly is representative of what the world actually is, and not merely representative of the parts which we like. Therefore, we ought to be willing that all the nations should be members without attempting to appraise closely those which are "good" and those which are "bad." Already that distinction is obliterated by the present membership of the United Nations.

Some of the present member nations, and others that might become members, have governments that are not representative of the people. But if in fact they are "governments"—that is, if they "govern"—then they have a power which should be represented in any organization that purports to mirror world reality.

If the Communist government of China in fact proves its ability to govern China without serious domestic resistance, then it, too, should be admitted to the United Nations. However, a regime that claims to have become the government of a country through civil war should not be recognized until it has been tested over a reasonable period of time.

If the United Nations membership were made substantially universal, that might end a preponderant voting superiority of the United States and its friends which, while pleasant, is somewhat fictitious.

Communist governments today dominate more than 30 per cent of the population of the world. We may not like that fact; indeed, we do not like it at all. But if we want to have a *world* organization, then it should be representative of the world as it is.[2]

Had Communist China been included in the United Nations at the time of the restlessness in North Korea, conceivably the uprising might have been averted, or, had it occurred, it might have been terminated earlier. This, of course, is speculative, but one point is plain—that the United Nations cannot be regarded as constituting a world government to the degree that the intervention can be construed simply as police action. It is also the conflict of two power blocs.

When one turns to the conduct of this and of every modern war, the gravest difficulties are encountered, for the more

[2] *War or Peace* (New York: The Macmillan Co., 1950), pp. 190-91.

war has improved at the point of technology, the more has it
deteriorated at the point of morality because modern weapons
are not only more deadly, but less discriminating. The code
of the just war calls for the sparing of noncombatants. Today
there are no noncombatants. This was brought home to me
poignantly during a discussion at the Yale University Divinity
School when sanctions against Italy were under discussion.
A speaker defended resort to military measures. An inquirer
put to him a question, "Would you then bomb Rome and
kill women and children?" "Why not?" he answered. "Is life
any more sacred because it is young?" The answer is, of
course, no. Life is not more sacred, but it is less responsible.
The civil law makes a distinction between the juvenile and the
mature offender, between the sane and the insane. War ob-
literates all such distinctions, and whereas civil government
has become more and more moral, war has become more and
more oblivious to morality.

The character of modern weapons has occasioned grievous
heart searching among the churches. Commissions have been
set up to report on the morality of atomic bombing. Those
who justify the use of such weapons argue that they are no
worse than others already in vogue. After all, planes did more
damage to life and property in Tokyo than did the atomic
bombs in Hiroshima and Nagasaki. And, again, we are re-
minded that the napalm jelly bombs are much more cruel
in the pain which they inflict. Thus, we proceed from one
weapon to the next. The introduction of each new instrument
of frightfulness occasions a shock. Then, after a time, we
grow inured and are ready at the next "advance" to say that
after all in principle it is no worse than the preceding.

This sequence may easily evoke cynicism, but there is a
validity in the argument that the morality of a weapon is not
to be measured in terms of the numbers it kills at one throw,
and perhaps not even in terms of the pain inflicted, since no
weapon is painless and death is the end of them all. The real
moral line lies not between one weapon and another but in
the manner of their employment. The ethical frontier was
passed in the shift from strategic to obliteration bombing. The
first struck only at military objectives. If some noncombatants

211

happened to be in the way, that was just too bad. The aim was not to strike at them, but rather to spare. With obliteration bombing, the case was altered. The civilian population became the object of attack. What this entailed I witnessed with my own eyes at Nuremberg. Here the munitions factories survived, while the residential section lay in rubble. I was talking with a G.I. about it, and he remarked, "We could not get at the factories because they were protected by antiaircraft, so we had to kill the people who worked in the factories." And that is modern war.

In Korea the atomic bomb has thus far not been used. The jelly bomb has been employed, and there is the charge that we have used bacteriological weapons. The accusation is denied on our side, and the evidence adduced in support of the incrimination is not very convincing. Yet we cannot deny that we have a department of bacteriological warfare and do not exclude on moral grounds the possibility of using such weapons.

One of the most frightful phases of modern war is its aftermath. So many of the normal facilities of life are disrupted —communication, food, shelter, and sanitation—that the deaths from malnutrition and exposure may well nigh equal or even exceed the casualties of battle. The *United States Strategic Bombing Survey* in 1947 reported that in Japan disability claims by reason of pulmonary tuberculosis rose from 13.6 per thousand insured persons in 1933 to 43.7 per thousand in 1941. The deaths from tuberculosis reached an all-time peak in 1943 wth a total of 171,474. The rate was 225 for 100,000 of the population as compared with 180 in 1932; this record shows an increase of 25 per cent. The rate in the United States in 1943 was five times lower than in Japan.[3]

A graphic picture of what war leaves in its wake is given by the British war correspondent Reginald Thompson, in his book *Cry, Korea*. He writes:

We lay together on the ridge of the hills, watching the air-craft diving with their rockets, and the bursts of the shells from the ships of Inchon. Yet it was a scene of peace. The smoke rose

[3] Pp. 217-19.

from the burned out villages as it might have risen from the fires of autumn, and those villages which had until now escaped, seemed like fairy circles of grey mushrooms under the tall poplars which spaced the broad valley plain. Far beneath we could see the peasants working placidly in harvesting the tall ripe sorghum, unmindful of the war which was about to envelop them. It was a scene both rich and beautiful, for the ripening grain and the green crops promised a harvest which was not to be fulfilled. In the early hours of the following day, the airfield of Kimpo was captured, and when I came this way again, an infantry division had moved up to take over from the Marines and had fanned out south and east. The brief respite had ended in death. The bright colors were gone from field and female under dust and pall. No longer the scarlet of pimentos, no longer the vivid green and crimson of silken clothes. Now the villages smoldered in the hollows and old men sat at the roadsides with the knowledge that the deluge of war, which had seemed for the moment to have passed them by, might now overwhelm them.[4]

One can understand why in Burma one Burmese is reported to have said to another, "Are you not worried for fear of a Chinese Communist invasion of our land?" To which the other replied, "I am, but there is something which worries me more, that we shall not be able to dissuade the United States from rescuing us."

This remark brings into play the consideration formulated by Thomas Aquinas that when recourse is had to arms, the foreseeable good must outweigh the foreseeable harm. One recalls the attitude of those in England who at the outbreak of the Second World War renounced their pacifism because they would rather lose their immortal souls than be parties by neutrality to the extermination of the Jews. Now one ruefully recalls that their intervention did not save six million Jews from extermination. Yet, they could have been saved if we had been willing to find for them somewhere else to go. Rather than take them in, we preferred to fight to compel Hitler to keep them, and now Hitler is gone and so also are they.

Another condition of the just war was the keeping of

[4] London: Macdonald & Co., 1951, p. 46.

good faith with the enemy. This meant primarily the observance of treaty commitments. Deception was allowed only in the case of ambush on the field, but such restriction of deception is impossible in war. Both sides cultivate espionage, and one wonders why the churches have not appointed a commission to deal not only with the morality of atomic warfare, but also with the morality of organized lying. We are very horrified by it when it is used against us. In the United States the death penalty has recently been imposed for giving military secrets to Russia. We might reflect that the judgments passed upon Nathan Hale and Benedict Arnold depend on the side which writes the history, and we might further reflect that wars cannot be carried on, whether cold or hot, without finding out everything possible with regard to the moves of the other side. However much we may dignify our operations under the caption of military intelligence, we cannot disguise from ourselves the fact that we, too, are engaged in the practice of deception. We endeavor to break down the integrity of those who can supply us with information, and no trade is too despicable to serve as a cover for espionage. After all, when nations trust ultimately to mass slaughter for their survival, is it surprising that they do not recoil from wholesale deception?

What all this adds up to is simply that the traditional ethic of the just war is no longer tenable save with grave modifications. Those Christians who feel that despite everything we cannot renounce war in an extremity, will say that the code, indeed, of the just war has gone by the board, but that the intention is still justice, peace, and love, and that the cause is at least relatively just. Others will feel that the whole business is becoming so monstrous that the Christian must witness against it in every way, including nonparticipation. No nation is likely to take this course. Probably no church will do so; even the historic peace churches are no longer unanimous on the point. The decision then rests with individuals. If they take their stand as conscientious objectors, their churches will give them moral and perhaps even financial support, and some of those who cannot agree with them will yet rejoice that their protest is a constant prick to the Christian conscience.

The attitude of the state toward the conscientious objector from the Christian point of view scarcely differs from that required by a liberal point of view. The state cannot well make of conscience an absolute, because the commission of a crime may under some circumstances be conscientious. The assassin of Gandhi was presumably conscientious, and Communists who conspire to overthrow by violence the Constitution of this country may be extremely conscientious. The question then comes to be not whether they are sincere, but how inimical is their conduct to the welfare of the community. Some restraints must be imposed if there is a danger. The object of the restraint should be only to ward off an imminent threat to the community and never to break down the integrity of the objector. This means that the penalty should not be punitive and should not be continued after the danger no longer exists. To deprive conscientious objectors of citizenship for life is political folly, for such persons in peaceful walks of life and even in politics in peacetime may be the most loyal and useful of citizens. One recalls that two British prime ministers were conscientiously opposed to two of Britain's wars: Lloyd George to the Boer War and Ramsey MacDonald to the First World War. Britain is wise enough to curb men only for an emergency and when it is over to employ them without prejudice even in the highest offices of state.

The treatment of the conscientious objector in the United States at the moment differs from that accorded during the Second World War. The objector may be assigned with pay to useful civilian employ instead of being relegated to civilian public-service camps where the work was often inconsequential and the absence of pay made the inmates dependents on their families or their churches. Those who wish to be informed as to the details of the present law and the various procedures should obtain a copy of the *Handbook for Conscientious Objectors* published by the Central Committee for Conscientious Objectors, 2006 Walnut Street, Philadelphia 3, Pennsylvania.

Yet, if those who indorse participation in warfare can enjoy no complacency in these times, neither can the conscientious objector take his position lightly and without much searching of heart as to the grounds. An objector among my friends tells me of the shock which he has recently encountered. During the Second World War he renounced his status as a divinity student and refused to register. In consequence, he served a prison term. On release he went out as a missionary to India and arrived at the time and in the place where the Hindus were massacring the Mohammedans. The latter were trying only to escape, but at the very railway stations they were mowed down by the Hindu police. Corpses were piled up by the thousands and carried away in trucks. In that situation two occurrences contributed to the restoration of order. The first was the assassination of Gandhi, which sobered the Hindus, and this certainly does show that the claim for the power of soul force is not illusory. Yet, this had to be reinforced by a second factor—namely, the arrival of Christian troops who were ready, if need be, to fire upon the Hindus. This missionary conscientious objector said that he had reached the point where he would prefer a military state to sheer chaos.

Now the action of these Christian troops which he described was not war; it was police activity. They were not in any sense participants in the quarrel. They came in strict impartiality with the sole purpose of restoring order. The amount of violence which they would need to use was minimal. Tear gas might ordinarily have sufficed. Certainly they would not have needed to bomb cities. Yet, in a given juncture they might have had to fire on the mob. They might even have killed some innocent bystanders. If pacifism be based on an absolute refusal to take life, such intervention would have to be ruled out. One may question whether New Testament pacifism is so extreme, for one recalls that Paul was willing to accept an armed guard to conduct him from Jerusalem to Caesarea Philippi. The situation in India is comparable. It was the action of a police force, albeit in military uniform. Yet, the whole episode shows the difficulty of drawing absolutely precise lines.

This at any rate is plain. The Christian church must regard

war as hideous, and every effort must be made for peace. The form of this endeavor will probably not be that of a mass refusal to engage in warfare. If peace is kept, it will be kept by those who are ready to fight in an extremity but will do their utmost to avoid that extremity. Those who refuse to participate do well to realize that their stand may make its ultimate contribution to a warless world, perhaps a century hence; but at this present juncture peace will be preserved, if it is preserved, by peace-minded nonpacifists. Their hands ought in every way then to be strengthened.

How much can be done concretely is difficult to know. One of the most disconcerting developments is that peace itself has become a weapon. We read that in Berlin the eastern sector will mail to the western sector thousands of doves, and the western sector will reply by returning doves with feathers ruffled by having passed through the Iron Curtain. This little story may be apocryphal, but we cannot question the peace offensives which emanate from the Communists and leave always the suspicion that these gestures are designed only to weaken and take advantage of the opposition. On the other hand there are many indications that the Russians do want peace. They must have peace if they are to rebuild after all the devastation of war. The problem is how each peace-minded group can convince the other of genuine intent, and certainly that is not easy when the governments of both countries are feverishly engaged in piling up atomic weapons. Our best hope for a decade may well be simply to keep the war cold.

In the meantime we can develop every device for increasing understanding. A group of English Quakers were recently permitted by their own government and by the Russian government to visit Russia. The report made on their return was not naïve enough to suppose that they had been shown all the festering sores in the Russian body politic, but it does say that they were accorded more freedom than they had expected. One fruit of their mission, at least, was the establishment of rapport on the personal level so that Russian scientists were willing thereafter to communicate with British scientists.[5] If our own government were sympathetic to such interchange, more might perhaps be developed.

The United Nations offer another channel, and here, too, the Quakers have been experimenting. They have a representative who explores and encourages every device looking toward mediation.[6] One of the interesting conclusions is a disagreement with Wilson's slogan that covenants should be openly arrived at. There appears to be, after all, a value in secret diplomacy at the initial and tentative stage. Responsible statesmen are fearful of making concessions and putting out feelers if the press will blare to the public every suggestion and pin them down beyond the point of any elasticity. Another interesting conclusion is that the techniques of mediation developed in labor disputes can be transferred to the political area.

Perhaps the churches might seek to assist government at the point of sound propaganda. Our own government has been singularly inept at this point. We assume that our way of life is better and everybody ought simply to recognize it. We are quite lacking in imagination and suppose that a movie showing bobby-soxers eating ice cream in a midwestern drugstore will be an antidote for Communism in China. Christianity, democracy, and Western culture must become aggressive in telling statements as to what our way of life means to us and what it can mean to others.

If that is to be done, the emphasis will have to be shifted from the material advantages which our system confers in any given set of circumstances to those principles by which our culture was forged and without which we may doubt whether it can survive. We forget that our system cannot be simply transplanted to another soil apart from the faith by which it was originally inspired. A widely traveled friend of mine, who grew up as a missionary's son in Central America, recently remarked to me that our economic pattern cannot be adopted by other peoples, let alone imposed upon them, unless our modes of behavior be also adopted. The point is that our econ-

[5] Kathleen Lonsdale, ed. *Quakers Visit Russia* (London, Friends' Peace Committee, 1950.)

[6] Elmore Jackson, *Meeting of Minds*, (New York: McGraw-Hill, 1952).

omy depends on credit, and credit depends on trust, and trust depends on integrity. If integrity be lacking, the structure crumbles. In this country we make contracts with the intention of keeping them, but there are countries where contracts are intended to be broken unless the law is invoked. Under such circumstances long-term relations are impracticable. The delivery of goods and the payment will be made to coincide as nearly as possible.

We see, thus, in one area what is equally true in many another—that certain moral qualities alone make possible our way of life. These qualities were engendered by Christian faith. Now in many quarters the faith which begat the virtues, which in turn produced the culture, has become simply faith in the culture. Whether that will suffice is extremely dubious.

In other words, the holding and the spread of our way of life by persuasion rather than by atomic bombs is contingent upon this revival of faith, and this is the major task of the churches, though in the meantime we should neglect no specific endeavor in the cause of peace.

14

The Church and World Political Order

Walter W. Van Kirk

The churches of christ in the united states are committed to the establishment of a world political order. It could hardly be otherwise. Christians are the divinely inspired propagandists of world community. They worship a God who is the creator of all men and the judge of all nations. They adore a Christ whose vision carried him beyond the confines of Palestine to the ends of the earth. Their Lord proclaimed the gospel of one world. The apostle Paul and the early disciples preached that gospel with such fervor and with such peril to the pretensions of the Roman Empire that many were thrown to the lions, while others were driven into the catacombs.

Having in mind this deathless devotion of the early Christians to the oneness of the human family under the fatherhood of God, the church historian Harnack said: "From the very outset Christianity came forward with a spirit of universalism, by dint of which it laid hold of the entire life of man in all its functions, throughout its heights and depths, in all its feelings, thoughts and actions. This guaranteed its triumph." Augustine's *City of God* set forth the vision of one who saw all races and nations subsisting under the governance of the Almighty. Many centuries before Briand expounded his thesis of European federation, a Dutch Christian by the name of Erasmus foresaw the need of establishing on that continent a federated community. Nor can it be forgotten that William Penn, more than 250 years ago, wrote an essay "Towards the

Present and Future Peace of Europe." In this essay Penn foresaw the need of creating in Europe an international order that would hold in restraint the sovereignty of competing nation states. Then there was Immanuel Kant, who, in 1795, in his essay "Perpetual Peace," recommended that "the law of nations shall be founded on a federation of free states." At a still later period Edward Everett Hale advocated the creation of the United States of Europe.

It is not possible within the compass of this chapter to cite the voluminous testimony of the scores of Christian leaders who, at the risk of life and limb, dared to challenge the concept of the divine right of kings and the boastful arrogance of princely potentates who, in their mad search for political power, set nation against nation in a succession of bloody Armageddons. The Federal Council of Churches, in its "Statement of Guiding Principles" (1942) said:

We believe that the principles of cooperation and mutual concern, implicit in the moral order and essential to a just and durable peace, calls for a true community of nations. The interdependent life of nations must be ordered by agencies having the duty and the power to promote and safeguard the general welfare of all people. Only thus can wrongs be righted and justice and security be achieved. A world of irresponsible, competing and unrestrained national sovereignties, whether acting alone or in alliance or in coalition, in a world of international anarchy. It must make place for a higher and more inclusive authority.

There is scarcely a church body in the United States, denominational or interdenominational, that has not, at one time or another, supported the idea of a world political order. Despite differences as to theology or doctrine, the Christian community in the United States is practically unanimous in its judgment that nation states must surrender to the organized international community whatever measure of their national sovereignty is required to establish peace and justice on a global scale. The statements of the Oxford and Amsterdam conferences could be cited to prove that Christians everywhere have made up their minds that isolationism as a pattern of national behavior is both politically suicidal and morally indefensible.

Nationalism, as a social and cultural dynamic, has asserted itself with increasing vigor for many centuries. As a political dynamic, nationalism has been and is a decisive factor in shaping the conduct of sovereign states in their relations with one another. Accelerated by the American Revolution, the French Revolution, and the Industrial Revolution, nationalism swept forward on many fronts. In the effort to establish its ecclesiastical and spiritual identity apart from Rome, Protestantism contributed in no small measure to the projection of nation states in western Europe.

In his *Essays on Nationalism* the eminent historian Carlton Hayes said: "The most significant emotional factor in public life today is nationalism." That was in 1926. What of today? Nationalism is in the ascendancy in Asia, the Middle East, and Africa. Indonesia, with its 76,500,000 people, has achieved its independence. India, with its 360,000,000 people, and Pakistan, with its 75,842,000 people, have thrown off the yoke of political bondage. The Philippines, with its 20,246,000 people, has lifted high the banner of national statehood. Ceylon, with its 7,742,000 people, and Israel, with its 1,516,000 people, are rejoicing in their newly acquired national sovereignty. Since the end of the Second World War more than 600,000,000 people have marched through the portals of freedom.

But this is not all. The creation of Libya as an independent political entity has inflamed the imagination of Africans from the Mediterranean to the Cape of Good Hope. The heady wine of nationalism is being quaffed by the Arab states—Iran, Iraq, Syria, Egypt, Jordan, and Lebanon. In all these areas the tendency is to exalt nationalism and to do this in a manner reminiscent of the Boston Tea Party. In Tunis and Morocco there are bloodshed on the city streets and rioting in the market places as the Paul Reveres shout their slogans of liberty, justice, and fraternity. The lights are burning low in the colonial offices of empire states as subject peoples everywhere clamor for their emancipation.

Now that a peace treaty has been signed with Japan there may well follow a rebirth of nationalism in that country. The patriotic fervor of the Japanese people will increase to the degree required to meet the threat of Communist aggression and to secure from the United States and other Western nations treaties of economic reciprocity. And with an Iron Curtain dividing Germany into two parts, the voice of Bismarck is invoked as the German people carry forward their drive for national unity. He who believes that Germans will be content forever with seeing the land of their fathers divided against itself have closed their ears to the whisperings of the ages. German nationalism, in the long run, cannot be destroyed by diplomatic pen-pushers. Either in peace or in war, Germany will someday be reunited.

Nationalism has triumphed in Yugoslavia, where Tito's armies stand poised to resist the Kremlin aggressor. Titoism is the voice of Yugoslavia protesting against absorption in the rapidly expanding Soviet Empire. What has happened in Yugoslavia may well happen in due time throughout all of eastern Europe. When the patriots of Poland, Rumania, Bulgaria, and Hungary rise from the underground with freedom in their hearts and weapons in their hands, the shots they fire will be heard around the world. In Russia, where the political theorists of the Kremlin proclaim the doctrine of a classless society in which the nation state will wither away on the vine of a dead past, there is manifested, by contrast, a militant nationalism that is positively frightening in its implications for the rest of the world.

A wave of nationalism is sweeping over Italy in protest over the loss of Trieste. In France a revival of nationalism is deemed to be the only sufficient answer to political rivalries in the Chamber of Deputies and to the threatened dissolution of the French Empire. Within the British Commonwealth of Nations, Canada, New Zealand, and Australia frequently exercise their national sovereignty in a manner disconcerting to Downing Street. And what shall we say of the United States? Here and there across our land is heard the voice of those who would have the American people hide behind a wall of bayonets. Others, fearful lest the admission of aliens to our shores will corrupt our culture, subvert our social order, and destroy our institutions of government, support restrictive immigration policies that are confessedly nationalistic in content and perspective. Still others, weary of being taxed for the economic recovery of the free world, tighten their purse strings as they make ready to go it alone.

No amount of wishful thinking by the academic prognostications of world government can fell the ghost of Machiavelli. This Italian patriot in his classic essay, *The Prince*, foresaw with what persistence men everywhere would cling to the concept of the sovereign state with a devotion akin to fanticism. Nationalism, in its cultural, economic, and political manifestations, is a force to be reckoned with, a force that molds history today, as in the ages past. No amount of sleight of hand by the wand-wavers of world government, can cause the sovereign state to vanish. Nor can the proponent of world order naïvely assume that nationalism is on the wane.

We come now to the baffling paradox of our times. Paralleling the rise and resurgence of nationalism is the movement for one world under law. In modern times the movement for world constitutionalism may be said to have begun with the convening of the Hague conferences in 1899 and 1907. Then followed the creation of the League of Nations and the establishment of the World Court of Justice. The Protocol for the Pacific Settlement of International Disputes (1924), the Locarno Treaty (1925), and the Kellogg-Briand Pact for the renunciation of war (1928) marked successive steps in the search for a world community responsive to the discipline of international law.

Impetus was given this movement long before Christ was born. As far back as the third century B.C., Asoka was proclaiming the gospel of world community. He did not spell out his philosophy in terms of an international organization, but he did envisage a world order that would advance the well-being of human beings regardless of racial or geographical considerations. King Philip of Macedon got quite excited about the "one world" idea, as did Alexander, albeit the "one world" with which their names are associated was to be achieved by the benevolent use of armed force. Then came the Caesars. They considered themselves to be the exponents of one world under Roman law, which law was to be enforced by the military operations of the Roman legions.

During the Second World War the golden words inscribed on these treaty parchments were washed away by the blood of the soldier dead. Despite all pledges to the contrary, war as an instrument of national policy and for the aggrandizement of nation states was resorted to with a fury unprecedented in history. Then followed the establishment of the United Nations, and the creation of such specialized agencies as the United Nations Educational, Scientific and Cultural Organization; the Food and Agriculture Organization; and the World Health Organization. Shortly thereafter, resolutions calling for the establishment of some form of world government were introduced in the halls of Congress. The Atlantic Union resolution suggested that President Truman summon the representatives of the seven originators of the North Atlantic Pact to consider the possibility of establishing a union among themselves. The World Federalists sponsored a resolution which would commit Congress to the eventual establishment of a world government with defined and limited powers.

More recently the federation movement has gathered momentum in Europe. The European Coal and Steel Community, popularly known as the Schuman Plan, offers promise that at long last the nations of Europe will bury their ancient rivalries. There was established under the Schuman Plan a High Authority to which the member government—France, western Germany, Italy, Belgium, the Netherlands, and Luxembourg—assigned regulartory powers over production, prices, and investment in the coal and steel industries. Also included in the Schuman Plan are such international organs as a Common Assembly, a Council of Ministers, and a Court of Justice. Said Foreign Minister Schuman in launching his plan:

The community of production which will in this manner be created, will clearly show that any war between France and Germany becomes not only unthinkable but in actual fact impossible. . . . By pooling basic production and by creating a new high authority . . . this proposal will create the first concrete foundation for a European federation which is so indispensable for the preservation of peace.

A European Defense Community is also being evolved. If and when the treaty setting up this community is ratified, the groundwork will have been laid for the merger of the armed forces of the signatory nations into a single European Army. The European Defense Community also provides for a Council of Ministers, a Court, and a Common Assembly composed of eighty-seven representatives drawn from the national legislatures of the member states. Pending the establishment of the European Defense Community, the Schuman Plan Assembly has assumed responsibility for drafting "a treaty constituting a European political authority."

Students of world affairs are rubbing their eyes in utter amazement as they observe this trend toward unification in western Europe. Perhaps the most dramatic step yet taken by any nation in support of the primacy of international law was taken by the Dutch Government in December, 1952. The lower house of Parliament, by a vote of eighty-six to seven, approved a constitutional amendment which would yield ultimate authority to supernational organizations. Under this amendment power is granted the government to intrust legislative, administrative, and judicial authority by agreement to international organizations. It is also provided that, where required by "the development of international legal order," the Dutch Parliament may by a two-thirds vote ratify treaties even when such treaties are in conflict with the Dutch Constitution. "The Netherlands Government," said the *New York Times*, "has put itself at the head of a procession leading not only toward the unification of Europe but toward a transformation in the idea of national sovereignty."

How shall Christians evaluate the comparative strength and durability of these seemingly opposing forces: national sovereignty and international authority?

It should be said at the start that nationalism "per se" is not contrary to the Christian ethic. Nationalism can be a force for good or for evil. When it is exploited by totalitarian tyrants, nationalism can debase the culture of a people and debauch its civilization. When invoked by statesmen who have regard for the rights and freedoms of peoples other than their own, nationalism can enrich the society of the sovereign state and exalt those qualities of life treasured by the Christian community. Nor need nationalism be a deterrent to the development of a wholesome and rewarding international order. Christians can strive for the ultimate creation of some form of world order and still hold fast to that which is noble and uplifting in their national heritage.

It is because Christians have dared dream of a political and social order that would transcend the absolute sovereignty of the nation state that they have given a wholehearted support to the United Nations. Here we have, if anywhere, a world political community. The United Nations is not a world legislative body. It can recommend economic and military sanctions against an aggressor, but it cannot enforce these actions except by consent. Member states, in a juridical sense, remain sovereign. The veto accorded the Great Powers is an acknowledgment of this fact. The United States, no less than Russia, insisted on the veto when the charter was drafted at San Francisco. Otherwise the charter would not have been ratified by the Senate. However, in practice, some abridgment of absolute national sovereignty is implied in the charter. Member states are pledged to "refrain in their international relations from the threat or use of force against the territorial integrity or political independence of any state, or in any other manner inconsistent with the Purposes of the United Nations." It is also provided that "all members shall give the United Nations every assistance in any action it takes in accordance with the present Charter." It is specified that "in order to ensure prompt and effective action by the United Nations, its members confer on the Security Council primary responsibility for the maintenance of international peace and security, and agree that in carrying out its duties under this responsibility the Security Council acts on their behalf." Member states agree "to accept and carry out the decisions of the Security Council in accordance with the present

Charter." Furthermore, all nations are obligated to give the United Nations an accounting of the condition of their dependent peoples. Under the trusteeship system the nations administering trust territories assume definite obligations for the well-being of native populations. But the authority of the United Nations is derived, in the main, not from the policeman's club but from moral compulsion.

Despite these restricted powers, the United Nations has functioned, in certain limited respects, as a world legislature. It transformed the status of Libya from that of a one-time Italian colony to that of a sovereign and independent state. The General Assembly in 1948, submitted to member states for their ratification a Convention on the Crime and Punishment of Genocide. A Universal Declaration of Human Rights has been approved, and the General Assembly now engaged in the process of drafting one or more covenants on human rights, which, when ratified, will establish in law the rights and freedoms of man.

As for its competence in maintaining international peace and security, the United Nations has functioned more effectively than its critics are prepared to concede. The United Nations stopped the Kashmir War. The issues related to this war have not been resolved, but the fighting has ceased, thanks to the United Nations. Otherwise, India and Pakistan might even now be involved in a military conflict with implications of threat to the peace of the entire world. The United Nations stopped the war in Indonesia. Through its good offices the Indonesian nationalists and the Dutch government agreed to sit down together at a round-table conference at the Hague. It was there that the United States of Indonesia was established. The United Nations stopped the war in Palestine. Here, again, the issue related to this conflict have not been entirely resolved, but a cease-fire was accomplished, and the Israelis and the Arabs did lay aside their swords. As for Korea, it can be said that the intervention of the United Nations in that war-torn land is the longest step yet taken by the world community looking toward the establishment of a system of collective security.

Despite these achievements the United Nations has fallen

upon difficult days. There are those who say that its days are numbered; that the shaft of marble hugging the shore line of the East River is hardly more than a mausoleum where repose the hopes nurtured at San Francisco that the swords of the nations would be sheathed forever. The criticisms directed against the UN underscore how difficult and how hazardous is the process of developing a world political order. Attacks on the United Nations are increasing in volume and intensity. Those who would establish a superstate with executive functions that would transcend the concept of absolute national sovereignty assail the United Nations for being too weak. Those who worship at the shrines of nationalism assail the United Nations for being too strong, since, as they say, the UN intervenes in matters of domestic concern.

In the United States the display of the United Nations flag is said by some to be derogatory of the Stars and Stripes. A resolution has been introduced in the House of Representatives calling for the withdrawal of the United States from the United Nations. Fifty-five Senators joined Senator Bricker of Ohio in introducing in the Senate a proposed amendment to the Constitution which would drastically limit the participation of the United States in the United Nations and which would rule out the possibility of our nation's ratifying such covenants as those on genocide and human rights. Others object to the United Nations on the ground that American participation costs too much. Scarcely a day passes that some radio commentator does not lift his voice in ridicule of the United Nations. Newspaper editors and magazine writers are increasingly hostile toward the United Nations. The fact that a few members of the Secretariat have been discharged as subversives has aroused much opposition to the UN.

It must be confessed that certain of the criticisms leveled against the United Nations are deserving criticisms. The UN has not bridged the chasm between East and West. The UN has not reached an agreement for the reduction and regulation of armaments, including atomic weapons. The UN has not solved the prisoner-of-war issue in Korea, nor has it been able thus far to effectuate its resolution calling for a free and independent Korea. There is a measure of frustration in the Security Council and much haranguing and name calling in the General Assembly. But to say the United Nations has failed, and is no longer entitled to the support of the American people, is utter nonsense. It is more than that. Such gossip is utterly irresponsible and positively dangerous to our peace and to the peace of the world. Where the United Nations is weak, let it be made stronger. Where the structure of the UN is lacking, let it be improved. Where the procedures of the UN are faulty, let them be brought into line with the needs of this solemn hour. If there are subversives operating under the cloak of the UN, let them be discharged, and quickly. But to abandon the United Nations is unthinkable. Churchmen who swallow hook, line, and sinker the misconceived and biased propaganda against the UN should be ashamed of themselves. At San Francisco the churches were heard in support of the United Nations. Pastors and laymen called for the ratification of the charter. Ministers summoned the faithful to their altars to pray for God's blessing on the United Nations. All this was a part of yesterday. Today, at a time when the United Nations is being kicked around by ill-informed critics, and by the unashamed propagandists of political and economic isolationism, the churches must again rally their forces in support of the United Nations.

I am among those who believe that the surest way ultimately to achieve some form of world government is through the United Nations. A super-world state endowed with constitutional authority and with sufficient police force to impose its judgments on sovereign nation states may come some day. But to believe that such a world government can or will be established in the foreseeable future, is to close one's eyes to reality. Those Americans who advocate world government on the assumption that the United States is prepared to subordinate its national sovereignty to an international authority would do well to read the *Congressional Record* of June 26, 1952. A debate on United States appropriations to the UN was under way. It was recommended that a limitation be put in this appropriation bill which would provide that none of the funds should be used to pay our contribution to any international organization which promotes the doctrine of one-world government and world citizenship. Accordingly, the following amendment was agreed to: "None of the funds appropriated in this title shall be used to pay the United States contribution to any international organization which engaged in the direct or indirect promotion of the principles or doctrines of one world government or world citizenship."

Where, it may be asked, were the Senators who, in July, 1949, sponsored a resolution calling for a world federation endowed with authority to enact, interpret, and enforce world law? A similar resolution was introduced in the House over the signatures of 104 Congressmen. To propose resolutions on world order is one thing. It is another and quite different thing for the Congress of the United States to commit itself and the American people to the principles of world government. More than once Senators have attached their signatures to petitions and affirmations extolling world government. But when the chips are down, and names and votes are publicly recorded, an amendment to an appropriation bill is agreed to which specifies that not a dime of the taxpayers' money shall be used, directly or indirectly, for the promotion of the principles of doctrine of one-world government.

Nor is there reason to believe that the Soviet Union is prepared, either now or as far into the future as mortals can see, to accept the binding authority of an international code. Quite the contrary. The Kremlin is a hotbed of rampant nationalism. Every effort of the UN to project itself into areas that impinge on the national sovereignty of the Soviet Union is vigorously challenged by the Russians. A nation that refuses to modify even to the slightest degree the veto privilege which it enjoys in the United Nations is not a nation favorably disposed toward world government.

What all this adds up to is that Christians, in the matter of world government, would do well to make haste slowly. This is not a counsel of despair. This is an appeal to reason. By all means let Christians constantly strive for a world community under law. But let them not be deceived into believing that world government can be achieved by oratory, or by the introduction of meaningless resolutions in the halls of

Congress, or by drafting blueprints of a world political structure. With all its shortcomings the United Nations is the one organization through which over the years a world community capable of achieving and maintaining peace with justice for all may be evolved. That is why continued support of the United Nations by the churches is so important.

Of still greater importance is the development of an international ethos. The present sad state of the world cannot be attributed to faulty international machinery. In spite of all its structural and procedural shortcomings, the United Nations could put an end to the arms race, ease the tensions between East and West, and facilitate the processes of peaceful change. Then why are not these things done? The answer is simple. What is lacking is not machinery, but the will to use the machinery for the fulfillment of the ends so eloquently set forth in the charter signed at San Francisco. The problem of world government, therefore, must be approached from deeper levels than that of political structure. It is fear that menaces the peace of mankind, and hysteria, and national pride, and the worship of guns, bazookas, and bombs, and the desire for conquest by military weapons or by subversive infiltration. The political scientist is not able to prescribe remedies for the spiritual sickness of the nations. The political scientist is not able to substitute the spirit of reconciliation for the spirit of recriminaton. Nor is he able to reap the fruits of peace from a seed sowing of distrust and dishonor.

It is precisely in these areas where the prophets ordained by God step into the breach. They, more than the political scientists, are the true peacemakers. Theirs is the task of bringing the lust for power and the craving for conquest under the judgment of God. Theirs is the task of establishing the conditions of peace. Theirs is the task of developing that spirit of world community which is prior to the establishment of world government. A world government that does not rest upon a common foundation of moral principles would, in all likelihood, become an instrument of dictatorial terror and oppression.

What, then, can Christians do to develop this international

ethos? They can promote the recognition and observance of human rights. The Senate of the United States has thus far refused to ratify the Convention on the Crime and Punishment of Genocide. Our nation stands before the world as a Christian nation. Our people have condemned the mass slaughter of political, racial, and religious minorities. But when an opportunity is given them to place this peculiar form of mass homicide under the ban of world law, they betray their heritage. The Christian-thinking people of America should exert whatever moral pressure is required to get this convention ratified.

The churches can do more than they have yet done to expound the principles embodied in the Universal Declaration of Human Rights. Christians can prepare themselves for the forthcoming debate on ratification of the projected covenants on human rights. They can participate in programs of technical assistance. They can evince a greater interest in the curative and creative endeavors of the UN Economic and Social Council. They can support with greater vigor the specialized agencies that are answering the plaintive call of human needs in various parts of the world. They can identify the missionary movement with the legitimate aspirations of native populations for political advancement and economic justice. They can support programs of land reform. If Christians everywhere were to engage in united effort to raise living standards and to combat the social evils by which human beings are degraded and the economic evils by which the masses are exploited, they would engender a sense of fellowship in the things of the spirit and thereby strengthen the moral foundations of the world community.

Christians also have it within their power to practice in their own life and work the gospel of co-operation which they proclaim for the nations. A cleric who condemns isolation as a political philosophy while practicing isolation as an ecclesiastical philosophy will have much to answer for in the day of judgment. Christians who are so jealous of their ecclesiastical sovereignty that they are unwilling to co-operate with their fellow Christians of another denomination would do well to cast out the beam in their own eyes before they undertake to cast out the mote in the eyes of the nations. It is when Christians move forward together in a united offensive ogainst the divisiveness of the secular community that they exert their maximum influence in the striving for world order. The National Council of Churches in the United States, and kindred bodies of co-operative effort in other lands, provide the nations with a much-needed object lesson of the unity of spirit that can be achieved when hands are clasped across the barriers of yesterday. Similarly, when 158 national churches from 43 countries unite to form a World Council of Churches, they strengthen the moral foundations of the world community.

American Christians can vastly improve their strategy in their search for world order if they will work in close co-operation with the Commission of the Churches on International Affairs jointly instituted by the World Council of Churches and the International Missionary Council. This commission is an agency which seeks, among other things, to promote the law and the progressive development of supernational institutions. The C.C.I.A. sponsored a proposal for United Nations Observer Commissions, and this proposal was unanimously approved by the General Assembly. It has made articulate the voice of the churches in support of the Universal Declaration of Human Rights. It has issued a statement of guiding principles to insure the success of technical assistance programs. It has followed with sympathetic interest the work of the Trusteeship Council. It has stressed the political and moral factors which must be taken into account in the effort to reduce and regulate armaments. It has assisted in the care and resettlement of refugees and displaced persons. The churches can take pride in the far-flung operation of the C.C.I.A. Its constructive efforts in support of world order have won high praise from officials of government and officers of the United Nations.

Above all else Christians can nurture the spirit of world community by keeping hope alive in the hearts of men. A third world war is not inevitable. To say that it is, is to yield to a philosophy of despair that denies the presuppositions of the Christian faith. It is not surprising if secular-minded statesmen whose moral insights are compromised by too great a reliance upon armies, navies, and air forces, should give way to despair. What is surprising is that Christian leaders should echo this despair and join the procession of those who are without hope. Christians ministers who tremble every time Malenkov speaks, or who go into a tail spin of abject terror every time a bomb is exploded on the proving grounds of the Atomic Energy Commission, should be unfrocked.

It is indeed true that the times in which we live are full of peril. Danger knocks at the door of every man, woman, and child. But this is God's world. He has not surrendered his sovereignty. Our God is still the Lord of history. It is he and not any earthly potentate who will reign forever and ever. In this knowledge let Christians be done with their weeping. Let them be done with their prophecies of doom and destruction. Let them proclaim from their pulpits and their pews the good news that if men will walk in the ways of God and do his will, there is no power on earth by which they can be destroyed.

15

The Church as an Agency
of Social Action

OREN H. BAKER

Thy kingdom come,
Thy will be done on earth.

OUR THOUGHT SHOULD BE CLEAR WITH RESPECT TO THE
PRECISE MEANING OF SOCIAL ACTION AS DISTINGUISHED FROM
the action of an individual. This can be illustrated by a relatively simple situation. A family suffers misfortune as the
result of prolonged illness ending in the death of the bread-
winner. Its members are in a state of emotional and economic
deprivation. A neighbor steps in, supplies their need from his
own stock, stands by them through the crisis, counsels them
about reorganizing their affairs, and guides them through the
period of readjustment. There are three significant things
about this example of typical individual action. First, it involves a person who has proper sensitivity to an existing human need. Second, it discloses a mature sense of responsibility.
Third, it affirms that the individual had under his control
resources adequate to meet the need in all the terms set by
the situation. These three conditions—sensitivity, responsibility, adequacy of resources—must be present in any kind
of action designed to meet human needs; and when they are
the possession of one person, individual action is relevant and
sufficient.

However, in the light of our general observation of the

contemporary human scene, we discover that some important modifications must be made to bring our illustration into line with actual experience. First, the kind of action described is increasingly rare, even among Christians. Second, we observe variations in the degree in which the three conditions are found to exist in combination for proper action. It can be said that all people have some sensitivity to the distress of their neighbors. Many have a mature sense of responsibiliy. But few people normally have in themselves and under their control adequate resources to meet the needs which surround them. A third fact is that times have changed. We have passed out of the age when an agricultural and craft economy set a social pattern in which individuals were self-sufficient with enough surplus to bring aid in a direct fashion to those in the grip of misfortune. Surpluses continue to appear, but individual action is inhibited by the further fact that human sympathy has been modified by an industrial and urbanized society which increases social dependency and engenders impersonal attitudes. People live in closer range with one another for better or for worse and sometimes defensively erect emotional barriers to provide a feeling of distance once guaranteed by geographical separation. In short, the increasing complexity of an interdependent social order demands action in a dimension beyond the capacity of the individual.

The issue will become clearer if we consider the problem of a group of families living in a city slum. Here is a congested area to which people have moved because of a progressive deterioration in their economic and personal adequacy. Left to their own resources, they can afford nothing better than a domicile in a tenement. An imaginative person standing outside the slum, viewing the plight of these inhabitants and the threat they present to social health, at once perceives that while he might do something singlehanded, his resources are quite inadequate to bring about significant change. Plainly this is a social problem requiring the joint effort of many individuals working through responsible channels in terms commensurate with the demands of the situation. Social action, then, is action by a group on a scale which can produce effective change in conditions which depress the living of many individuals. It is action directed toward the liberation of those who are unable to extricate themselves from circumstances that block the road to full, self-competent, personal attainment. The objectives of such action vary with the dimensions of the problems presented and range from the type of situation we have used for illustration to the needs of a whole society, a nation, or the world. There is a sense in which our modern civilization is a gigantic social problem with many focuses of human need and aspiration but one implicit goal—the release of all humankind from constricting social structures and the building of "more stately mansions" to house an emerging human soul that can respond freely to the wide diversities of mankind and live in all the abundance of a brotherhood made rich by universal sharing. Athwart our path to this goal stand the last bastions of resistance doomed to fall before an advancing global solidarity. The futility of our wars is now patent in the fact that they are frantic efforts to maintain fluid boundaries against an inevitable social interpenetration on a world scale. In other words, human relations in our kind of world have become compact with a degree of mutual impingement that was formerly unknown and with a resulting sensitiveness and tension not unlike the impact of molecules forced to unite under compression. Earth space is contracting. Effective isolation is gone. People thus thrust together are tempted to run or to fight. But to run is cowardly and to fight in the modern manner is to invite ruin. We halt between the alternatives, realizing that apart from others our manhood cannot be made perfect, that what we do to them and what they do to us will settle the destiny of all.

With this understanding of the conditions which give rise to social action and the varying objectives involved in a free society, we turn to the chief concern of this chapter—the nature and method of *Christian* social action.

First of all, it should be recognized that the church does not occupy a position that is parallel to that of any other institution. It can be studied from the outside as Wach and many others have studied it, and there is profit in that approach. Judged, however, by its central and controlling purpose, the church cannot be placed alongside the state, business, the school, or even the family. All these institutions are uniform ways by which a society satisfies needs and guarantees survival. But their several activities directed toward these ends are never independent of one another. They are interrelated in ways which serve the whole group. In a complex and changing society such as ours, not only has this interrelatedness increased, but functions of one institution tend to pass imperceptibly into others. Schools take over responsibilities of the family. Government erstwhile barred by the mores from business moves into business under pretext of social change called "emergency." Once depending upon the charity of neighbors and the initiative of local communities, the federal political establishment is now acquiring the characteristics of a "welfare state." Taxes, especially levies on income and provisions for social security, inform every citizen periodically that he must share his wealth.

When the church looks at itself thoughtfully in the light of these conditions and re-examines its distinctive function, certain attitudes immediately appear. First, it rejects the status assigned to it by sociological analysis based upon so-called objective observation of characteristic phenomena. It reverts to its inner, motivating genius rooted in the historic event of God in Christ reconciling the world unto himself and, upon reflection, emerges with the conviction that this event, though it occurred at a specific time and place, had a depth and relevance to the human situation that makes it an inexhaustible source of insight and direction. The mandate of the Christian gospel issuing from the Word of God made flesh, strips the labor union, the employers asssociation, the schools, and the family of their intense occupation with immediacy and thrusts the claims of ultimate destiny into their perspectives.

Second, the church in its concern for individuals caught in the toils of this world cannot be content to limit its activity to the art of cushioning its members against the hard facts of circumstance, or to increase their tolerance for frustration. A temple of refuge for broken hearts, the church most certainly is. A sanctuary where people present themselves in penitence and adoration, a church by definition is. But in its work of healing, the aim of the church is to restore the wounded soldier to the field of action in the unending war against the evils which inflicted his injuries, not to hospitalize him as an invalid to be nursed in peace of mind by liturgical sedatives. Worship is indeed the heart of religion, and prayer is the heart of worship, but it is the function of the heart to energize brain and muscle for action. Orientation toward life as a whole, centered in God and venturing forth in faith as a worker together with God in carrying forward his creation, is the essence of the religious way. Mahatma Gandhi, with all his emphasis upon private prayer, confesses in his autobiography that God was never quite so real to him as during the days when he was actively identified with the struggles of the poor farmers in the north of India. To work for a cause is to pray. Christian social action summons the church to actualize in daily deed the words of Jesus,

> *Thy kingdom come,*
> *Thy will be done on earth.*

Third, all this means that the church is not a "pressure group" seeking ends in competition with other groups. It must at times espouse particular causes as steps intermediate to the fulfillment of its mission. But in all these undertakings it will be evident that its reach exceeds its grasp. The step that is taken is dictated by a goal much farther on. Christian social action is the application of the spirit of reconciliation to human relations and is directed toward the achievement of an inclusive community of all men in which each in the value of his individuality shall become mutually participant in the values and goals of others through the redemptive work of God in Jesus Christ. The three words "redemption," "reconciliation," and "inclusiveness" express the means and the goal of the kind of action the church may undertake as a part of its distinctive task. Redemption is the process by which the individual undergoes the change necessary to membership in the Christian community. Reconciliation refers to the activity of the redeemed person in removing the barriers which separate men from one another. Inclusiveness expresses the ultimate range of the Christian objective.

JUDGING THE ISSUES AND SEEKING THE GOALS OF CHRISTIAN SOCIAL ACTION

The previous chapters of this book have examined in detail the nature of our society and suggested areas in which social action is needed.

The first step of the local congregation will be the selection of an alert and competent committee on Christian social action which will work co-operatively with other churches in the community. It should be emphasized that the very nature of the task, as well as our criterion of inclusiveness, requires the collaboration and united effort of all congregations in a given territory. A starting point can be found wherever interest, vision, intelligence, and zeal exist, but ultimately all constituents of the Christian mind should become involved. A complete inventory of the major social needs will then be taken and made available to all working units. This done, we are ready for planning and action. The basis of judgment in all cases will grow out of inquiry about how any set of conditions is affecting human beings, limiting or perverting their development as persons. If pursued far enough, this principle will lead to an examination of the whole range of human experience at home and abroad, but the problems nearest to the local church are those associated with the threats to the vitality and integrity of the family. Exploration of the needs in this area with active assumption of responsibility for them is an excellent way to develop the habit of social thinking in the minds of church members. Health is a closely related field. No one needs to argue this point to a generation that is as health conscious as ours, but certain questions can be asked that will stir people out of their complacency. From these areas, it is natural to move to others. How do members of the community spend their leisure time? Where do young people go for recreation? Are taverns and poolrooms exploiting them with enticements of drink and gambling? Who are the underprivileged on account of economic status? Is education available to all? Is the local government honest and efficient? What outreach has the community for the larger world beyond itself? These are bare samples of the kind of questions which identify opportunities for social action.

The next step is an appraisal of the adequacy of organizations already at work on social problems. The concern of the church in doing this is twofold: first, to inspire and support existing agencies which, though not operating under church auspices, are in reality its extended helping hand; second, to arrive at an exact determination of neglected areas where social effort is needed. Often a church stands in its own light by not recognizing its children in the "good works" undertaken by other groups in the community. Actually the altruism on which a mature religion is built has its roots in the natural pity and sympathy which the average human being has for his kind. Though limited in their range, these feelings nevertheless enter into the motivation of social action. More often than not, however, the church will find that some of the most effective of these agencies are being administered by its own members in a way that enhances their Christian witness. A council of social agencies, operating under support of a community chest, is a good example. The three basic elements compounded to produce this organization flow directly from Christian teaching: the desire of a community to provide care for those who are unable to take care of themselves; the desire to conserve resources through a unified and efficient administration of the gifts of the participating citizens; and the desire to preserve the self-respect of those who are dependent upon community generosity through an intelligent distribution of benefits and services. In its accounting of its influence, the church may legitimately look upon this kind of social action as an expression of its own spirit, and the absence of direct ecclesiastical control as a part of its own philosophy of losing life to find it.

This does not mean, however, that the church as such surrenders responsibility for these services. Quite to the contrary. It will review the conduct of the agencies, the manner of their administration, the standards employed, the adequacy of the services themselves at the point of actual contact with need. It will be alert to discover signs of favoritism based on prejudice and special pressures exerted on administrative personnel. On the more positive side, it will endeavor to judge the need in the community and urge more adequate support by the citizens to meet deficiencies.

In like manner, the church may adopt the good works of organizations which are seeking better government, better human relations in industry, better education for mature living, greater equality for good housing, and the improvement of all conditions which enable human beings to develop their maximum potential. *Wherever there is an issue for personality, a threat to the abundant life, there the church has a stake; and wherever that life is being advanced, the church acknowledges its partnership.* Particular responsibility for these functions will be located in committees on Christian social action, but concern for the ends approved by the Christian conscience will be diffused among all members with a growing sensitiveness to need and an increasing zeal to bear the Christian witness in all relationships.

By selecting those objectives and activities which look toward the growth of community in human relations, the church renders its judgment upon them. It states what it can approve and encourage. It leaves out what has no potentiality for advance toward the kingdom. With respect to good works under nonchurch auspices it goes as far as it can on the logic of Jesus, reported by Luke, that "he that is not against you is for you" (R.S.V.). Such a strategy offers far more promise for progressively Christianizing the social order than periodic, sometimes spasmodic, agitation in behalf of some particular cause of transient consequence. Human beings are deeply involved in the complexities of social living, and the leaven of the gospel must find as many points as possible to affect all conditions. We are looking for the kingdom, but in every community there is a sense in which it is at hand. Indeed, it is at hand wherever there is potentiality for a good that the spirit of Christ can use in lifting men to the level of loving their neighbors as themselves.

CHRISTIAN SOCIAL ACTION AS EVANGELISM

It has been a presupposition of the treatment of our subject that any program of social action worthy of support by the church must spring from grounds indigenous to the Christian gospel. We now make that assumption explicit in the affirmation that Christian social action is evangelism in that it undertakes to *direct change* in human relations through an orientation toward life as a whole and toward the ultimate destiny of the human race. We come to this position with an almost overwhelming conviction of the engagement now upon us. For it would seem that the door of opportunity for which the church has been waiting is now opening, albeit it may be slammed in our face by the onward march of Communism. The frustrations and sufferings of this century have brought down upon us the judgment of mankind that, claiming so much for our gospel, we have been all but impotent in holding back the evil powers which have engulfed the world and carried millions down the road to ruin. Our own nation, once acclaiming itself Christian, once looked up to and copied by peoples near and far, now finds itself in growing disfavor around the globe. We know our record and can be thankful that it is not worse. But we cannot forget that with the exception of our losses in battle casualties, we have not only come out of two world wars unbombed, unscathed, but have entered upon a period of material prosperity unparalleled in our history. The parable of Dives and Lazarus is not without somber meaning for us—with a footnote, of course, stating that whereas Lazarus found solace in Abraham's bosom, his modern counterparts are rejecting our charity and clamoring for a place on Malenkov's knee. Two billion people look at us today with querulous and hungry eyes, many with downright hatred in their hearts. But what is more appalling is the fact that with the black stain of Hiroshima on our souls we continue to feed the world with promises of worse things to come if it does not watch out!

Yet, in spite of this dilemma, we dare to say that this is the day of opportunity for the church. Why? Because we know beyond the shadow of any doubt the main reason for our failure in the past, the reason our gospel has not saved the world from its present, desperate plight. The plain fact is that while Protestantism began its history by rejecting the separation of religion from life, it has in recent times drifted into a new monasticism in its emphasis upon individual salvation. Unwittingly, yet with theological rationalization, it has adopted the fallacy that saints can be made in a social vacuum.[1] It is now clear that no man is saved until all the relations he bears to others, *relations which are the very substance of his being as a person*, have been brought under the rule of Christ. That is what we mean when we speak of Christian social action as evangelism. We shall discuss this theme in its practical aspects under four headings—the source of initiative, the process of decision, the nature of the objective, and the means of social evangelism.

The Source of Initiative

Action by the church, with respect to social conditions, is a response to the divine directive in history. The appearance of the church itself in human affairs is neither accident nor the result of merely human will. Its existence is the outcome of the initiative of God and expresses his provision for making articulate his active purpose in the world. This purpose has manifested itself among many peoples, but it took hold of the Hebrew mind in a unique and remarkable way. On the heights of prophetic judgment and vision it transformed national destiny into a world mission by which the suffering Servant would bring all peoples together under the sovereignty of the one, eternal God. But this vision dimmed, and the purpose lapsed until the day the Roman conqueror marched his legions through the streets of Jerusalem and a young Galilean rose in the synagogue at the crossroads of the Gentiles, opened the Scriptures, and read:

The Spirit of the Lord is upon me,
because he has anointed me to preach good news to the poor.

---

[1] Having been engaged for more than a quarter of a century in relating psychology to pastoral work, I cannot avoid stating that this new interest contains the danger of continuing the individualistic fallacy in religion. There is a sense in which "pastoral psychiatry" is an escape from the tougher job of social redemption. The warning is that pastoral concern must not submerge the prophetic function, for without the prophet the pastor cannot be made perfect. Both were strongly combined in Jesus.

He has sent me to proclaim release to the captives
and recovering of sight to the blind,
to set at liberty those who are oppressed,
to proclaim the acceptable year of the Lord.

(R.S.V.)

The church came out of that. It was born in a pure heart that could see God and say, "Today this scripture has been fulfilled in your hearing" (R.S.V.) Still the centuries marched. Up the years in the travail of challenge and response, to use Toynbee's phrase, Western man took his course, often muddling through in his own strength, sometimes led by the hand of God in insight and courage. Again, in our time, the issue is joined—whether we shall emerge from the shadows that mark the dawning of a new day or linger on in the continuing darkness where men, camouflaged by rival ideologies and battle cries, grapple with one another to the death without knowing who they are until their blood cries from the ground in the mockery of Cain, "Am I my brother's keeper?" Shall this be the final cynicism with which to drape the ruins of the atomic age?

The answer is, No! Again the good news comes! That old vision of the prophet accented by Jesus returns in historic fact. *God hath made one all nations and races.* By an inescapable interdependence he has brought the most diverse types of humankind to one another's doors. We are shocked to realize it, but the great thing has happened without our knowing it. While we, by the magic of our science, are annihilating distance and exploiting the resources of the earth for our own advantage, a neighbor on the other side of the globe pokes his head into our tent and says, "Me too!" By that we know that God is no respecter of persons. By that too we know that he, all through the days of our preoccupation, has been setting up the conditions for a new age of man. Self-obsessed, we lose our identification with the human race. We multiply words to explain ourselves. We wall ourselves in with rationalizations reinforced by dogmatic bluster and threats, knowing full well that if a fox should go up against that wall, it would fall. All the levees erected to keep the stream of life in restricted racial and nationalistic channels are being inundated by the flood of intermingling peoples. The tides of interdependence are bearing us onward toward an end fraught with catastrophe but freighted also with high hope of possibilities for good beyond anything eye has seen or ear heard.

It is the mission of the church to witness to the meaning of the divine initiative in the midst of the contemporary scene. It brings the insight of Paul that "the whole creation groaneth and travaileth in pain together until now" and "the earnest expectation of the creation waiteth for the revealing of the sons of God" (A.S.V.). That is the good news of God in Christ at this very hour of history—the revealing of all men to one another as sons of God with the consequent removal of barriers of separation, the freeing of captives everywhere, and the emergence of an advancing brotherhood. Christian social action is the response of the church to the divine initiative in the actual conditions of our world here and now.

The Process of Decision

The Christian social evangelist will make his decisions in the light of four major convictions. First, the affirmation that God is in the midst of the human struggle today as realistically as he was on that primeval morning when the earth was without form and void and darkness was upon the face of the deep. His Spirit broods over our disorder and confusion to make all things new through the power of the divine image in Christ, in whom all life holds together as a new creation. "For in him all the fulness of God was pleased to dwell, and through him to reconcile to himself all things" (R.S.V.). This conviction affirms the availability of power for the task.

The second conviction is the sense of urgency arising from man's threat to himself and the consequent obstruction of the fulfillment of the divine purpose in man. Doom more real than the hell of yesteryear hangs over the modern world. But the crisis is not the working of a devil from Dante's inferno. We see more clearly than ever that it is the power of the beast in man himself, a power that on occasion moves him to wipe out whole populations of his kind in fires ten thousand times hotter than a Dante could imagine. The real issue is made explicit in Mark's simple account of the temptation of Jesus—"And he was with the wild beasts" (A.S.V.) All our decisions are made with a beast clutching at our hearts, and it is only by the ministry of angels that we are saved for the better possibility. This is the constant crisis of man, and it was never more acute than now.

But sobering as this is, there is a third conviction that stirs the evangelist. It is the fact that over against the threat of destruction stands the high promise of a new earth wherein "dwelleth righteousness," the actualization of the will of God for our time. The very powers which men turn to self-destruction can be converted into forms that will serve the higher life in Christ. This conversion is the work of evangelism, for the change that must come is not a change in things but a change in man himself that will guarantee a change in the use of things. Things are incidental and instrumental. The perfection of man in true sonship is the goal toward which God is working. The older evangelist knew that man does not live by bread alone. The social evangelist knows that man does not live alone. He lives in joint relations with his kind; and if he would rise to a higher life, the social forces compounded of individual and collective sin must be converted to the higher purpose. The superindividual forces of evil must be conquered if the personal is to survive and attain unto its full stature in a regenerated community.

The fourth conviction contributing to the decision of the social evangelist is the realization that he must begin where he is, where he can most realistically establish contact with social conditions which need conversion and purification. He sees the whole world in his parish and his parish as the way to influence the wider society. The parish is the grain of mustard seed. If it be quickened in responsiveness to God, its power will be felt beyond its physical boundaries. This was never more true than now. For the vast system of communications incessantly at work brings the whole world to every fireside. Nowadays a common human dwelling is an international house in which every kind of voice near and far states the issue of the day. And that issue—how well we know—may mean the sending of a member of the household to do duty on the other side of the globe. But this system of communications is a two-way affair. No true servant of God does his work to be seen of men, to gain a cheap publicity; nevertheless a city set on a hill cannot be hid, and a clear light will be a guide to those who sit in darkness. Therefore, let no pastor feel that he works in a corner cut off from the rest of the world, that he is powerless to effect change on the far horizons. If he does his work at home as social evangelist, if he develops witness to the power of God to reorder life, that will be good news welcomed by others in distant parts who are looking for the day of the Lord. Lest we be discouraged, we need constantly to remember that it was a little band of men living in a land one hundred miles long and less than fifty miles wide who started a movement that still has the vitality to shape the course of events in our own troubled time. The parish is the cell of the universal, Christian social organism.

The Nature of the Objective

Much of the objective of Christian social evangelism has been implied in the foregoing paragraphs. It remains to focus attention on the distinctive character of the Christian mission in contrast to the claims of rival and competing ideologies. First, as valuable as the social sciences are in giving us technical equipment for our task, our concern and function cannot be identified with them. For the most part they are descriptive and statistical, presenting the facts about social changes which have already taken place. As evangelists, our task is to project goals for change, decide what direction this change should take, and set about bringing it to pass. It is significant in this connection that the men who have attained the stature of Christian social evangelists in our time entered upon their work without benefit of scientific sociology. Walter Rauschenbusch, Washington Gladden, and Francis J. McConnell began their careers as pastors. Basically their orientation was derived from the intimacies of those social relations where life appears whole in the full context of the hopes and fears, aspirations and deprivations of the human heart as it searches for the good, the beautiful, and the true in back street and country lane. Descriptive sociology has no power to institute change.

249

Social experience must pass through the alembic of prophetic insight and pastoral concern, acquire the warmth and depth of a divine empathy, before it can become creative. It is out of this that the social evangelist formulates his objective.

Another contrast is necessary to disclose clearly what the central aim in social evangelism is. Put directly and simply, as we have already intimated, this aim is community under God. This kind of community is fundamentally different from the philosophy of collectivism, which is a grouping of people drawn together by the intensity of some specific need such as that which we see in the labor union organized for collective bargaining, or in a military alliance with Russia to win the war against Nazism. The collectivist ideal, especially in the Marxist form where economic determinism reduces life to a single factor, induces the individual to subordinate himself in all the variety and possibility of his total being to a single, limited need and allows him to be manipulated by those who acquire power over him through that need. Community in the Christian sense is like the family. It embraces human beings in all their diversity, both freeing and uniting them in the joint undertaking of mutual self-realization. For this reason the Christian social evangelist sees life whole and joins his purposes with that of the eternal Father, whose will is that not one of these little ones shall perish under despotic structures which destroy the freedom to grow. Only in such community that includes the total range of human need and possibility can the best of all possible worlds, the kingdom of God, be realized. Only under such conditions can the Christian objective be attained in the revealing of the sons of God who are brothers in one human family.

The Means of Social Evangelism

What now are the means by which we may move toward the high ends set before us in this book? How may we enter the promised land of the new age that opens out in prospect before us?

First, we must recover the power of the prophet in preaching. During our generation it has been said frequently, even by ministers, that the day of preaching is ended. Were we disposed to diagnose this mood, we might suggest that it reflects the presence of more pathology than theology in the pulpit. Be that as it may, the plain fact is that the doubt about preaching is rooted in the irrelevance of so much of it. Too often it is the voice of a man bewildered rather than a voice crying in the wilderness and making new paths straight. Such preaching of course is vain. If all a man can do is to take a "nice" idea, break it down into three parts, and talk entertainingly for twenty minutes once or twice a week, then let us say that preaching has fallen out of the great tradition and should be discarded. Real preaching, however, is the voice of the centuries, past and future, speaking to the hours. It is the sweep of eternity through the human heart, not the shaking of reeds by the winds of the transient and inconsequential. It is judgment inviting to change, conversion, dedication to a crusade. It is the translation of the Word of God into the vernacular of everyday challenge without robbing it of its awful meaning. It is the voice of a man who is in travail with his generation, bearing its infirmities and weaknesses, and emerging with a vision of a new world in the making under God. It is a report of what God is doing now and a declaration of what men must do if God through them is going to advance his purpose before they sleep in the dust. Make no mistake about it—words have power when they are a report on the movement of the spirit of God in the soul of a man who has become his instrument. Preaching is not homiletics. It is the utterance of the prophet-pastor baptized in concern for a lost world, a world blundering toward the abyss, hoping for a miracle when the common sense of repentance would suffice.

But such preaching cannot end with the benediction, or even with an altar call. It must justify its mission in the action of the total congregation. If the impact of the gospel is to be felt on the frontiers of the community in the redemption of human relations, the best intelligence must be combined with the highest devotion. Just as the older evangelists organized prayer meetings for "unsaved" individuals, so now must all the members of a church share their observations about social evils, exchange their judgments, gather facts, reach agreements, plan the course to be followed, develop a strategy for dealing with opposition, withal seeking the wisdom of God in their undertakings. In short, Christian social action should be incorporated in the normal evangelistic program of the local church by the simple logic that no individual can be separated from his environment and that ultimately in an interdependent world all must be saved together if we are to be saved at all. And in measuring the success of this evangelism we shall count not only the number of individuals who "join the church" but the number of social evils challenged and destroyed.

Preaching, however, is not the only means to the ends before us. The social meanings of the Christian life must emerge on all the levels of the educational program of the church. Children and youth must discover that Christianity is not a private affair but a cause; that one's own life attains fulfillment only in joining with others in the service of goals beyond oneself. Actual participation in terms of graded experience will induct the youth of the church into an adult wisdom that will insure a competent leadership for the church tomorrow. But the educational concern of the church will extend beyond its own walls. It will inspire public education, including higher education, with the ideas which sustain responsible living in a free society based upon equality of opportunity and a disciplined intelligence. Such a program will become not only the bulwark of the nation, the prophylaxis against totalitarianism in all its forms, but prepare the way for reconditioning the human mind to live creatively in the presence of the vast human diversities of this earth.

As pertinent as all this may be to our subject, the most fundamental requirement of such a program remains to be mentioned. The objectives of Christian social action must be included in the conditions of membership in the church.[2] None

---

[2] Specifically this means that those who confess faith in Christ and join the church are committed to the work of Christianizing the family, preventing delinquency and crime, promoting good health through education and medical care for all, removing all forms of discrimination and human exploitation, and abolishing war, to mention only a few of the great social needs. *But this commitment will not be real unless the church program actually incorporates these ends and new converts understand that they are a normal part of Christian obligation.*

of the goals we have examined can be attained unless those who make up the Christian community are willing and ready to move in the direction our thought has led us. This is where the real rub comes. For most of the disciplines prescribed for the new convert in current practices of the churches are limited to the development of personal piety. To be sure, in a vague sort of way we talk about service as the outcome of faith in Jesus Christ. The judgment rendered here is not that these purposes are wrong or inept, but that they do not adequately define the mission of the church or the responsibility of the individual Christian. The monastic view of Christian living must be abandoned. It must be emphasized that goodness of any kind is not a private affair but a mode of action directed toward redeeming human relations from the power of evil. To put it cryptically, to be good means to be good for something. To be Christian means to be an agent of redemption—the salt of the earth, the light of the world. It follows that members of the church who are nonredemptive have lost their savor, and their witness will be trodden under the feet of men. Indeed, this is actually what is happening today throughout wide stretches of the earth.

With this insight before us, and so vividly obvious, it is almost amazing that we have delayed our response to it so long. Blame cannot be attached to anyone or to any group. In fact, our present plight is not so much the result of specific negligence as the outcome of certain prevailing attitudes. One I have already mentioned in my reference to a subtly rationalized monasticism which has continued the individualistic stereotype set by the revivalism of about a century ago. Another should now be considered. This is the fear on the part of church leaders that Christian social action will be called social reform and not identified as the normal objective of religion. This charge of course is the result of poor education about the meaning of our faith and is found to be groundless when the mission of the church is fully understood. That mission, we repeat, is not reform but redemption. The difference needs to be kept clearly in mind. Reform is directed toward some organized evil from the outside. Its objective is to restrain a group from aggressions which jeopardize others.

253

There is a place for constructive reform in a free society, and the church will certainly not be indifferent to it. But the real genius of the Christian approach through redemption is the concern to bring about change at the source of human motivation, ultimately a change in the inward character of the very men who are engaged in the evil, not merely the gross repression of their evil acts. The point can be made sharper by the contrast between the reformer and the prophet. Usually the reformer organizes his forces against some particular evil and wages his campaign until some institutional act, such as the passing of legislation, secures his objective. The prophet works under the power of a divine directive that affirms the relevance of the will of God for the control of life through devotion to that will. In short, in the work of redemption the church expresses the divine concern for the persons who practice the evil as well as for those who are the victims of the evil that is being practiced. Redemption and reform may coincide in certain limited situations, but their orientation and method amount to a fundamental difference in the character of their respective undertakings.

If we are to make progress toward our goal, the church must recover the compelling sense of cause inherent in the very idea of a mission, the conviction of being called by God and sent by him to do something which accords with his eternal purpose. Nearly all the feelings of frustration, not to say futility, which harass our churches, and at times make them exaggerate tidbits of achievement, are due to an eclipse of a basic sense of cause in the dimensions of the opportunity and challenge of our time. This condition is especially poignant just now when people are turning to the churches as they have not for more than a generation. We face the embarrassment of having no explicit cause to offer them that will engage all their powers. Their coming to us is due, without doubt, to the anxieties which afflict men everywhere. But the major question of the hour is: How shall we meet this event, this sudden turning of the multitudes to the enfolding arms of the church? Shall we yield to the temptation merely to ease their pain, offer them a transient relief from the fears which besiege their hearts, or *shall we inform their faith and*

mobilize their courage for creating the next age in history?
Shall we present to them, as we now restore for ourselves, the
call of the Master to seek first the kingdom, knowing that in
dedication to his cause anxiety about things of time and sense
will flee away as night before the day?[3]
This is a fateful time for those who lead the church. For
without a cause to serve there can be no effective discipline
for the individual. A Christian without a mission which com-
mands his total devotion is the very acme of paradox. Purity
of heart and personal rectitude are not ends in themselves but
the preparation required for the purification of a corrupt
world. The time has come again when church members must
sanctify themselves not for purposes of individual sainthood
but for a work of atonement in all their contacts with the
social order. In this emphasis, Christian social action expresses
the very essence of the doctrine of the cross in Christian theology, for as one great teacher has said, all the sins which killed
Jesus were social sins, sins of the group—militarism, bigotry,
corruption of justice, graft and political power, mob violence,
and class contempt. Neglect of the superindividual evils by
the Christian church is no longer possible except at the cost
of its distinctive witness. Christian social action is therefore
the test of our sincerity when we pray

> *Thy kingdom come,*
> *Thy will be done on earth.*

Suggested Curriculum
for Education in Christian Social Action
General

Alexander, Will W. *Racial Segregation in the American Protestant Church*. New York: Friendship Press.

Arndt, Christian O., and Everett, Samuel, ed. *Education for a
World Society*. New York: Harper & Bros., 1951.

Beaver, Gilbert A. *Christ and Community*. New York: Association Press, 1950.

---

[3] It is a fact that many people who are emotionally ill would become well
if they could find a cause that would take them out of themselves and release the powers which swirl in the vortex of morbid guilt and anxiety.
Losing one's life in constructive social action is the very essence of mental
health.

Bennett, John C. *Christian Ethics and Social Policy*. New York: Charles Scribner's Sons, 1946.

Demant, Vigo A. *God, Man, and Society*. New York: Morehouse-Gorham Co., 1934.

Fletcher, Joseph F., ed. *Christianity and Property*. Philadelphia: Westminister Press, 1947.

Landis, Benson Y., ed. *Religion and the Good Society*. New York: National Conference of Christians and Jews.

Leiper, Henry S. *Blind Spots*. New York: Friendship Press, 1944.

Marrow, Alfred J. *Living Without Hate*. New York: Harper & Bros., 1951.

Mays, Benjamin E. *Seeking to Be Christian in Race Relations*. New York: Friendship Press, 1946.

Oldham, Joseph H., ed. *The Oxford Conference*. Official Report. Chicago: Willett, Clark & Co., 1937.

Poteat, Edwin M. *Last Reprieve?* New York: Harper & Bros., 1946.

Temple, William. *Christianity and Social Order*. New York: Penguin Books, 1950.

Trueblood, D. Elton. *The Predicament of Modern Man*. New York: Harper & Bros., 1944.

Pamphlets and Study Courses

"The Social Creed of the Methodist Church" from *The Discipline of The Methodist Church*, 1952, Paragraph 2020.

Why a Social Action Committee? Board of Education, The Methodist Church, 1001 19th Avenue South, Nashville 3, Tennessee.

Facing Issues; the Why, How, What of Social Action Conferences. Board of Education, The Methodist Church.

Learning for Life; a Study Program for Adults in the Church. The International Council of Religious Education, 206 South Michigan Avenue, Chicago, Illinois.

Christian Action; Graded Lessons for Older Youth. The Board of Education, The Methodist Church.

Dare We Be Christian? Lesson Series for Junior High Age. Boston and Chicago: The Pilgrim Press.

The Christian Churchman in Politics. Board of Education, The Methodist Church.

The Christian Churchman in Industrial Relations. Board of Education, The Methodist Church.

Conversations About Industrial Relations. Board of Christian

Education of the Presbyterian Church, U.S.A., Witherspoon Building, Philadelphia 7, Pennsylvania.

The Races of Mankind; Public Affairs Pamphlet No. 85. Public Affairs Committee, Inc., 22 East 38th Street, New York 16, New York.

Building Bridges—Between Groups That Differ in Faith, Race, Culture (Revised 1948). The National Conference of Christians and Jews, 381 Fourth Avenue, New York 16, New York.

Bridges of Brotherhood; Stories of Practical Projects in Interracial Good Will. Board of Education, The Methodist Church.

Racial Differences and Human Resemblances. Douglas G. Haring, University Bookstore, Syracuse University, 303 University Avenue, Syracuse 10, New York.

Know—Then Act—Race Relations. Margaret C. McCulloch. Friendship Press, New York.

World Christian Citizenship Through United Christian Youth Action; A Guide to "Open House to the World." National Council of the Churches of Christ, 79 East Adams Street, Chicago 3, Illinois.

How Shall We Pay for Health Care? Public Affairs Pamphlet No. 152.

The Christian Home—Monthly. The Graded Press, The Methodist Church, 810 Broadway, Nashville 2, Tennessee.

Let's Get Down to Earth; Manual of Christian Social Action for Town and Country Churches. Council for Social Action, Congregational Christian Churches, 289 Fourth Avenue, New York 10, New York.

These Rights Are Ours to Keep; Public Affairs Pamphlet No. 140.

BIOGRAPHICAL NOTES

EDDY ASIRVATHAM was born in Madura, South India. He received the B.A. degree from the American College, Madura. Then with the help of Dr. Sherwood Eddy he studied at Hartford Theological Seminary, where he received the B.D. degree and was awarded the prize in systematic theology. He did graduate work at Harvard and at Edinburgh University, where he received the Ph.D. degree. After having been pastor and teacher of theology at Pasumalai and senior lecturer in political science at Lucknow University, in 1937 he became head of the department of political science and public administration at the University of Madras, India. In 1945 he became professor of missions and Christian international relations at Boston University School of Theology. In 1953 he has been invited to the headship and professorship of the department of political science at Nagpur University, Nagpur, India. Dr. Asirvatham has written *Political Theory*, *Spencer's Theory of Social Justice*, *Forces in Modern Politics*, *A New Social Order*, and *the Future Constitution of India*.

ROLAND H. BAINTON, Titus Street professor of ecclesiastical history at Yale University Divinity School, has been a member of the Yale faculty since 1920. He served as instructor in church history at Yale from 1920 to 1923, when he became an assistant professor. In 1932 he was promoted to associate professor and in 1936 to Titus Street professor of ecclesiastical history. An ordained Congregational minister, he received his education from Whitman College (B.A.) and Yale University (B.D. and Ph.D.). He has received the D.D. degree from Meadville Theological Seminary and from Oberlin College. In 1948 the Doctor of Theology degree was bestowed upon him by the University of Marburg, the oldest Protestant seminary in Germany. Among his books are: *Here I Stand*, a biography of Martin Luther; *Concerning Heretics*; *The Life of George Lincoln Burr*; *The Ref-*

ormation of the Sixteenth Century; and *The Church of Our Fathers.*

OREN H. BAKER, dean and professor of pastoral theology at the Colgate-Rochester Divinity School since 1945, holds degrees from Denison University (Ph.B.), the Colgate-Rochester Divinity School (B.D.), and the University of Chicago (Ph.D.). He was a pastor for fifteen years, after which he became professor of applied Christianity and pastoral counseling at the Colgate-Rochester Divinity School and subsequently dean and professor of pastoral theology. Dr. Baker is the author of *Albert W. Beaven: Pastor, Educator, and World Christian,* a study in the art of being a minister, and many articles. He is a member of the editorial board of *Pastoral Psychology.*

L. HAROLD DEWOLF, professor of systematic theology at Boston University School of Theology, was born in a Methodist parsonage in Nebraska. He received the A.B. and S.T.D. degrees from Nebraska Wesleyan University and the S.T.B. and Ph.D. degrees from Boston University. Before assuming his present duties, he served for thirteen years in student and full-time pastorates and for ten years in university teaching of philosophy and psychology. He is the author of two books, *The Religious Revolt Against Reason,* published in 1949, and *A Theology of the Living Church,* published in 1953. In addition, he has contributed to several volumes of multiple authorship and to many religious, philosophical, and educational journals.

ROBERT ELLIOT FITCH is dean and professor of Christian ethics at the Pacific School of Religion. Born in 1902 in Ningpo, China, he is the son and grandson of American Presbyterian missionaries. He received the A.B. degree from Yale University, the B.D. from Union Theological Seminary, and the M.A. and Ph.D. from Columbia University. He spent one year of special graduate study at the University of Paris. Dr. Fitch has taught philosophy in colleges and universities, both in the eastern and in the western sections of the United States, for twenty years. Before he went to the Pacific School of Religion, he was professor of philosophy and dean of Occidental College, Los Angeles. He is the author of many articles for religious and philosophical publications.

CAMERON P. HALL attended Williams College, Williamstown, Massachusetts; New College, Edinburgh, Scotland; Mansfield College, Oxford, England; and Union Theological Seminary,

New York. He has served as associate pastor of the Broome Street Tabernacle, New York; pastor of Christ Presbyterian Church, New York; and pastor of the University Presbyterian Church, Madison, Wisconsin. In 1939 he became director of the Department of Social Education and Action of the Board of Christian Education of the Presbyterian Church, U.S.A. Among his duties were the editorship of *Social Progress* and the director-ship of the World Order Movement. In 1946 he became executive director of the Department of the Church and Economic Life, National Council of the Churches of Christ in the U.S.A. He is the author of *What Churches Can Do About Economic Life; Economic Life: A Christian Responsibility; The Christian at His Daily Work; Religion in the Day's Work;* and other books.

JOSEPH HAROUTUNIAN was born in Marash, Turkey, of American parentage. He was graduated from the American University of Beirut. His father was a Congregational minister and a professor at Marash Theological Seminary. Dr. Haroutunian came to America in 1923. He received the B.A. degree from Columbia University, the B.D. degree from Union Theological Seminary, and the Ph.D. degree from Columbia University. In 1949 he received the Doctor of Divinity degree from Lawrence College, Appleton, Wisconsin. From 1932 to 1940 he taught biblical history at Wellesley College, and in 1940 he went to McCormick Theological Seminary to be professor of systematic theology. He is a regular speaker for the Faith and Life seminars of the Presbyterian Board of Christian Education. He is the author of *Piety Versus Moralism, Wisdom and Folly in Religion,* and *Lust for Power.*

GEORGE HEDLEY is chaplain and professor of sociology and economics at Mills College, Oakland, California. He received the A.B., M.A., and B.D. degrees from the University of Southern California and the Th.D. and D.D. degrees from the Pacific School of Religion. Prior to his assignment at Mills College, where he is in his fourteenth year of service, he taught at the College of Puget Sound, the Pacific School of Religion, and Hartford Theological Seminary. In 1927 and 1929 he was recorder and photographer for the archaeological expedition of the Palestine Institute at Tell en-Nasbeh, Palestine. He has been active in labor-relations work and in labor education. Among his recent books are: *The Christian Heritage in America, The Sym-*

bol of the Faith, and *The Superstitions of the Irreligious.* A new work, on Christian worship, is appearing in the autumn of 1953.

DONALD M. MAYNARD received the A.B. degree from Ohio Wesleyan University, the B.D. degree from Garrett Biblical Institute, and the Ph.D. degree from Yale University. He served pastorates in Florida and Wisconsin before going to Florida Southern College as professor of religious education. In 1931 he went to Scarritt College in a similar capacity, and since 1948 he has been professor of religious education at Boston University School of Theology. Dr. Maynard is a member of the board of directors of the Religious Education Association and is one of the representatives of the Methodist Church to the General Assembly of the Division of Christian Education of the National Council of Churches of Christ in the U.S.A. He is the author of *Your Home Can Be Christian.*

WALTER G. MUELDER received the B.S. degree from Knox College, Illinois, and the S.T.B. and Ph.D. degrees from Boston University. He has also studied at the University of Frankfurt, the University of Wisconsin, and Harvard University. From 1934 to 1940 he held a professorship at Berea College. Later he was a professor in the Graduate School of Religion, University of Southern California. In 1945 he became dean and professor of social ethics at Boston University School of Theology. He delivered the Lowell Lectures in Boston in 1951. In 1952 he was a delegate to the Third World Conference on Faith and Order. In collaboration with Laurence Sears he has written *Development of American Philosophy. Religion and Economic Responsibility* is Dr. Muelder's latest book.

DONALD T. ROWLINGSON, an ordained Methodist minister, received the A.B. degree from Allegheny College and the S.T.B. and Ph.D. degrees from Boston University School of Theology. In 1932-33 he attended the University of Berlin. He has been instructor in religion and alumni secretary at Allegheny College; professor of Greek and New Testament at Candler School of Theology, Emory University; and, since 1950, professor of New Testament literature at Boston University School of Theology.

S. PAUL SCHILLING has just become professor of systematic theology at Boston University School of Theology, after serving from 1945 to 1953 in a similar capacity at Westminster Theological Seminary, Westminster, Maryland. A native of Maryland, he holds the B.S. degree from St. John's College and the A.M., S.T.B., and Ph.D. degrees from Boston University. He also did graduate study at Harvard and the University of Berlin. He served for thirteen years in pastorates in Virginia, Maryland, and the District of Columbia. Dr. Schilling is a fellow of the National Council on Religion in Higher Education. From 1948 to 1953 he was president of the board of education in the Baltimore Conference of the Methodist Church, and a member of the board of directors of the Maryland-Delaware Council of Churches.

WALTER W. SIKES has been associate professor and head of the department of philosophy of religion and Christian ethics at Butler University School of Religion since 1952. He received the B.A. degree from Hardin-Simmons University; the M.A. degree from Vanderbilt University; and the B.D., S.T.M., and Th.D. degrees from Union Theological Seminary. He came to his present position after six years as national director of social education in the United Christian Missionary Society of the Disciples of Christ. From 1936 to 1946 he was associate professor of philosophy and religion at Berea College, Berea, Kentucky. He had previously taught Bible at Abilene Christian College and had served pastorates in Tennessee and in New York City.

ANSON PHELPS STOKES was graduated from Yale in 1896 and began in 1900 twenty-one years of service as secretary of the university. For several years he served as canon of Washington Cathedral (Protestant Episcopal). He was also chairman of the Family Service Association and of the Interracial Commission of the Federation of Churches. Since his retirement he has lived in Lenox, Massachusetts, and has completed his three-volume work *Church and State in the United States,* published in 1950. Dr. Stokes has been active in interracial work as president of the Phelps Stokes Fund and has served as trustee of various educational and philanthropic foundations, including the Brookings Institute, the Rockefeller Foundation, the General Education Board, and the Institute of International Education. Among the many honors he has received are the Legion of Honor from France, where he served during the First World War, and the "Churchman of the Year" award for 1951.

WALTER W. VAN KIRK is a graduate of Ohio Wesleyan University and Boston University. The degrees Doctor of Divinity, Doctor of Laws, and Doctor of Humanities have been conferred upon him. From 1925 to 1950 he was executive secretary of the

Department of International Justice and Goodwill of the Federal Council of the Churches of Christ in America. In 1951 he became executive director of the Department of International Justice and Goodwill of the National Council of the Churches of Christ in the U.S.A. He has a wide international background and is active in the United Nations. He is the author of *Youth and Christian Unity, Highways to International Goodwill, Religion Renounces War, Religion and the World of Tomorrow,* and *A Christian Global Strategy.* In February, 1951, he was Earl Lecturer at the Pacific School of Religion.

INDEX

265